Richard J. Perry

APACHE RESERVATION
Indigenous Peoples and the American State

University of Texas Press, Austin

Requests for permission to reproduce material from this work should be sent to Permissions, University of Texas Press, Box 7819, Austin, TX 78713-7819.

∞ The paper used in this publication meets the minimum requirements of American National Standard for Information Sciences—Permanence of Paper for Printed Library Materials, ANSI Z39.48-1984.

Library of Congress Cataloging-in-Publication Data

Perry, Richard John, 1942–
    Apache reservation : indigenous peoples and the American state / Richard J. Perry. — 1st ed.
        p.   cm.
    Includes bibliographical references and index.
    ISBN 0-292-76542-8. — ISBN 0-292-76543-6 (pbk.)
    1. Apache Indians—History. 2. San Carlos Indian Reservation (Ariz.)—History. 3. Apache Indians—Government relations. 4. Apache Indians—Social conditions. I. Title.
    E99.A6P45   1993
    973'.04972—dc20   92-37253

To Rick, Jaya, and Travis,
with love

Contents

Maps

Photographs

Preface

This book is about the peculiar American institution known as the Indian reservation. It explores the broad processes that produced the reservation system through examining the history of one Native American population—the San Carlos Apache of Arizona.

Among other things, a reservation is a nexus of relationships between a small indigenous population and the global system that encompasses them. Every reservation is unique in many ways, but in some respects the history of San Carlos is a history of United States Indian policies, with their daunting complexities and implications, acted out in southeastern Arizona. In dealing with the relationship between the San Carlos Apache and the American state, this book is as much about one as it is about the other.

I was an eastern college student on a summer job with the Bureau of Indian Affairs when I first set foot in San Carlos. That was 1963. As the drone of the Greyhound bus faded in the distance, I listened to the silence close in and smelled the hot air, savory with the aroma of desert brush baking in the sun. I walked along the blacktop road that curved off toward the horizon among broken hills, scrub, and cactus. A tiny lizard startled me, darting over the rocks under a brittle bush. The crunching footsteps sounded like a raucous affront to the stillness as I trudged along the gravel shoulder. Eventually I heard the hum of tires behind me, and an Apache man and woman in a pickup truck stopped to offer a ride.

In the decades that have passed since that day, I have spent a good deal of time trying to understand more about San Carlos. I returned in 1970 for my doctoral research in anthropology and have gone back several times since then. The processes that have made San Carlos the way it is continue to raise provocative questions—about the people themselves, about the nature of an "Indian Reservation," about change and persistence, and about American society.

Initially the most intriguing problem, it seemed, was to reconcile what I knew or thought I knew about Apache history with the people I saw talking, laughing, and going about their business around me in the San Carlos community. Somehow, images of the past and the present did not seem to fit. The Apache past involved a Subarctic heritage tempered through centuries of existence in the volatile arena of the Southwest. Knowing that the ancient forebears of these people had lived in the Subarctic, it seemed important to fathom the deep processes of culture change that had operated in their odyssey to the Southwest. This was the focus of another book (Perry 1991). But this and other reservation communities today raise still more significant and compelling questions. To grapple with some of the issues, we must perceive the reservation as part of a larger system of relationships.

The Apache now find themselves enmeshed, like the rest of us, in a global system of capitalism. They remain distinct within this context, but their existence is fraught with problems and issues that seem rife with anomalies, paradoxes, and contradictions. Many of these arise from the very nature of the reservation and its relationship to the larger sociopolitical system. This is the central focus of the book.

I have begun with a simple assumption. I assume that human beings tend to act pragmatically. Rather than simply judging whether actions have been good or bad, it seems more useful to examine the conditions in which these actions appeared rational to the people who took them. The history of the Western Apache abounds with heroes and villains, but to identify one or the other amounts to description, not explanation. We can achieve more by exploring the processes that have led apparently rational individuals to make the decisions they did.

On the San Carlos Reservation today, about ten thousand Apache live on a 1.8 million acre tract. Government agents in the late nineteenth century demarcated the region in what they considered to be an essentially worthless part of the territory. Apache lands now verge on a booming region of the Southwest whose rampant economic and population growth is among the highest in the country.

In little more than a lifetime, the changes in southern Arizona have been almost too extreme to comprehend. An aged Apache man who, in his youth, had scouted for the army during the times when the government still felt it necessary to hunt Apache renegades, died only a few years ago. But for hundreds of thousands of people today, Arizona's central valley means fast food chains, glass-walled office buildings, and jet noise. The Phoenix Cardinals play football in their home stadium only a few hours' drive west of San Carlos. The historic image of the Apache has become commercialized in the interim. In the sprawling expanse of south-central Arizona one can shop at an

"Apache Plaza," buy a rug at "Apache Carpets," bowl at the "Apache Lanes," and at the end of the day relax in a pool or watch color television at an "Apache Motel."

Apache people are far from oblivious to this, and some, to the extent they are able, take part in it. But out in the desert, the people of San Carlos continue to speak in Apache, observe a kinship system with ancient rules of etiquette and obligations, and interpret their experience through precepts and premises quite foreign to the surrounding population. The home of the San Carlos Apache has little in common with the "Apache Land" of fountains, sprinkled lawns, and golf greens of the Phoenix suburbs.

There is no attempt here to speak for the people of San Carlos; they are more than capable of doing that for themselves. This book is written from the perspective of one who is not a member of that community but a member of the nation state that created Indian reservations. Nor is it intended to be a detailed ethnography of San Carlos Apache culture. Keith Basso's *Cibecue Apaches* (1970) is a good, accessible work on the Western Apache community on the Fort Apache Reservation north of San Carlos, and his other works (1979, 1990) are a mine of information and insights into contemporary Western Apache society. Grenville Goodwin's classic *Social Organization of the Western Apache* (1969) remains essential reading for anyone who wishes to begin to understand something of Western Apache culture. In the future, no doubt, a member of the San Carlos community will write a study that lends far deeper insight into the life of the people than any outsider could produce.

The intention here is not to portray a cultural system at a particular moment in its history but to describe a historic process. The book is offered as an attempt to understand how the Apache have maintained their existence within the global system. It examines the ways in which the people selected strategies from their cultural repertoire and altered their patterns over several centuries in the face of shifting circumstances. The pages that follow explore some of the factors that shaped those circumstances. My greatest hope is that the book will be of interest to the people of San Carlos and in a general sense, at least, meet with their approval.

Many people deserve thanks for their help in this enterprise, but none shares any responsibility for whatever mistaken interpretations I may have developed. I offer my deepest gratitude and respect to the people of San Carlos for their patience and kindness. Faced with crushing problems, they have been victims of a ponderous system without a face—but in a sense that system has had thousands of faces, many of which look like mine. The people who took us into their lives and treated our children as their own gave me something I can never repay. The elderly woman who in 1963 asked me to call her *shiwoye*, "my grandmother," and who offered me her kind and patient instruction remains one of the most significant figures in my life. Her warm humanity offered me a place in her large joint family, and I regret that I can never repay her.

Many aspects of life on a reservation are difficult to discuss, and I have no wish to intrude on the lives of the people. Most of the information I have used regarding San Carlos is a matter of public record, gleaned from published materials, public documents, and manuscript collections that have been made available to researchers. Many of the quotes and observations amplifying this information date from almost twenty years ago, and some of the people who shared these comments are no longer alive. I have taken care to respect the anonymity of people in San Carlos who discussed these issues with me.

I am grateful to the late Marshall Durbin. I met Marshall in San Carlos when he was doing linguistic research for his doctoral dissertation, and he helped me to find a place to live with an Apache extended family. In long hours of conversation, Marshall taught me a great deal about linguistics, about the Apache, and about enthusiasm for anthropology. There are other people, too, who took the time to share information, interpretations, and insights and, as a result, enriched whatever value this book might have.

I would like to thank Mr. Buck Kitcheyan, former Chair of the San Carlos Tribal Council, for sharing some of his thoughts and concerns. I would also like to thank Mr. Marvin Mull, another former Chair of the Tribal Council, who granted me permission in 1970 to work in San Carlos and suggested some issues to pursue. Mr. Joe Sparks, former San Carlos Tribal Attorney, also was very kind, not only in suggesting issues of substance, but also in pointing out some of the pitfalls in the path of writing such a book. I hope that I have managed to avoid at least some of them. And I must express my special debt to the late Philip Cassadore, an extraordinary, kind, and wise man whose life exemplified his belief in the promotion of understanding through the sharing of views.

Dr. Alice Pomponio, Associate Professor of Anthropology, provided excellent advice on the manuscript. Thanks also to Dr. Veronica Kann, Assistant Professor of Anthropology at St. Lawrence. Dr. Donna Searles, who did extensive field work in San Carlos in the late 1980s, provided numerous points of information and insights and saved me from several errors of omission.

Ms. Jen Reisch, undergraduate assistant for the Department of History at St. Lawrence, did some valuable archival research for me. Ms.

Chris Marin, Director of the Arizona Room at Arizona State University's Hayden Library, was extremely helpful. Dr. Elizabeth Brandt, Associate Professor of Anthropology at Arizona State University, and Dr. Philip Greenfeld, Associate Professor of Anthropology at San Diego State University, both of whom have done linguistic research among the Western Apache for many years, provided assistance I greatly appreciated. Mr. Peter Steere, archivist at the University of Arizona, was extremely helpful and congenial. In writing this book, I have drawn together and tried to reconcile a range of information, some of it contradictory. None of these people should be held responsible for the conclusions I have drawn.

My doctoral field research in San Carlos was funded by National Institutes of Health fellowships 1 F01 MH43646-301A1 and 3 F01 MH43646-01A1S1 from the National Institute of Mental Health. I would also like to express my appreciation to St. Lawrence University for the Faculty Research Grants which allowed me to return to San Carlos after many years to update information and test my impressions against the realities of the present.

Apache Reservation

CHAPTER 1

The Reservation

On the section of U.S. Route 70 that runs from Safford to Globe in southeastern Arizona, a billboard proclaims the land of the San Carlos Apache. It seems natural to scan the countryside in search of something different about this area from the region back up the road. But there is not much. Rolling, sun-scalded hills mottled with brush recede toward the mountain ranges and mesas that sprawl into the distance. Probably the most significant difference is what is not there. The towns, irrigated cotton fields, and orchards that verged on the highway a few miles back are gone. This is, indeed, "Indian country."

A couple of lifetimes ago this countryside and much of the vast territory beyond it, now scattered with towns and fields, belonged to the Apache. They had not negotiated for it or bought it, nor did they ever sell it. But for centuries they maintained control over it and drew their subsistence from the game and wild plants that live in the multiple niches and zones of the region. Until the mid-nineteenth century this part of *Apachería*, as the Spanish and Mexicans referred to it, was practically unknown territory to outsiders.

Few other peoples have inspired such an exhaustive range of perceptions, from romantic fascination to hatred. Outsiders have characterized the Apache as superhuman and subhuman, crafty and innocent. Popular opinion has portrayed them as "cruel savages." Yet in the past, people they captured and adopted often chose to spend the rest of their lives with them.

The people who provoked these reactions seem as elusive to history as they were to the Spanish, Mexican, and Anglo-American adversaries who hunted them over the broken terrain of the Southwest. Some of the greatest admiration and respect for the Apache appears in the writings of military people who fought them. Some of the most vitriolic hatred spewed from people who contested them for their resources. U.S. Route 70 bisects land that once was the domain of a few

Desert terrain on the San Carlos Reservation

thousand people whose impact on history and popular thought in Europe and America is astonishing in proportion to their numbers.

The road continues westward toward Globe and passes the hamlet of small houses at Bylas, an Apache community. Twenty-some miles down the highway, Apache houses built through government programs sprinkle the hillsides. A turnoff leads north into a vast range of hills and mesas toward the reservation hamlets of Peridot and San Carlos, out of sight a few miles away.

Route 70 continues westward toward Globe, a community of almost seven thousand with modern supermarkets and the wide main street of an old western town. The venerable Old Dominion Hotel, which Pancho Villa shot up in a raid north of the border in less settled times, accidentally burned down a few years ago. Globe, a mining town with a predominantly Anglo-American population and many people of Mexican descent, serves as a major buying center for people from the San Carlos Reservation.

Twenty miles east among the mesas, San Carlos looks peaceful in the afternoon. Clusters of small frame houses and a few old-fashioned dome-shaped, brush-covered dwellings dot the hillsides.

The earth between them is packed bare and dusty from the tread of daily activity. Dogs who spend their lives outdoors doze in the shade, and here and there, women work quietly under flat-roofed *ramadas*. Washing machines stand outside a few of the houses. Many of the houses have no plumbing, and in some, corrugated cardboard nailed to the inside walls provides meager insulation against the extremes of cold and heat.

Across the sandy, flat bed of a dry wash, the beige buildings of government agencies stand out with sharp edges in the Arizona sun. The offices of the Bureau of Indian Affairs, the Tribal Council, and the tribal store form a community core with sandstone permanence. The jail and Public Health Service hospital stand nearby, just out of sight.

The great-grandchildren of some of the most fiercely independent people in the history of the world—the few thousand Apache who dominated an area about the size of France and raided at will over a far greater region—now live at San Carlos, Peridot, Seven Mile Wash, and Bylas. After more than three centuries of sovereignty in the Southwest where they hunted, grew their gardens, and lived in small camps in their strongholds in the mountains, they finally lost control over that vast region and relinquished possession of most of their territory. A wider global political and economic system immersed them at last and drew them in. Today most of the people known as Apache live on reservations in Arizona and New Mexico. San Carlos is one of the oldest and largest of these.

An "Indian reservation" is a strange phenomenon. In many ways it is much like other communities. Usually there is at least one population center where government offices cluster with small businesses and, perhaps, a medical facility. The military restrictions of the past ended long ago, and people can come and go as they choose. The inhabitants are citizens by law, and theoretically they have most of the legal rights of other citizens.* Most people on reservations speak

*The extent to which the Constitution applies to Native American communities has been a matter of some ambiguity. As Charles Wilkinson points out: "Indian tribes are part of the constitutional structure of government. Tribal authority was not created by the Constitution—tribal sovereignty predated the formation of the United States and continued after it—but tribes were acknowledged by the Constitution in the reaffirmation of previously negotiated treaties (most of which were with Indian tribes), the two references to 'Indians not taxed,' and the Indian Commerce Clause" (*American Indians, Time, and the Law*, p. 103). This has come to mean that the internal workings of Native American groups do not automatically fall under the purview of the Constitution, but they can be addressed through Congressional legislation.

English, although not necessarily as a first language, and the mass media continuously expose them to American popular culture. Even in the early 1960s, television antennas towered over many Apache homes, and Apache children were acquainted with the same television characters as children in Chicago, the Bronx, Los Angeles, and Akron.

In other ways, though, a reservation is different from other communities. For one thing, its population is legally defined on an ethnic basis. This is a consequence of the historic process that led to the designation of reserved areas for Native American populations who had become incorporated by the state. The right to be a member of such a community is defined on the basis of "tribal" (or, for practical purposes, genealogical) relationships. Associated with that right, on most reservations, is access to communally held resources such as a place to live and perhaps the use of farming land.

In many reservations the structure of local government and even the concepts of community and tribe are products of incorporation within the state. This is true of San Carlos. And in many cases, the processes of daily existence involve contradictions and compromises between the formal structure and older modes of living.

Population Enclaves: The Concept of Reservations

The idea of reserved areas for indigenous populations within a nation state—usually groups who have been defeated through force or who have submitted under the threat of force—is not unique to the United States. The problem of what to do with surviving aboriginal peoples is common to most states associated with invading populations.

The incorporation of indigenous peoples into the state often is a lengthy process and has often stopped short of completion. Many factors have tended to inhibit it. Not the least of these is that groups already holding power within the state may work to exclude indigenous peoples. Perhaps more commonly, less powerful interests may perceive threats to their own tenuous position from indigenous populations who might compete with them. In many cases, indigenous peoples themselves have resisted such incorporation. The result has often been the creation of enclaves that lie within the state's hegemony but that are not wholly a part of the state itself.

The English in the seventeenth century set up reserves for Celtic tribes on the Scottish and Irish borderlands (Bolt 1987:29). Late in the eighteenth century the Spanish in northern Mexico set up "peace establishments" for the Apache (Griffen 1988:3–5). The Spanish state never succeeded in extending hegemony over the region, and although the Apache were somewhat receptive, they saw no sufficient reason to comply with the program for very long. The Spanish eventually abandoned that policy.

In the past century the idea of the "Indian reservation" has become familiar to most Americans. But like many commonplace ideas, its familiarity masks profound contradictions. In some cases, particularly in the East during the early years of the American nation state, Native American groups negotiated for reserved territories from a position of relative strength.

Government documents during that period generally referred to Native American populations as "nations." Subsequent shifts in the balance of power often led to renegotiation, generally to the detriment of the weaker party. In the early nineteenth century, as the United States became increasingly self-conscious of its own nationhood, government documents more often referred to Native Americans as "tribes"—a diminutive of "nation" in some respects and a reflection of the changing relationship.

In the era when Americans were most intensely pursuing the "winning of the West," many voices objected to the establishment of reserved areas for indigenous peoples. Some argued for their annihilation and, at times, attempted to implement such a policy themselves. In 1864 the Arizona Territorial Legislature unanimously adopted a resolution advocating the killing of all Apache. This measure had some precedent in the Southwest, where earlier in that century the Mexican governments of Sonora and Chihuahua had offered bounties for Apache scalps, with varying payments for men, women, and children. In 1862, the American General James Carleton set a "no prisoners" Indian policy in New Mexico Territory, which at the time included what is now Arizona. Even later in that century after reservations had been established, Arizona vigilantes mounted occasional attacks on Apache communities. General Philip Henry Sheridan's remark at Fort Cobb, Indian Territory, in 1869—"The only good Indian I ever saw was a dead Indian"—reflected more than an isolated opinion.

This raises inevitable questions. Why did the process of annihilation stop? Why did proponents of genocide manage to see their policies pursued at certain times but fail at others? Why, after the bloody history of conflict set in motion by the European invasion of North America, are there reservations at all? We cannot disregard humane concerns for Native Americans that played a role throughout this process, but American history offers little evidence that such sympathy governed relationships between Euro-Americans and indigenous peoples with any consistency. The extent to which native peoples were perceived as a threat must also have been a factor, but this does not account for all cases. American history is filled with attacks on peaceful Native American populations.

To approach the issue as a tale of bad people harming other people may have some validity, especially in particular instances, but this does not take us very far. Throughout the nineteenth century and other periods, a varied assortment of scoundrels and humanitarians has always been available. Why have certain voices succeeded in influencing policy on particular occasions?

To address this problem, we might start by examining some of the overt rationales for reservation policies in the United States. In the nineteenth century, some advocates of the reservation concept presented it as a means of protecting indigenous peoples who had lost their land base and been weakened through war and disease. In this view, the state should help these people develop the capacity to survive on their own, particularly through economic enterprise. By now, though, it has become clear that the reservation system has not usually led to economic viability. After generations of government supervision, most reservations are burdened by staggering poverty and lacerated by the social problems that poverty engenders.

Other early proponents of the reservation concept assumed that in the wake of frontier expansion, Native American populations would soon die off. A popular theme at the time, often expressed in literature, was the sad but inevitable end to a "noble race." From that perspective, reservations were to be refuges where hapless and somewhat anachronistic populations could live out their last days in peace (see Sumner 1906). Once again, though, history has invalidated that perception, and most reservation populations have expanded far beyond their numbers at the turn of the century (see Snipp 1989:64).

A more sanguine view assumed that if Native Americans survived, the reservations would be a temporary expedient until their populations blended into the wider society (see Hoxie 1984). Government and church programs attempted to hasten this process through such measures as removing children from their families and sending them to distant boarding schools. Yet after generations of coercion intended to wean Native Americans from "traditional ways," many Native Americans' sense of cultural identity seems at least as strong as ever. Indeed, some of the most outspoken proponents of Native American sovereignty are people who have gone through such programs or who have been separated from reservation communities most of their lives.

Contradictory Aspects of the Reservation Concept

When all of this is taken into account, the Indian reservation in the United States presents a range of anomalies and contradictions. Supposedly the reservation was a refuge for dying peoples, but their populations increased. The reservation was supposed to be a means of assimilating indigenous peoples into the wider society, but Native Americans' consciousness of ethnic distinctness seems at least as acute as ever. The reservation was rationalized as a measure to protect Native American peoples from exploitation, but it became a device for the chronic and systematic divestment of their resources. It was touted as a means of promoting economic development, but reservations today are pockets of some of the most extreme poverty in North America. Reservations were part of the process of bringing Native Americans into the wider society as self-sufficient citizens, but their structure inhibited the people's capacity to exert control over their own affairs.

Is it possible to make any sense of these contradictory aspects? The disparity between the ideals and realities of reservations is enormous. What is a reservation really all about?

The reservation model has altered a great deal through this historic period. Reservation policies have evolved from treating Native Americans as prisoners of war to dealing with them as semi-independent communities. Periodically, state and federal legislators have sought to abolish reservations altogether—a move that Native American peoples have bitterly opposed. And the histories of different reservations vary in significant ways. Throughout this process the reservation has been the primary point of articulation between Native American populations and the nation state. Reservation policies, and the form the reservation has taken in various cases, reveal much about that relationship.

We could approach these issues at a number of different levels. We might begin by examining some of the pertinent aspects of nation states and the processes that affect their relationships with indigenous peoples. Ultimately, any historical process is a result of myriad individual choices and actions. But persons make these choices within the context of existing situations that entail their own ground rules. Individuals exercise options within the constraints of the possibilities they perceive and the consequences they anticipate. People often make choices in competition with other actors in the arena. Before examining the reservation system at close focus, therefore, it will be useful to step back and consider some of the larger, more impersonal, or collective, dynamics that have framed such choices and actions.

Reservations, Nations, and States

In conventional understanding a state incorporates a large, often heterogeneous population with a governmental structure of some sort. But a state involves more than the formal apparatus of government. It is an intersection of institutions and interest groups which often are not formally a part of the government itself but whose concerns and pressures affect government policies (see Poulantzas 1980).

At various historical moments, Euro-American states have embraced such interest groups as "the church," "plantation interests," "the Crown," "mining interests," "big business," "the military," and many others. Critical journalists often decry the ways in which powerful lobbies influence the actions of the state, as if this were illegitimate. In one sense it is. The legitimacy of the state rests on the myth of its independence from such interests. In another sense, however, the state does not exist over and above such interest groups; it exists in the tensions among them. A state may advance the interests of one group or another, but the state is not identical with any one of them in particular. It is such a ponderous, multifaceted, complex phenomenon that confronted the Apache and other Native American peoples.

This conjunction of forces, pressures, influences, and constraints may override the will of particular individuals or populations. Interest groups may promote certain government policies, but such interests must operate within preexisting conditions. Persons might occupy pivotal positions that allow them to tip the balance in favor of one course of action over another, but the key players are not the most salient factors in understanding the historical process. A more fundamental issue is the process by which these persons, interesting as they may be, came to occupy such roles.

The concept of nation is somewhat different from that of the state. In the words of Benedict Anderson (1983), we might consider a nation to be an "imagined community" in the sense that the population perceive among themselves a common essence of some sort. As Anderson points out, in many parts of the world this phenomenon has been associated with the spread of printed literature in the vernacular which promotes a sense of shared referents and identity.

Clearly, a state can exist without such a sense of common identity among the populace, while a population can possess a sense of nation without having an independent state. The contemporary world is full of examples of "separatist nationalism" among ethnic populations who seek independence from the hegemony of existing state systems and who specifically lack a state conforming to their sense of nation (see Hobsbawm 1989:121).

The idea of nation, in the sense of nationalism, is a relatively recent historical development, and in most cases it seems to have arisen in one of two ways. State power holders have sometimes endeavored to promote a sense of commonality over a population as a means of strengthening hegemony. Alternatively, populations within a state have developed this sense of collective identity to resist state hegemony, often in hopes of creating a state of their own (Anderson 1983).

The concepts of state and nation, in that sense, have tended to be associated, but although they may be combined, they are not coterminous. In the United States and elsewhere, the state's hegemony engulfs many diverse populations, but the predominant power is held by a population which accepts the proposition of collective identity.

From these perspectives, such populations as the prereservation Apache were neither nations nor states. They were not states because they were not internally differentiated in a socioeconomic sense with competing interest groups and they had no overarching governmental structure. As Morton Fried puts it, "In some definitions, such as those contributing to or inspired by Marxist theory, the state coincides with all societies composed of two or more classes involved in relations of dominance and subordination, primarily in the sphere of economics, but also in other sectors of social life" (1968:144). Nikos Poulantzas, in the same vein, observes that "whenever there is class division and thus class struggle and power, the state already exists as an institutionalized political power" (1980:39).

The Apache had an egalitarian social organization with no all-embracing political mechanisms to subsume local aggregates of people. They occupied a vast region and shared common language, perceptions, and social understandings, but they were not a nation because the local clusters of people were all but independent of one another. Social cohesion resided in networks of individual kin ties but did not involve any operational sense of group identity or corporate political boundaries. Ironically, perhaps, the extent to which the Apache more recently have begun to coalesce into interest groups may stem from their collective resistance to the encroaching state.

In other parts of North America indigenous groups did show many of the attributes of states. Eventually even these were overcome in the extension of Euro-American state hegemony, usually through violence. Nation states have tended to extend their hegemony through the extension of economic control, often through outright territorial claims involving the expression of power through violence. The process requires a state either to eliminate the indigenous inhabitants or incorporate them.

For hegemony to be realized, indigenous populations must be prevented from acting effectively as sovereign groups with full control over their own resources. Instead, they become interest groups within the state. Although they may retain some capacity to act as interest groups after having been incorporated within the state, they are unlikely to compete successfully with more powerful, entrenched constituencies within the same arena.

Antonio Gramsci underscores the necessity of consent for the full extension of state hegemony (1971). This may have been significant at a later phase of Native American existence within the state, but it seems less applicable to the earlier period which involved the exertion of power to achieve their incorporation. To the extent that consent occurred, it resulted historically from violent coercion.

The state, on behalf of its more powerful constituents, is likely to confiscate resources held and controlled by aboriginal populations. Sometimes states have separated the people from their former resource base by relocating them to a different, reserved territory of little apparent value. In other cases the state has achieved this without removal, merely by taking over control of the disposition of local resources. Usually the rationale for such policies has been the alleged need to administer such resources on the behalf of the indigenous people.

In the American case, one result of this has been the systematic expropriation of resources on most reservations. When reservation lands have contained copper, coal, water, oil, grazing land, uranium, or other valuable commodities, outside interests have extracted them with the assistance or acquiescence of the government. Usually this has accrued little benefit to the indigenous population, and generally it has transpired without the possibility of their exerting control over the use of their holdings.

As in other parts of the world, the state has promoted the establishment of local reservation governance structures which, in many cases, have legitimized the extraction of resources while creating the appearance of indigenous consent. Much of the political conflict on reservations today has to do with questions of tribal governments' valid representation of the will of the population.

In a few parts of the world, invading populations have abbreviated this process by annihilating aboriginal peoples. Europeans on horseback hunted native peoples in Tasmania for sport (see Davies 1973; Travis 1968; Roth 1890). But an indigenous population can also disappear as a collective entity if its individuals are assimilated into the broader population of the state. In either event, the original inhabitants' resources become accessible to other interests.

On the face of it, assimilation implies equal participation within the state. But assimilation neutralizes the capacity of indigenous peoples to operate effectively as interest groups in competition with other constituencies to influence state policy. If an indigenous population dissolves as a collectivity and becomes a mere scattering of individuals, or "citizens," rather than a group with its own special interests, the peoples' impact on the actions of the state is bound to dissipate.

After a population has been incorporated into a state, long-term measures to promote assimilation usually continue in the attempt to individualize the population. But assimilation programs usually afford only restricted access to the larger system, generally at the level of minimally paid labor. For this reason, such programs may actually inhibit tendencies for populations to assimilate because they relegate access to the system to the most powerless levels. Racial or ethnic discrimination in its various forms often plays a role in this restriction.

Michael Burawoy notes that racism often involves "a particular mode of reproduction of labor power and . . . 'powerlessness' is not so much the defining as a necessary condition for racism" (1983: 1083). In the United States, employment training on reservations normally emphasizes manual labor rather than education leading to professional, high-status positions that might provide easier access to power within the state.

As a result of these factors, reservation populations often remain in a situation of chronic impoverishment after being deprived of their former means of subsistence. This creates and maintains their need to take employment whenever the opportunity arises. They find themselves dependent upon a market economy with no commodities at their disposal but their own labor and with little leverage to bargain for its price. They become a surplus pool of labor. They might be called upon for the occasional needs of employers, or they may simply be kept in reserve, perpetually underemployed, as a threat by which employers can exert leverage on existing labor.

Some Comparative Cases: Australia, South Africa, and Canada

The history of the Australian reserve system exemplifies a number of these phenomena. Aboriginal populations were driven from large tracts of territory with the expansion of the sheep industry, and for a time they were used as labor on ranches (Elkin 1951). The Australian reserve system expressed and reinforced a social distinction between aboriginal and Euro-Australians. Native Australians were inhibited from either assimilating at higher levels of the social order or fully providing for their own needs with access to their former territories. As a consequence, the labor of indigenous peoples tended to be relegated to the marginal and least-rewarding sectors of employment or to be left unutilized altogether.

When Australia became independent in 1901, the British government made no provisions for federal oversight of Aboriginal affairs, leaving policies to the various states. This was maintained by the Australian Commonwealth Constitution of January 1, 1901. As G. Sawer, an authority on the Australian constitution, notes, "It was widely thought that the Aborigines were a dying race whose future was unimportant" (quoted in Morse 1984:22).

The Australian situation has evolved considerably since that time. The Constitution Alteration (Aboriginals) Bill of March 1, 1967, transferred more authority over Aboriginal affairs to the federal government, and since that time further legislation has been passed to restore land to indigenous peoples and recognize Aboriginal customary law. The full effect of these changes remains to be seen, however.

A *New York Times* article on January 26, 1988, reported on celebrations marking Australia's two-hundredth anniversary: "The past two centuries have been a period of annihilation, dispossession and now poverty for the aborigines, who today number perhaps 160,000, only about half of their population before the advent of white settlers . . . Today they are outcasts in their own land, living on reservations or in urban slums, suffering an infant mortality rate three times the national norm and earning half the average national wage of $310 a week . . . Prime Minister Bob Hawke has offered to sign a treaty acknowledging 'grave injustices' against the nation's indigenous people. His Government, in a mostly symbolic gesture, has returned some of their lands, including Ayers Rock, a giant monolith in the center of the outback that is sacred to the aborigines."

In South Africa, designated black polities within the nation state provide labor in mines and other industries that support the economic structure of the state system. Michael Burawoy comments that "the ghetto, like the Bantustan and the Mexican town or village, is a definitely located institution whose function for the capitalist economy is the allocation of the renewal [of labor] process to areas where renewal costs are low" (1983:1083). Cultural distinctness, racial laws, and the purported independence of the Bantustans, or "homelands," serve to rationalize the exclusion of these large indigenous populations from access to the resources controlled by the white minority. In this case, the ability of indigenous populations to exert effective pressure on state policy has dissipated further through violent conflict among themselves, often covertly encouraged and even instigated by more powerful interests.

In Canada, where vast territories remain inhabited almost solely by native peoples, many indigenous populations were articulated to the wider economic system centuries ago through the fur trade. In this case, for native peoples to retain possession of their territories and provide furs for the market was to the advantage of the most powerful economic interests within the state (see Tanner 1979). Although the invading population failed or declined to occupy much of the Yukon, Northwest Territories, or even much of northern Ontario and Quebec, the extension of economic hegemony began early through trade for the international market in beaver furs.

The nature of this relationship tended to avert direct violent conflict of a sort that has characterized conquest in other parts of the world. Nonetheless, where direct competition for local resources did occur, as in the prairie provinces or on the Pacific Coast, aboriginal populations became enclaves on designated reserves through processes similar to those that occurred in the United States.

In the prairie provinces of Canada and elsewhere, there was some amalgamation of native and Euro-Canadian populations, particularly Cree and French. But rather than bringing about an assimilation of the native population into the wider sphere and thus effecting their disappearance, this process gave rise to yet another distinct population known as Métis ("Mixed"). A local minority, they came to occupy a role within the state similar in many ways to that of indigenous peoples.

The Canadian state has tended to circumvent the issue of native control of resources by consistently refusing to recognize aboriginal prior ownership of lands, with a few notable exceptions. The government has restricted its recognition of claims to the principle of prior use, for the loss of which the state might choose to pay compensation, as a courtesy.

The Canadian state has continued to adopt an ambiguous posture regarding the sovereignty of native peoples, possibly because until recently the competition for resources has not been particularly intense, except in a few regions. The Canadian state has recognized the distinct status of indigenous peoples with whom it has treaty agreements. Those who have not signed formal treaties or otherwise been formally acknowledged—perhaps an equivalent number—are not officially recognized as native peoples. Hence, even though they might retain distinctive languages and cultures, they do not exist legally as

"Indians" and have no formal claim to resources as such. As for those "status Indians" who *do* have rights to the use of reserve land and other resources, the Canadian state has employed various means of promoting assimilation which would cause them to disappear into the national milieu. Prime Minister Pierre Trudeau underscored this aim in his White Paper of 1969, asserting the equality of all Canadians within the nation state regardless of ethnic identity. In the past, measures to promote assimilation in Canada have included laws extinguishing the native status of women who married nonstatus persons (whether these persons happened to be indigenous or not), cash incentives for relinquishing status, and the exclusion of status Indians from voting (Asch 1984).

By the 1970s, state hegemony in some regions of Canada began to change character. The Cree of northern Quebec had retained possession of their vast territory since the early days of the fur trade and had interacted with the wider sphere mainly through a few trading posts. In the 1970s, however, energy interests in the south perceived Cree territory as a source of hydroelectric power. This led to the James Bay project, the largest hydroelectric project in the world, which flooded thousands of square kilometers of hunting territory to produce electric power for metropolitan areas in Canada and the northeastern United States. The Province of Quebec contracted with New York State for the sale of much of this resource.

In the process, the Cree collectively found themselves in the role of an interest group within the state. They created the Grand Council of the Cree to represent the scattered bands. The ensuing treaty, a product of long negotiation, set aside designated areas for the exclusive use of the indigenous peoples and provided for various forms of compensation, including cash payments. The James Bay Cree remain in northern Quebec, albeit on diminished territory, but before the episode ended, they had become an indigenous enclave within the hegemony of the state in direct competition with other constituencies for the disposition of their resources. As of spring 1992, negotiations were underway for the major expansion of the James Bay project.

As in Australia, the situation for indigenous peoples is rapidly evolving. On December 16, 1991, the Canadian government announced that the Inuit population would be granted political domain over 770,000 square miles of land in the Northwest Territories. The region is to be known as Nunavut, "Our Land," and some government representatives have suggested that it might eventually become a province. According to the *New York Times* of December 17, 1991, John Amagoalik, principal negotiator for the Tungavik Federation of Nunavut, stated that "we have been saying for 20 or 30 years now that the Inuit really wanted to become full Canadian citizens, and the granting of self-government and the recognition of our rights in the north will result in that."

This appears to be a major reversal of previous Canadian policies, although as of this writing, the details remain to be worked out. The agreement gives indigenous people mineral rights to only fourteen thousand square miles. The mineral disposition for the rest of the 770,000 square miles will rest with the government, with royalty payments to the Inuit. The *New York Times* adds: "Another group that has taken a keen interest in the negotiations has been Canada's resource companies, many of them United States–owned. For them, development may have been eased by the Eskimo's acceptance of a principle that Ottawa calls 'extinguishment,' meaning the surrender of the claim some native leaders have made to all land, water, and resources in their regions." Nonetheless, the agreement seems to represent a major recognition of aboriginal rights, while at the same time defining their limits.

Whether or not native peoples of Canada, or "First Nations," as many choose to refer to themselves, are formally acknowledged in the future, they are likely to remain firmly within the hegemony of the state, and they will find themselves in competition with powerful interest groups within the same arena.

Reservations and the American State

In the early years of reservations in the American West, the military, missionaries, and civilian officials competed for authority over the local populations. Erratic policies, inefficient administration, and corrupt officials are such standard aspects of the history of most reservations that they have become clichés. As we shall see in later chapters, the history of San Carlos is one example.

Aside from the vagaries and fortunes of particular administrations, the most consistent aspect of a federal "Indian reservation" is that it is administered from outside. In most important ways, a reservation is supervised by agents of constituencies external to the community rather than by the inhabitants. It differs from other communities in this fundamental way.

How is it controlled? If people on a reservation are free to come and go as they choose, in what sense is control exercised?

For one thing, many decisions affecting the local population are made by representatives of the federal government or subject to their veto. While in a sense the reservation "belongs" to the Native American populace—they have certain exclusive legal rights with regard to it—they do not have full sovereignty. If by "own" we mean the right to use and dispose of something, the government, in a de facto sense, is at least a joint owner of reservations.

The limited sovereignty of Native American communities was affirmed in Supreme Court Justice John Marshall's series of "Cherokee Nation" decisions in the early nineteenth century (see Deloria and Lytle 1983:27–33; Wilkinson 1987). The Non-Intercourse Acts of 1790 had already established that the inhabitants of a reservation cannot sell its parts or resources without government supervision. When such transactions do occur, the government generally oversees the disposition of the proceeds. In many cases the inhabitants of reservations have been unable to prevent the government from presiding over sales of land and expropriation of other resources. All of this has had profound implications for the lives of people who live on reservations.

The federal government, in its capacity as administrator of reservations and overseer of resources, has negotiated agreements with outside firms on behalf of Native American populations for the sale or lease of water rights, grazing land, coal, oil, timber, uranium, and a range of other commodities (see Jorgensen 1978, 1984). Yet the government—and more specifically, the Department of Interior—does not merely represent Native American populations. The Department of Interior includes the Bureau of Mines, the General Survey, and the National Park Service as well as the Bureau of Indian Affairs. These divisions with their many agencies respond to an array of constituencies and interests. Some of them are conflicting, and many of them are capable of exerting powerful influences on policy. This is partly because the federal agencies are funded by Congress, which in turn responds to a still broader spectrum of concerns. Within this competitive arena a reservation community of a few thousand indigenous people may not command primary consideration.

As executor for native peoples, the federal government has negotiated for them in such matters as royalty payments for mineral extraction, and often this process has not brought the most lucrative possible returns for reservation populations. Mineral royalties have been set at rates far below market value and contracted in ninety-nine-year nonadjustable leases. And meager as the returns may be, the government often holds them in trust, which means that the money may be released in increments on the basis of criteria that seem appropriate to the persons who happen to represent the government in that capacity at the time.

By the usual standards, most reservation communities are impoverished. C. Matthew Snipp notes that, on fifteen of the sixteen largest reservations, "from one third to over one half of all Indian families residing on these reservations had incomes below the official poverty line" (1989:259). In half of all reservations in 1979, 43 percent of families with children had incomes below the poverty level (Plantz and Stinson 1987:27). Whatever conventional criteria one chooses to apply—per capita income, household income, unemployment figures, property ownership—Native American communities on western reservations are at the bottom of the scale. Most are located in areas where few local employment opportunities exist. Even if this were not the case, people who have grown up on reservations are likely to be ill-prepared to compete successfully for good jobs. Hence, their access to independent sources of personal income is minimal.

If the tragedies of individual poverty are vivid, the collective consequences of poverty among the populace are staggering. In the rates of infant mortality, average life span, alcoholism, violent crime, suicide, and a range of diseases commonly associated with being poor, reservation communities lie toward the most appalling reaches of the spectrum.

As custodian of reservation communities, the government has provided health care, agricultural advice, and schools. It has also attempted to alter indigenous cultural patterns, taken children away from their parents, and sent elderly people away from their communities to "rest homes" in cities. Although many individuals in government service have spent their careers in the attempt to alleviate the severe problems of reservation communities, Native Americans have not thrived under government supervision.

The San Carlos Case

The people of San Carlos face many of the problems that afflict other Native American populations, and in San Carlos some of these are especially severe. E. E. Dale, writing of San Carlos in 1947, reported that "the health situation is, on the whole, discouraging" (Dale 1949:243). While some serious problems of the 1940s such as tuberculosis have lessened somewhat, others have continued or even become more severe.

Most people in San Carlos have inadequate income. Unemployment estimates over the past three decades have hovered between 50 percent and 80 percent. And in a peculiar way, San Carlos is a violent community. The homicide rate is far above the national average, and this violence seems strangely self-directed. Rarely are outsiders the victims of attack. More often the victim is a close relative or a spouse. Michael Everett refers to homicide on the nearby Fort

Apache Reservation as "the most persistent of all aboriginal patholo-
gies" (1980:167). This impression of internally focused violence in
San Carlos is further borne out by the suicide rate, which is tragically
high—especially among teenagers. In 1953 and 1954, San Carlos
Apache tribal convictions for all crimes were almost ten times the
national average and one fourth higher than the average for all Native
American populations (Stewart 1964).

Yet San Carlos is not merely an anarchistic aggregate of despon-
dent people living amid the remnants of a shattered heritage. Their
networks of kinship still provide meaning and support. Apache is
spoken throughout the community and remains a preferred language
for most. Ancient concepts and perceptions of reality still color life in
San Carlos. And the people season their lives with humor. They
laugh often and easily in the face of material problems that would
cause many in the wider society to sink in despair. Mired in troubles,
San Carlos is a place of vitality and deep strength, resilient human
spirit, and pride. It is also a place of anger.

The Apache Background

The people of San Carlos, with those of the Fort Apache Reservation
adjoining them to the north, often are referred to as Western Apache.
They speak dialects of a language included within the Athapaskan
phylum, which is one of the most widespread language groupings in
North America. Linguistic evidence indicates that the Apache share
an ancient common past with other Athapaskan speakers in the
mountains of Alaska, the Yukon, British Columbia, and the barren
grounds of the Northwest Territories of Canada. They are also linked
to small populations on the coast of Oregon and northern California
(see Krauss 1973, 1979).

The Western Apache were associated more recently with other
Apache groups of the Southwest and the Plains: the Jicarilla, Lipan,
Mescalero, Chiricahua, Navajo, and Kiowa Apache. Many of these
peoples have continued to share features of their common heritage.
This past has colored their present and continues to be a part of their
reality.

This ancient heritage had a significant effect on the ways Apache
populations adapted to the circumstances in which they found themselves. For the most part, the strategies they developed and the options they chose were not inevitable or dictated solely by the environment but were consistent with preexisting perceptions and patterns.
The San Carlos Reservation community is a product of intricate com-
binations, clashes, and reverberations among all of these factors.

Map 1. Distribution of Athapaskan and Eyak populations

When the Apache came into the Southwest, they encountered other indigenous peoples with ancient and unique histories of their own who had developed finely tuned adaptations to the region. Some of these were village agriculturalists with elaborate political and ceremonial systems who had established themselves on the land over a thousand years before. Apache interactions among these peoples, the arrival of still others, and the ways in which they all dealt with one another constitute immensely complex phenomena. To fathom the processes that led to the modern reservation community, it will be necessary to understand something about these events.

Our approach to the San Carlos community takes into account the deep cultural background of the Western Apache, including what is known of the prehistoric phase in the Subarctic. This ancient "Proto-Athapaskan" setting gave rise to the fundamental strategies of hunting peoples in a sparse mountain environment—the free, unimpeded movement of small groups, a value on individual independence, concepts of a capricious and unpredictable universe, and other widely shared Athapaskan features.

Later chapters discuss the Apache migration into the Southwest and the changes that occurred through the periods of Spanish, Mexican, and Anglo-American presence, with attention both to the culture of the Apache and the circumstances they confronted in successive eras. The establishment of the reservation, the evolution of its administration and policies, and the structure of relationships between the Apache and the wider society are essential facets of Apache reality, reverberating with the dynamics of Apache culture throughout the process.

The complexity of these historic processes is daunting. How can we best approach it? Often the answers we find have a good deal to do with the questions we ask. What questions should we ask about San Carlos?

Approaches to Considering the Western Apache Case

We could apply a range of theoretical perspectives to the San Carlos Apache case. Each has its assets and liabilities. To what extent can any of them help us make sense of the situation?

To begin, it will be useful to sort out an array of possible considerations and approaches. If we hope to develop any reasonable understanding of the San Carlos situation, for example, we must consider Apache culture.

Anthropologists and others have used the term "culture" in many ways. Some have treated it as if it were an entity with a life of its own.

Some—particularly when the topic has been Native Americans—have tended to imagine "traditional culture" as something stable and coherent, a pristine way of life that was intact before European contact but was damaged or even destroyed in subsequent times.

But to reify culture as a coherent phenomenon with its own dynamics and trajectory removes us too far from ground level where human experience is played out. We might better conceive of culture as a reference to the orientations, perspectives, patterns of shared behavior, and interpretations of reality that characterize people and flow through their lives as a result of a collective common experience. Language is a part of culture. So are etiquette, concepts of propriety, beliefs about what foods are good to eat or disgusting, and a sense of the way human relationships are structured.

Culture in this sense is not particularly stable, nor is it a matter of absolute consensus among members of a population. The knowledge and perceptions that constitute culture are distributed unevenly, even in a small society (see Keesing 1987). Although generation after generation might perpetuate these ideas and ways of behaving from an ancient past into the future, they are not fixed or stable. The concept of culture refers to a summary of what individuals do and think.

Since people at any time can decide to do things differently and are liable to change their beliefs and revise their interpretations of events, culture is inherently volatile. On the other hand, people in any population tend to do things just about the same way they have done them before. And generally they do things the way others do them, perhaps because that is the "normal" way, or because it is the "right" way, or because it seems to work. We tend to see things the way we have learned to see them and to share with our associates a general understanding of reality. Thus, although culture is intrinsically changeable, it tends to be fairly consistent within a population through time and space.

People with different cultural backgrounds may very well see events differently, value different things, have vastly different convictions about the ideal nature of human interaction, disagree about whether grasshoppers, dogs, or fish are good to eat, and vary in their opinions of how the universe works. These concepts and ideas affect the choices people make and the ways in which they are likely to react to events or to cope with situations.

We might choose to focus on Apache culture as the sole unit of analysis. This would give full attention to the people whose situation is, after all, what we are trying to understand. But although an examination of Apache culture is crucial, it is not enough. To focus on the culture alone, as if it were an isolate, affords little attention to the systemic interrelationships between the Apache population and surrounding peoples. A perspective emphasizing collective patterns also might lead us to overlook the strategies and choices individuals have made in response to particular events—choices that had significant repercussions on their fortunes.

We also need to understand something about the conditions and constraints arising from factors outside the Apache sphere of control. In some respects the Western Apache have responded to situations in the way almost anyone would have. In that respect, we could say that the *circumstances* of the Apache situation are significant, and perhaps even primary, considerations in understanding what has happened to them. Many aspects of Apache circumstances, though, cannot be understood without taking the culture itself into account. Apache responses, choices, and initiatives have been informed by their own perceptions of reality. Often, these actions have not been the same as one could have expected of people whose culture is different. External relationships, the distribution of power, the issue of hegemony, and strategies adopted with regard to other groups are especially important in trying to understand the Apache experience in the historic period.

The concept of "underdevelopment" is one way of viewing cases in which ethnically or culturally distinct populations are beset by serious economic problems. "Modernization" is a complementary term associated with the same perspective. A central aspect of the concept of underdevelopment is that the community in question has not succeeded in developing adequate or effective economic institutions.

Theoretical perspectives are grounded in certain assumptions about reality, whether explicit or not. The idea of underdevelopment entails an inherently evolutionary model with teleological implications. A state of *under*development implies the expectation of a subsequent and superior state of *development*. The teleology here involves a movement from "less so" to "more so" on a scale that, in practice, usually idealizes capitalist principles. It suggests a single direction of desirable change which may or may not be appropriate in particular cases.

This also tends to be true of "modernization," which refers to a desirable state toward which nonmodern or less-than-modern "traditional," or "primitive," societies presumably should aspire. From the perspective of modernization, there is a tendency to lump the diverse social systems of the world into the alternative categories of "modern" and "traditional," or "premodern," perhaps subdividing the latter into "Third World," "Fourth World," and so on. The specific cultures of populations outside the "modern" category may receive little attention, except insofar as they are likely to promote or inhibit change toward modernization (see for example McClelland and Winter 1969).

Underdevelopment or modernization models may lend themselves well to quantitative measures of social characteristics, particularly economic data. This framework is less useful, though, in accommodating other less accountable aspects of the quality of life in diverse social systems. It also tends to underplay historic processes because of implicit assumptions that development proceeds from a stable traditional base.

In practice such models also tend to have an ethnocentric bias. Certain characteristics of industrialized capitalist societies, such as the nuclear family, often have been treated as signifiers of modernness. The converse implication is that alternative forms, such as extended families, are signs of backwardness. Such "traditional" features as indigenous kinship systems or local ceremonial practices come to exemplify premodern stages and thus appear as problems to overcome in bringing about change for the better. Policies based on such views, when implemented, have generated considerable disruption and resistance among "target populations" (see Bodley 1982, 1983).

Probably we could reach a consensus that certain phenomena are undesirable and define them as problems. Severe poverty, insufficient nutrition, and high mortality rates create misery. Underdevelopment models generally attribute these problems to inadequacies of the indigenous social systems and assume their incapacity to meet essential human needs.

When we consider that the ancestors of the Western Apache survived difficult circumstances for millennia before the reservation period and held out tenaciously under the onslaught of invading armies for over three centuries, we might question assertions about the inadequacy of their traditional social organization. The available evidence suggests that, if anything, the prereservation Apache population were healthier, better fed, and lived longer than their descendants do today. Clearly something else is involved here other than inherent capacities of the indigenous system to meet human needs. The issue seems more precisely to be the capacity of indigenous systems to operate effectively within the present context, which is dominated by a global system of capitalism.

Other theoretical approaches attribute the problems of underdevelopment to external relationships. Dependency theory, for example, emphasizes the exploitative nature of relationships between Third World and developed areas and takes the position that underdevelopment is a result of these dynamics. André Gunder Frank points out that in a dependency relationship resources flow from "satellite" areas for the benefit of the elite in "metropolises," where raw materials are converted to commodities to be sold, in turn, for the profit of metropolis-based interests (see for example Frank 1972).

At a fundamental level, this relationship is established and maintained by the use of force. It entails profits for small but powerful concerns while inducing the progressive impoverishment of satellite populations. People in the satellite regions draw little benefit from the extraction of their resources, for which they typically supply the labor. As a bitter irony, they are left with little choice but to buy the goods produced from these resources, thereby profiting the metropolises further at their own cost. In this view, underdevelopment is less a manifestation of the inadequacies of the indigenous systems than a product of exploitation.

World systems theory develops this concept further. Immanuel Wallerstein has argued that the expansion of a world system of capitalism, beginning in the sixteenth century, resulted in a complex global division of labor among the world's populations (1974, 1975). Wallerstein underscores a crucial distinction between populations of the "core" and those of the "periphery," similar in many ways to Frank's metropolis and satellite.

These perspectives lend useful insights into the San Carlos situation. Louise Lamphere has applied a dependency model to the Navajo, depicting the role of the government in allowing powerful corporations to extract coal at great profit, which has left the Navajo population impoverished while despoiling their lands and ground water (1976). Later chapters will discuss the comparable appropriation of Apache resources, including copper-bearing lands, in more detail.

A major shortcoming of dependency and world systems approaches, though, is that they often pay little attention to the nature of indigenous cultures. An emphasis on power disparities between core and periphery or metropolis and satellite may imply that the details of local culture make little difference.

None of these approaches is sufficient in itself, but jointly they embrace a range of considerations that we must include if we hope to understand much about San Carlos. Dependency and world systems approaches lend powerful insights into the effects of the wider context on the Apache population. San Carlos Apache culture, society, and history also demand attention. We can draw the pieces together using insights from a historical materialist perspective to examine changes and processes that have occurred within the Apache population itself and explore the effects of external forces. With this approach, it will be especially useful to consider the repercussions of subsistence on other aspects of the Apache's lives.

From the prehistoric phase well into the nineteenth century, the people controlled their own territory and consumed what they were able to produce without accumulating a surplus. They distributed their resources through the medium of kinship without relying on the exchange of goods as commodities among themselves, and their social system was fundamentally egalitarian. For centuries in the Southwest, they were able to maintain control over their base of subsistence—the territory known as *Apachería*—until the forces associated with an encroaching state wrested it from them.

Apache raiding for subsistence, which came to complement their hunting base, eventually became a factor in their demise. In its early phases, raiding was a highly successful method of supplementing their subsistence needs, but raiding had implications that led finally to a breakdown of the social system. One of these was the need to exploit the productivity of nearby populations, taking livestock from Mexican villages while refraining from driving the villagers away. Eventually this developed into far bloodier and more destructive warfare.

Yet Apache relationships with other populations in the Southwest were far more complex. From early times they traded in petty commodities with other populations—tanned hides, stolen livestock, and even slaves for cloth, ammunition, and other goods they did not produce themselves but for which they had direct use. This represented a somewhat different use of resources than the direct production-for-consumption subsistence pattern of hunting, gathering, and gardening, although the items generally were traded for their use value rather than as commodities for further trade in a market system. Later chapters discuss why the Apache inability to accumulate surplus helped them to avoid becoming dependent on a market.

In the nineteenth century the Apache engaged in a final contest for their territory with a growing Anglo-American population represented by prospectors, miners, frontier settlers, and the army. The people who claimed lands and built towns and ranches in *Apachería* came to use the local resources in a way that was fundamentally different from the Apache pattern. Operating on the basis of a market economy fueled by the growing industrial capitalism far to the east, the incoming foreign population were motivated by incentives appropriate to the context from which they had sprung—particularly acquiring wealth and accumulating capital.

The turbulent period of the "Apache Wars" of the nineteenth century also is intelligible in materialist terms. In the nineteenth century, selling supplies to the army, whose presence was justified by the perceived Apache threat, came to be the major enterprise in Arizona. As a result, peace with Apache bands posed a danger to the economy. The balance tipped around 1870 with the heightened demand for the rich copper ore in the area. For industrial interests to benefit from this resource, the wars had to stop. A policy of peace came to predominate in the late nineteenth century, initiated by an abortive peace commission followed by a short and severe escalated military campaign to pacify *Apachería*.

The establishment of the reservation represents the most profound change in the history of the Apache. In their migration from the Subarctic to the Southwest, their ancestors had adapted to myriad local situations, populations, and circumstances. But this was qualitatively different. For the first time they lost their autonomy and access to their means of subsistence. With the establishment of the reservation, they had neither control nor possession of most of their territory.

The subsequent period up to the present has involved the people's attempts to adapt to a modern context dominated by global capitalism. In the early years of the reservation the Apache worked for wages as scouts and sold some farm products. By the turn of the century they constituted the major unskilled work force in the Southwest. With the influx of Mexican labor, particularly after the Reclamation Act of 1902, this began to change (see Barrera 1979:60). With the Depression, unemployment became one of the chronic facts of life in San Carlos. The Apache became a "surplus army of labor," kept in poverty and available for work—if employers found their current employees recalcitrant—but mostly left idle. Subsequent chapters deal more fully with the persistence and adjustment of Apachean culture throughout these times.

The sweep of events through which the Apache persisted invites us to examine large, impersonal trends and factors, but much of great importance rides on human concepts, ideas, emotions, and perceptions. This is particularly so in the Apache experience, where the local arena for centuries was quite small and the actors few. A rich array of characters took part in this drama—human beings who played remarkable roles, even though they may have operated within a context whose scope they did not fathom, constrained by forces they did not fully understand. As Eric Williams pointed out almost half a century ago in his book *Capitalism and Slavery*, "The various contending groups of dominant merchants, industrialists, and politicians, while keenly aware of immediate interests, are for that very reason generally blind to the long-range consequences of their various actions, proposals, policies" (1944:210).

In the San Carlos Apache case, as elsewhere, there have been people over the years who were malevolent, scurrilous, and reprehensible, people who were courageous and self-sacrificing beyond belief, and many who merely played the game as best they could. The cast of characters operated within a situation of daunting complexity.

CHAPTER 2

Apache Origins:
The Subarctic Base and the
Odyssey to the Southwest

The Apache are heirs to an ancient past. The culture of the Western Apache in the arena of the Southwest was built upon a social system that had developed much earlier in territory far to the north. The ways in which the population had dealt with the problems of subsistence in the past and the social arrangements that resulted comprised the cultural repertoire with which they met the challenges and opportunities that confronted them in Arizona. The complexity of countless human experiences that preceded the modern Apache population has blurred with time. Unrecorded events have faded and disappeared as they recede into earlier centuries. But we do have enough information to construct a general outline of Apache origins. Much of this comes from language.

The Western Apache speak a dialect of a language that they share with the other Apachean peoples of the Southwest and Plains. Their speech is most like the dialects of the Chiricahua Apache to the south, the Mescalero Apache to the southeast, and the Navajo to the north. But these dialects are not too different from the speech of the Jicarilla Apache of northern New Mexico or the Lipan Apache who once occupied the broken country of West Texas and ranged north to the Panhandle region. Farther out on the Plains, the Kiowa Apache speak a dialect that differs still more and, in fact, is just about equally different from the rest (Hoijer 1971).

What does this mean? Languages change with time, and as they change they become more distinct from one another. When a population separates, the speech of the divergent peoples eventually becomes more and more different. Unless there is close communication, languages do not become more alike as they change. The distribution of the Apache dialects tells us that the ancestors of these people once were a single population who later split into several groupings. The Kiowa Apache apparently separated before the rest did, since their dialect is the most different and is equally divergent from all of them (Young 1983; see also Davis 1988).

Other clues from language about the Apache past extend farther back in time. All of the Apache dialects are included in a widely dispersed language family known as Athapaskan. Athapaskan languages have an ancient relationship with Eyak, a language spoken on the north coast of Alaska. This tie is even older than the splits among the Athapaskan languages themselves. The Apache dialects, therefore, are part of a linguistic grouping known as Eyak-Athapaskan (Krauss 1973). This is one of the most widespread of all Native American language families.

Eyak is almost as different from Athapaskan as English is from Greek. After Eyak and Athapaskan diverged, the ancestors of Athapaskan speakers probably still constituted a single population. Some linguists believe that the earliest splits among Athapaskan languages themselves could have been as recent as two thousand years ago. The most remote differences among them are roughly comparable to the difference between English and Swedish, and some are about as similar as the various dialects of Spanish.

Most of the Athapaskan languages in North America are spoken in the western Subarctic in a territory ranging from the Alaskan interior to Hudson Bay. There is also a small pocket of Athapaskan speakers on the Pacific Coast in southern Oregon and northern California. For these and other reasons, it seems clear that the original North American homeland of Athapaskan-speaking peoples, including the Apache, was somewhere in the western Subarctic. But where?

The Athapaskan Homeland

One reason for thinking that the Athapaskan dispersion began in the western Subarctic is that the Athapaskan languages within that vast region are as different from one another as any Athapaskan languages anywhere. Some of the greatest differences, in fact, show up among languages that are spoken in neighboring territories (Krauss 1973; Krauss and Golla 1981; Dyen and Aberle 1974:380–383). Such a situation usually indicates an area where separations took place deep in the past (see Adams, Van Gerven, and Levy 1978). On the other hand, all of the Apache of the Southwest still speak dialects of a single language.

Linguists refer to different patterns of speech as dialects if the speakers of each can understand one another. Dialects come to be considered different languages when they no longer are mutually intelligible. Within the Subarctic, the process of transition from dialect to language shows up in varying degrees. There is a tendency for people who live nearby to influence one another's speech, which complicates matters (see Krauss and Golla 1981). But the differences and similarities among Athapaskan languages do help to narrow the search for the Athapaskan homeland.

Most of the Canadian Athapaskan dialects comprise one or two languages (Dyen and Aberle 1974:10–15). In Alaska, on the other hand, there are several distinct Athapaskan languages, some of which are extremely different from one another and apparently have been separated for a long time. Somewhere in Alaska the ancestors of Athapaskan speakers began to expand their territory, increase their numbers, and split into various local populations. Centuries later, one section of that population would migrate into the Southwest.

What else can we discern about these early beginnings? If we project back far enough, the antecedents of the Apache lie in Asia. Some of the cultural features most Athapaskan peoples shared, such as the symbolic importance of femaleness, death customs, and other beliefs, are characteristic of certain northern Siberian peoples (see Czaplicka 1914). Early Athapaskans came from somewhere out of the huge circumpolar milieu stretching from Scandinavia to Siberia. The various Athapaskan languages may have begun to separate shortly after they arrived in North America.

The two sides of the Bering Strait are fairly similar in many ways. On both, mountains and conifer forests give way to barren tundra, and both sides of the strait support just about the same kinds of game: reindeer on the Asian side, for example, and caribou in Alaska. The crossing between Siberia and Alaska is not particularly difficult for people who are used to living in that part of the world. On a clear day, one shore is visible from the other. The Oblate priest A. G. Morice, early in this century, wrote that "a sheet of water the shores of which can be seen with the naked eye by anyone standing on either of them can be no serious impediment to intercourse" (1914). People who hunted for a living there routinely ventured on journeys at least as challenging as crossing the strait. There are plenty of examples of communication between inhabitants of both sides. The relaxation of political constraints between Russia and the United States allowed Yupik-speaking peoples on both sides to revisit old friends and relatives.

Regions on either coast of the Bering Strait provide little plant food, and in that part of the world agriculture is out of the question. This alone tells us something about the early Athapaskans. They had to hunt and fish in a sparse environment to stay alive, and that placed some fairly severe constraints on their range of feasible strategies. We can fill in parts of the picture by exploring their ecological possibilities, considering the archaeological evidence of the region, and taking note of the ways in which more recent Athapaskan peoples in the same area have handled the problems of survival.

Clear evidence of Athapaskan peoples in the western Subarctic does not appear in the archaeological record before the first couple of centuries A.D. Before that time a type of stoneworking that produced small edged tools, or microblades, occurs throughout much of the Subarctic. Local tool styles in various places eventually developed from this tradition. But Athapaskan artifacts are quite different. They seem to represent an incursion of new people into the region, rather than a development from earlier local microblade technologies (see Shinkwin 1977).

For one thing, Athapaskan peoples tended to use large numbers of bone points, typically with the barbs cut along one side. Other Athapaskan hallmarks, such as a distinctive type of stone point, bone drinking tubes, and copper implements, occur throughout vast areas of the western Subarctic, and where they do occur, they denote an Athapaskan presence. But nowhere do they show up in archaeological levels earlier than the first few centuries A.D. There is no doubt that Athapaskans were present in the western Subarctic by that time. Earlier than that, as far as the evidence goes, they might well have been somewhere else—perhaps even on the Asian side of the strait.

Given the ecological situation they confronted, early Athapaskans could not have lived in large permanent villages. Food in the western Subarctic is far too sparse, scattered, and erratic in its occurrence to have allowed such a stable situation. Athapaskan peoples there in later times have had to be able to move easily and often to take advantage of opportunities for food.

From the craggy Alaska Range in the north, major mountain chains stretch like a spine to form the Rocky Mountain system. On the Pacific drainage side of this Cordillera, rivers cascade down to the coast, and salmon migrations provide a rich source of food. But these runs are seasonal. In historic times people congregated in fish camps in order to take advantage of the salmon runs, but they had to disperse at other times to search for different game. They clustered again in still other places for collective caribou hunts, driving herds into enclosures to be killed, then dispersed or moved on again to exploit other possibilities. No single local source of food could support people for very long. Without some opportunism and flexibility, life for hunters in the Subarctic would have become impossible (see Hosley 1981).

Not only do land animals and fish move from place to place, but their numbers fluctuate from year to year. Species that are plentiful at one time may become rare for a time and rebound a few years later. This may be a result of the short food chain. The number of species in the Subarctic ecosystem is relatively meager compared to other regions to the south, and as a result, minor shifts in conditions often have amplified repercussions. Whatever the complex reasons for this instability of game species, no group of people who specialized in a single source of food could have survived for long (see Burch 1972).

Hunters in such an area had to be able to seize chances when they occurred and to cope somehow with the unreliability of the game. This probably is one reason why Athapaskan peoples have tended to be associated with mountainous areas. The high Cordillera, with its bare, rocky tundra above the tree line, wooded slopes, sheltered valleys, and rushing salmon rivers, is a good place for hedging one's bets. It encompasses a range of ecological zones within a minimal distance, and the Athapaskan mountain orientation is attuned to the advantages of that environment. In later centuries the Apache would follow the mountain chain southward, utilizing these ecological features, until they confronted the northern outposts of the Spanish empire in the sixteenth century.

Other aspects of historic Athapaskan life in the Subarctic Cordillera suggest something about early Athapaskan patterns. Although permanent villages were not feasible, base camps in certain favorable localities acted as regional centers where people could coalesce periodically. A small Athapaskan group might comb thousands of square miles in their quest for food, but they would also be likely to gather at a particular camp or seasonal village for months at a time (see Holmes 1971). This has much to do with the Cordillera's multiple ecological zones, which allow hunters to set out in various directions from a single camp to exploit different possibilities. In the Athapaskan case, this involved other phenomena that had implications for the roles of men and women and the conception of gender. Many of these patterns were constituents of the Apache cultural heritage.

Repercussions of the Subsistence Pattern

Like most hunting societies, Subarctic Athapaskan peoples observe a gender-based division of labor that invests men with the primary responsibility for hunting. The ability to bring in game is a crucial requirement for males. It is a matter of life and death for the people who depend on the outcome. Hunting success in the Subarctic is subject to special anxiety because of the predominant factor of chance in this sparse environment. Not only is the food supply more meager here than in other regions, but it also is less predictable and beyond direct human control. No matter how skillful and assiduous a hunter may be, his luck may not hold; the game may not be there. Throughout the Subarctic, Athapaskan peoples have told tales of past starvation (See for example Krech 1978). Hunting was ridden with anxiety because its success depended on factors beyond the ability of humans to manipulate, and its failure meant catastrophe.

Historic Athapaskan peoples responded to this in much the same way people elsewhere have dealt with the stresses of existence. Beyond honing their practical hunting skills, they coped with the shortfall of human physical capacities by developing a concept of the hunter's influence over animals. This influence, a vital aspect of hunting success, also showed itself through luck in gambling. No doubt this is one reason why, even in recent times, gambling has had more than a purely social or recreational aspect for these hunters. Gambling is a means of testing the strength of personal power (see McDonnell 1984; Tanner 1979). In gambling as in hunting, influence could be fleeting.

This power of a hunter to project his will on game animals, causing them to give themselves up to be killed, is a crucial issue. Since hunting was an essential component of the male role, it was associated with maleness. And being tenuous, it was subject to being weakened or even nullified by its complementary opposite, femaleness. As a consequence, historic Athapaskan cultures show a range of practices and beliefs that emphatically separate femaleness from hunting. These practices were especially linked with such distinctively female phenomena as menstruation and childbirth.

These female-associated aspects of life were considered especially dangerous to men, probably because they connote a heightened degree of femaleness. A menstruating woman was not supposed to touch a man's hunting weapons because this would cause them to lose their effectiveness. Young women menstruating for the first time usually were secluded in a separate hut. If a woman were to look at a young man at such a time, it might result in his being killed on his next hunting trip (Townsend 1963).

Women in menstrual seclusion wore their hair combed down over their faces or had their eyes covered with hoods. In many cases they were cautioned not to look out over the woods because their gaze would offend game. All of this acted to maintain a dissociation of women from hunting. Women butchered game and prepared meat after it was killed, but these avoidance practices guarded the delicate, uncertain process of the hunt itself in which male luck and power was so crucial, from the nullifying influence of femaleness (see Jenness

1937; Helm 1981:301; Savishinsky 1974:320; Honigmann 1964:125; Nelson 1983:25; McKennan 1965:58; Gillespie 1981).

It is important to keep in mind that this recognition of femaleness as an abstract power did not necessarily indicate much about the social status of women as persons among historic Athapaskan peoples. Femaleness was considered a powerful essence or quality that existed above and beyond women as individuals. This quality was dangerous to men simply because it was the conceptual opposite of maleness, not because of any imputed malevolence or inherent evil associated with women as persons (see Perry 1977).

These factors of Athapaskan life interacted in an intricate way. The separation of male and female roles in the context of the base camp situation and the scattered distribution of resources meant that men often were absent for extended periods of time and that women did not usually accompany them. The people who remained at the base camps were those who did not hunt. These included older men, perhaps, but especially women and children.

Consequently, women formed the stable domestic core of the base camps. Since men often were away while women remained in each other's company, one of the most congenial arrangements was for women to remain with their own relatives rather than with strangers. Those relatives not engaged in hunting would primarily be their sisters and mothers. This is the essence of matrilocal (or uxorilocal) residence, in which women continue to live near their mothers and sisters, and their husbands move in from other groups (see for example Gough 1962).

Children who grew up in that setting lived with the people related to them through their mothers. Typically, the other children around them were their own brothers and sisters and the children of their mothers' sisters. Their mothers' unmarried brothers might still reside in the camp when they were not hunting, but often they, too, would be away. When these men married, they would leave to live with their wives' people, where their children would live also, with their own mothers' groups.

Other likely members of a child's most intimate social universe would be the mother's parents, her adult sisters, and their husbands —all people whose relationships were linked to the child through the mother. This kind of living pattern is compatible with the idea that interpersonal relationships are most appropriately defined in terms of ties though women. Matrilocal residence, in other words, is often associated with the idea that descent through women, matrilineal descent, is a more appropriate or significant criterion for defining interpersonal ties than descent through men. Almost all Athapaskan-speaking groups, including the Apache, observed matrilocal residence, and many had matrilineal descent. Many researchers believe that these features characterized early Athapaskan populations (see for example Dyen and Aberle 1974; Bishop and Krech 1980; Perry 1989).

What we know about recent Athapaskan peoples can help flesh out the earlier culture in other respects. In the beliefs of most Athapaskan peoples the universe was capricious, filled with unpredictable entities who could either help or harm human beings. Cornelius Osgood, for example, writes that the Bear Lake population lived "in a world of multitudinous spirits which influence or control their destinies" (1932:81). Annette McFadyen Clark notes that the Koyukon have "a belief that all humans and animals as well as many inanimate objects also had spirits, which could be turned to good or evil practice at the whim of their owners" (1981:593). She notes elsewhere that the people believed that all objects have spirits with a whimsical or unpredictable nature (1970:80). According to Richard Slobodin, "the Kutchin were encompassed by myriad supernatural beings, friendly, hostile, and unpredictable" (1981:527). Such concepts imply acknowledgement of human vulnerability in the face of erratic forces. They seem to echo the vagaries of a hunting existence in harsh regions and the anxieties associated with it.

Distinctive ways of dealing with death were also characteristic of Athapaskan speakers. The body was disposed of as quickly as possible, and generally it was taken from the dwelling through a hole in the wall rather than through the door. Many Athapaskan peoples believed that the human soul had two parts, one of which was malevolent and lingered near the corpse. Mourners buried the personal belongings of the deceased with the body. Often they broke or damaged them in some way, and they burned or abandoned the dwelling in which death had occurred. People avoided mentioning the name of the deceased for fear of calling the malevolent ghost (see for example de Laguna 1981; Goddard 1916; Jenness 1937; Honigmann 1964 and 1946; McKennan 1965; Osgood 1936).

Subsistence and Social Organization

These are some of the things we can attribute to the ancestors of the San Carlos Apache. Many of them continue to affect modern Apache life, and they are part of a common heritage the Apache share with other Athapaskan speakers throughout western North America. But the reservation community of San Carlos is vastly different from the social milieu of the Apaches' ancient forebears in the Subarctic. To begin to understand the relationship between past and present and take into account the changes as well as the continuities, it will be useful to go beyond the thumbnail description of early Athapaskan culture and try to link some causes with effects.

The reconstruction of early Athapaskan culture and social organization provides a basis for exploring subsequent changes in the Apaches' circumstances (see also Perry 1991). The primary needs of the early population—to survive in the western Subarctic—entailed a number of fundamental constraints and imperatives, including limits on population size and the need for mobility. Human efforts could exert only slight influence over these environmental factors. People might develop the most effective possible means of capturing the resources of the area, but no matter how efficient they might become, the available food was finite and meager. Unlike agriculturalists, people who rely entirely on wild foods have few effective means of expanding production.

The "feast or famine" nature of hunting encouraged widespread redistribution rather than hoarding of food resources. The resource base did not afford much possibility of accumulating storable surplus. They could lay away caches of meat for later use, but they could not store perishable food indefinitely. This strategy had limited potential and few possibilities for an unequal distribution of resources. A person might experience long episodes of scarcity punctuated by occasional overabundance of food, but one can eat only so many pounds of caribou before the meat begins to rot. A more effective strategy is to distribute the meat widely and strengthen interpersonal ties that one might call upon to secure fresh meat in the future. Wealth, if the term has any meaning in that context, was as much the possession of the personal skills and power to acquire food as it was possession of food itself. To amass and hoard food in any large quantities would have been pointless.

Subarctic hunting, by promoting the extensive sharing of food, fosters an egalitarian quality in the social organization. Egalitarian social organization in such circumstances is a rational strategy. The sparseness, mobility, and fluctuating quantity of game mean that one can never be sure of hunting success. Even though a hunter might exert personal power over game, since this power was tenuous and unstable, no one could survive for long without being able to rely at least occasionally on others, and in the long run this reliance was mutual and reciprocal. It enhanced everyone's probability of being able to stay alive. The food quest involved production for consumption, and interpersonal sharing relationships contributed to the maintenance of the social network.

When resources change hands in that manner, they are not exchanged as commodities. That is, their worth is not derived from their value as items that could be exchanged for other things. As Duncan Foley writes, "a commodity is the form products take when production is organized through exchange" (1983:86–87). The value of meat was based directly on its use as food and mostly limited to that. And just as these resources did not acquire value as a medium of exchange, their value as food was not particularly associated with the amount of effort or labor the hunter expended in stalking or killing animals. A caribou brought down by an easy shot near camp was no less tasty or esteemed than an animal that had eluded a hunter for days. In the context of Athapaskan beliefs, in fact, an easy kill might be a far more significant validation of the hunter's personal power.

Prehistoric Athapaskan peoples did trade for items other than food. The archaeological record shows that obsidian, the black volcanic glass valuable for making cutting tools and weapon points, was dispersed throughout Alaska from a single source (Clark 1977). But exchange of this sort is unlikely ever to have amounted to a predominant activity for any northern Athapaskan population. Unlike gold or silver in other parts of the world, obsidian's value stemmed directly from its use. Not until the days of the fur trade around the beginning of the nineteenth century did northern Athapaskan peoples become heavily involved in the exchange of commodities.

Another interesting question regarding the use of resources involves the sexual division of labor that excluded women from hunting. Certainly beliefs about the powers of femaleness underscored this division of labor. We might interpret this as a situation in which women were somehow exploited by being denied direct access to one of the most vital resources. But if there is any validity at all to this interpretation, it is far more complicated.

Men expended the labor of hunting and produced or procured the meat. Women expended the effort involved in preparing it. But the meat itself was shared by everyone. The situation was reciprocal and complementary, and it is difficult to discern evidence that one gender profited unfairly from the labor of the other.

For times of extreme scarcity, the possibility of differential access to food is less clear. Among some non-Athapaskan Inuit hunters on the Arctic Coast, men had primary access to meat when it was scarce. This custom was rationalized by reference to the role of men in procuring the meat—not because the meat was considered "theirs" or because they were more assertive than anyone else, but because of their need to function adequately in order to obtain more meat for the group. But there is little evidence of such gender-based distinctions among Athapaskan peoples.

Other aspects of the subsistence pattern reinforced the social standing of women. The quest for game, which often took men away from base camps, permitted women who were close relatives to form a stable domestic core and had the potential of allowing women to establish and maintain a strong social and political base. That seems to have been the case in Athapaskan societies, including the Apache, in historic times.

Although life would not have been idyllic in the Subarctic, before the fur trade era the people drew their livelihood directly from the territory and had the full use and benefits of the products of their own efforts. Athapaskan cultural patterns were attuned to egalitarian social and economic relationships. Customs and beliefs relating to death tended to inhibit property inheritance by stipulating that the belongings of the deceased should be destroyed. The belief that a ghost, the malevolent aspect of the soul, lingered around the property and could threaten the living if the items were kept by the survivors, reinforced this. Destroying the dwelling and abandoning the site stimulated mobility and militated against the possibility that concepts of property ownership or territorial claims could develop.

The prohibition on speaking the names of the dead had the effect of keeping genealogies shallow, stressing the importance of person-to-person relationships among living relatives, rather than permitting corporate lineages to form based on descent. The sense of an uncertain universe inhabited by capricious, unpredictable, and often dangerous powers reflected and perhaps helped to maintain a way of life that called for pragmatic, flexible responses to opportunity.

The Movement Southward

One of the perennial questions about the Apache past has to do with how, why, and when they ended up in the Southwest. On the face of it, Arizona and New Mexico seem to have very little in common with the Athapaskan homeland in Alaska. On the other hand, it is useful to remember Athapaskan peoples' basic ecological orientation to mountainous regions. A glance at any topographical map of North America will reveal that from the Alaska Range and the Subarctic Cordillera southward, the Rocky Mountains stretch as a corridor to the Colorado Plateau and the Sangre de Cristo Mountains of New Mexico.

In historic times the distribution of northern Athapaskan peoples extended from the Brooks Range of northern Alaska to southern Alberta—a range of more than two thousand miles. In contrast, the distance from southern Alberta to northern New Mexico and Arizona is only about half that far. Once early Athapaskans had adapted successfully to the mountains of the Subarctic, they may have spread as far as they could within that niche. The mountains running north and south through the continent were less a barrier to migration than a pathway for their expansion (see Perry 1991).

In the first few centuries A.D. the climate of northwestern North America was colder than it is today. A gradual warming trend began about two thousand years ago (Bryson and Wendland 1967; Harp 1978). Caribou, a major game animal for northern Athapaskan peoples, is essentially a Subarctic species, but in the early twentieth century caribou were seen as far south as central Idaho (Hall and Kelson 1958). In colder times this animal's range could have extended still farther south. Athapaskan peoples who hunted caribou would have had good reason to extend their activities as far south as the animal was available. A more puzzling question is why northern and southern Athapaskans separated.

The generalized subsistence pattern of Athapaskan peoples suggests that they hunted not only caribou but also a variety of other species as well. As the climate warmed and the range of caribou receded northward, some of the Athapaskan population probably followed them north in response. But since few of these people could have relied entirely on caribou even in the best of times, when caribou became harder and harder to find, the southern section of the Athapaskan population would have shifted their attention to such game as mountain sheep and goats in the high elevations, deer and elk at the middle altitudes, and buffalo and antelope on the Plains to the east.

The archaeological evidence from the mountains extending from southern Alberta to northern Colorado reveals that several new hunting techniques appeared after the first few centuries A.D. Probably many of these were associated with new groups of people entering the region. The data offer little hope of identifying Athapaskan speakers with any certainty, but the circumstantial evidence is very suggestive (see Perry 1980, 1991).

One of these populations moved into the Jackson Hole region of Wyoming fifteen hundred years ago and hunted the various altitudes and niches of the mountain range, setting up base camps at a number of different elevations (Wright 1984). This pattern had long been typical of Subarctic Athapaskans of the Cordillera.

Farther south, at sites in Wyoming known as Wedding of the Waters Cave and Spring Creek Cave, the evidence is still more suggestive. There, where dry conditions preserved materials that otherwise would have rotted away, archaeologists found the remains of arrows conforming almost exactly to the historic Apache types (Frison 1962, 1978:59). The Spring Creek Cave site is dated at about A.D. 225, with a considerable margin of error (Frison 1965). The arrow parts include stone points set into foreshafts of hardwood with pitch. The foreshafts, in turn, would have been set into a main shaft wrapped with sinew at the juncture. A fragment of a hollow mainshaft was among the remains at the site. They look like typical Apache arrows. The Chiricahua sometimes made theirs out of a simple wooden shaft, but they wrapped it, nonetheless, where the foreshaft would have joined in order to make it look the same (Goodwin and Basso 1971:229).

Farther south in Colorado just north of Denver, hunters a few centuries later used game-drive structures similar to the Subarctic pattern at high altitudes above the tree line (Benedict 1975a, 1975b). The people who built and used these structures camped in lower elevations, and like the hunters at Jackson Hole, they exploited a variety of niches in the mountainous zone.

By the time the Apache became established in north central Colorado, they already were practically in the Southwest. For untold centuries Athapaskan peoples had routinely traveled remarkable distances on foot. Small groups in the Subarctic exploited thousands of square miles of territory in their quest for food. In the Southwest, nineteenth-century Apache sometimes walked forty miles a day for weeks at a time (Clum 1936:207). For generations they raided hundreds of miles into Mexico and drove livestock on foot back to their camps in the mountains of eastern Arizona. For such people the two hundred miles or so between northern Colorado and New Mexico's Sangre de Cristo Mountains would have presented no barrier.

Although the archaeological evidence for the northern Rockies and the northwestern Plains is intriguing, all we know for certain is that, by A.D. 1500 or so, the Apache had long since moved out of that area and were at least on the fringes of the Southwest. After A.D. 1300 the inhabitants of the Wyoming region were Shoshoni who had migrated in from the Death Valley area to the south. The skills and strategies of the Shoshoni were adapted to hot, lowland conditions—a very different orientation from the Apache's (Wright 1978). In historic times the Shoshoni rarely exploited the high elevations unless they were in extreme difficulties. Still later, the area was contested by other populations who spoke Siouan and Algonkian languages—Crow, Atsina,

Blackfoot, and others. But by then the Apache already had established a stronghold in the Southwest and had maintained it for several generations.

Although the Apache went through many changes in their odyssey from the Subarctic, they retained a great deal of their ancient heritage. The traces of their past are clear in the features they continued to share with other Athapaskan speakers. Their common past and cultural similarities with other Athapaskan populations had been associated with a Subarctic subsistence base. Changing ecological conditions had significant effects on their lives and the strategies they chose, but the kinds of environmental situations that attracted them had a great deal to do with the conditions in which they had operated successfully in the past. This was a major reason the mountains became a corridor for them into the Southwest.

The experiences that led the Apache from the Subarctic to the mountains of Colorado had molded and tempered early Apache culture when they reached the borders of the Southwest. It is somewhat frustrating to lose sight of the Apache's ancestors in their transition from the Subarctic. But from what we can surmise about early Athapaskan culture, we can draw some conclusions about what they were like when they approached the Southwest. We know a great deal more—though still not nearly enough—about the Apache when they became established at the southern end of their migrations and when Europeans saw them for the first time and described them in writing.

A population distributed in autonomous, small joint family clusters who had exploited wild foods for tens of centuries, they now found themselves amidst people living in sparsely scattered agricultural villages. These villagers, whom Europeans came to know as "Pueblos" after the Spanish word for their towns, would become significant in the lives of many of the Apache for centuries to follow. So, too, would the Spanish—people who represented a stratified state system with roots in Europe which accommodated and balanced the interests of a powerful institutionalized church and a hereditary elite.

Apache fortunes would impinge upon those of other peoples of the Southwest and become entwined with them. Many of the Apache populations would interact closely with Pueblo communities. Upland Yumans lived in the western region of Arizona, and one of these populations, the Yavapai, eventually became allies of the Western Apache. Pimans to the south were to become their enemies—largely through political policies of the Spanish.

Eventually the Mexican state succeeded the Spanish, and the Anglo-American state succeeded the Mexican. Throughout this long history in the Southwest, the Apache had remarkable success in maintaining possession of their territory and control over their affairs. Toward the end of the nineteenth century this changed, and with the establishment of the reservation system, much of their sovereignty was lost. But before examining the reservation in sharper focus, it will be useful to look at the processes that led to it.

CHAPTER 3

The Apache and the Spanish State

The ancestors of the Apache had learned to be at home in mountainous terrain long before they followed the range of crags, slopes, and valleys toward the south. Their social organization was classless and egalitarian, and their values stressed individual autonomy. A capacity for the free and easy movement of small groups and individuals was a central aspect of this way of life. They had nothing resembling any centralized political structure beyond the ephemeral clusters of people who chose to associate themselves with successful, respected leaders. Relatives had strong and complex obligations to one another, but in the sixteenth century, the Apache were a population of free individuals linked only by kinship ties and common language and culture.

The early sixteenth century is a reasonable guess for the time of their arrival in the Southwest (see Dyen and Aberle 1974:213–214; D. Gunnerson 1974:5; Opler 1975:187). The very first Spanish expeditions in the region failed to mention them, but not long afterward they had become a significant presence. Early Spanish expeditions did encounter a variety of native peoples in the area, however. In many cases they did not learn very much about them or describe them in detail, and to be sure that none of these groups were Apache would be difficult (see Forbes 1959).

In a sense, though, the issue of the Apache's presence or absence may be misleading because of their capacity to cover vast distances on foot. Even when their base camps were in the mountains of central Colorado, the areas now known as northern Arizona and New Mexico were easily within their range.

Early Spanish accounts that refer to Apache with more certainty give the impression that they were a large population. One report describes them as "many and warlike" (Bolton 1916:183). But we should not take Spanish assessments of Apache numbers during this period too literally. In early historic times the numbers of Native

American peoples did decrease greatly from what they had been centuries earlier. Europeans introduced diseases that devastated many Native American populations (see Dobyns 1983). But Spanish accounts giving the impression that the mountains and plains north of the farming villages of New Spain were teeming with Apache might also have been a reflection of the scattered, freely moving nature of local groups who continued to follow the strategies they had developed farther north. The dramatic social and political impact of the Apache no doubt affected European perceptions of their numbers. During the eighteenth and nineteenth centuries there were times when Apache livestock raids into Mexico so terrorized villages in Sonora that small parties of three to a dozen Apache raiders caused the populations to flee in panic (see Spicer 1962). In general, Spanish chroniclers during the sixteenth century were in no position to provide an accurate estimate of Apache numbers.

Despite later hostilities, a primary aspect of Apache-Spanish interaction during the 1500s and early 1600s, in fact, was trade—usually in Santa Fe or in one of the pueblos the Spanish occupied. Most of these interactions were with the eastern Apache. The Spanish conquest of the Rio Grande Pueblo communities during the sixteenth and seventeenth centuries was probably far more violent than their interaction with the Apache.

Once the Spanish established a presence in these sedentary Pueblo communities, they made a few early exploratory ventures into the Plains and encountered buffalo-hunting Apache who traded hides. Before horses became common on the Plains, some of the eastern Apache hunted buffalo so successfully on foot that they could trade the dried or jerked meat and buffalo robes to eastern Pueblo in exchange for woven cloth, corn, and other village products (see Gunnerson and Gunnerson 1971).

These early encounters were not particularly adversarial compared to the interactions the Spanish often had with other Native American peoples, although the peaceful relationships were highly tentative. In 1601 Juan de Oñate, who encountered some buffalo-hunting Apache on the Plains, wrote that "we were not disturbed by them at all, although we were in their land, nor did any Indian become impertinent" (Bolton 1916:253).

The Spanish practice of kidnapping peaceful local inhabitants to act as guides through the regions they visited had a detrimental effect on their subsequent reception. Before the mid-seventeenth century, though, most hostile Apache interaction with the Spanish seems to have been in direct response to Spanish slave raids (Forbes 1960:121). The earliest recorded Apache attack on the Spanish was in 1629, long

after these peoples had first encountered one another. Apache forbearance during the early decades of the 1600s is remarkable—especially considering their later warlike reputation.

There is substantial evidence that the Apache persistently sought
ways of achieving peaceful coexistence with other populations in the
Southwest, from these early years through the nineteenth century
(Griffen 1988:76). Spanish lieutenant José Cortés, in his report of
1799, wrote of the Apache: "It has been and continues to be our absurd and foolish belief that they are impossible to force into peace
and the customs of a rational life, but this is a most patent fallacy.
They love peace and hate to lose it" (Cortés 1989:28). The general
failure of peaceful interactions raises important issues regarding the
dynamics of interaction among the various populations and interest
groups in the Southwest.

Although some small Apache groups ventured into close, albeit
fleeting, association with Spanish settlements, most of the Apache
with whom the Spanish dealt had secure possession of their vast territory and moved freely over thousands of square miles of plains and
mountains. The western section of their broad population was remote
from the Spanish bases along the Rio Grande and in Mexico to the
south. Perhaps this is why Spanish estimates of the number of
Apache range wildly, from references to a few thousand to statements
that they were "infinite in number," as Juan de Oñate wrote in 1599
(Forbes 1960:91). Long after the Spanish lost control over Mexico
early in the nineteenth century and even after Mexico had relinquished its claim on the area to the United States in 1848, Western
Apache territory remained almost unknown to outsiders.

Changes in Apache Strategies

We could view the Apache's initial movement into the Southwest as
a consequence of a mode of subsistence that had succeeded for many
centuries, using the mountains as a base from which they extended
their activities to exploit surrounding regions. Even the eastern
Apache, who drew a major portion of their resources from the buffalo
herds of the Plains, spent much of the year in the mountains (D.
Gunnerson 1974:126–137). José Cortés, writing in 1799, states: "They
also consider that they have found some places to be better than others according to the seasons of the year. But these changes of location
occur without leaving the mountain ranges that they recognize as
their own territory" (Cortés 1989:62).

The records from the Espejo expedition of the late 1500s mention a
"mountain people" near the Ácoma Pueblo community who "came

to the aid of the settlements and traded salt and game, particularly deer and rabbit and tanned hides in exchange for cotton *mantas*" (Schroeder 1974a:188). Joseph Jorgensen asserts that the Apache were the only Southwestern people who used tanned-hide clothing (1980:151).

As the Spanish seized control of many of these pueblos, they too entered the system of trade because of their interest in the robes. By the late seventeenth century, some of the eastern Apache had essentially become commercial hunters to supply this market (D. Gunnerson 1974:141). According to Spanish accounts of Pecos pueblo in the late 1500s, buffalo robes were so commonly traded that the villagers all wore them during the winter (D. Gunnerson 1974:80). Cortés in the late eighteenth century noted: "The extent of their arts and industry is limited to the thorough curing of the skins in which they dress and which they use in trading at Spanish posts. The best of this work is done by the Mescaleros, Lipanes, Xicarillas, and Yutas, but the Navajoos manufacture frieze, blankets, and other weavings of course wool" (1989:60).

But even these eastern Apache did not become fully dependent on this market and continued to feed themselves from the hunt. When occasional outbreaks of hostilities interrupted trade, they fared perfectly well in their own territory without it. When trade was lively, however, they killed far more buffalo than they needed for their own consumption and used the rest as commodities for exchange.

The Spanish describe these people as "dog nomads," referring to the hundreds of pack dogs which they used to transport the buffalo hides (D. Gunnerson 1974). Northern Athapaskan hunters and the other Apache groups had few if any dogs, probably because dogs compete with humans for meat. Most Athapaskan-speaking peoples view dogs with some ambivalence. But when the buffalo hunters were killing large numbers of animals for the market, the dogs became useful for transport and affordable because of the excess of buffalo meat.

In later centuries, horses allowed buffalo hunting on the Plains to become the basis for a complex and specialized way of life among many Native American groups. When the Apache acquired their first few horses is not certain. It may have been as early as the late sixteenth century. But the early buffalo-hunting Apache with their dog pack trains did not rely on horses and hunted buffalo on foot.

They may have used the technique of stalking at buffalo mud wallows. According to one account, Apache hunters covered themselves with mud and lay still while the beasts rolled in the mire, silently killing one at a time with bow and arrow without alarming the rest

(D. Gunnerson 1974:143). Another Spanish account suggests that they used the ancient game-drive technique, which Athapaskan peoples had used for centuries in the north to hunt caribou, stampeding the animals over cliffs or into enclosures where they could be killed (Hammond and Rey 1953:400). The western section of the Apache population, in the mountains far from the buffalo plains and the Spanish, did not take part in this exchange of buffalo hides.

Moving into the Southwest led to other changes for the Apache. Many of them added agriculture to their range of subsistence. They may have encountered agriculture for the first time when they entered the region, but eventually most of the scattered local groups of Apache adopted it to some degree. A few did not bother to plant crops at all, but by the end of the sixteenth century, eastern Apache near Taos pueblo had established small irrigated farms and were living in masonry dwellings. Spanish accounts depict them as "peaceful farmers tending their fields" (J. Gunnerson 1969).

Between these extremes, most of the Apache had a few farm plots here and there among their scattered encampments in the mountains, but they relied heavily on other sources of food. Cortés in 1799 wrote: "The Coyotero Indians sow a small amount of corn, beans, and some vegetables. The Navajoos, in season, sow corn, squash, and some fruits and vegetables. They harvest all this in great abundance and keep their stores throughout the entire year. The Xicarillas also plant corn, beans, squash, and a little tobacco in the mountain valleys they inhabit" (1989:60). Cortés also asserted, though, that "the Apache temperament is little suited to agriculture, and with the gathering of wild grains they satisfy their present needs" (1989:60).

Farming usually was a supplement, an addition to the preexisting subsistence mode, rather than a radical departure. Grenville Goodwin notes that, even in the late nineteenth century, the Western Apache could have given up their gardens at any time and lived on wild foods (Opler 1973). Apache agriculture still amounted to production for direct consumption rather than trade, and it did not interfere with their possession or control of the territory in which that production took place.

By the late seventeenth century most of the Apache also had adopted the pattern of raiding sedentary villages for food, especially livestock. Unlike agriculture, raiding did eventually have profound implications for them.

When raiding began as a general Apache pattern is not clear. They may have carried out small-scale sporadic raids soon after they arrived in the Southwest, but the Spanish records up to the 1630s provide no substantial evidence of this (Forbes 1960:98, 121). Trade seems to have predominated in whatever relationship they had. This seems consistent with other cases in which adjacent populations exploit different ecological zones. Each has something the other needs or wants.

The sort of raiding for which the Apache later became famous, and in which they developed an expertise that approached a perfection of the art, resembled an older pattern that first appeared much farther south among native peoples in Mexico. As early as 1554 the Spanish discovered gold and silver in Zacatecas and advanced in search of more mineral wealth. By 1560 they had established mines in Chihuahua. This invading presence provoked responses by non-Apache peoples of the area, who carried out numerous raids on the Spanish and made off with livestock. The Apache refined this pattern generations later, but apparently they did not introduce it to the region.

The ancestors of the Apache in their northern homeland would have had no particular incentive for subsistence raiding, since there was little surplus for them to take. Athapaskan peoples did, however, have a longstanding pattern of taking advantage of subsistence opportunities. This strategy arose from generations of survival in harsh and uncertain environments. Livestock and other food stores in the villages of the Southwest were potential resources. Raiding in that sense was as much a transformation of their existing mode of subsistence as it was an innovation.

Subsistence raiding had multiple aspects. In one regard it was an aggressive pattern, but generally, at least until the nineteenth century, it was not carried out with the intention of killing or driving away the villagers. Without them, the supply of food would have disappeared. The Apache did not carry out unremitting raids on the Pueblo peoples of Arizona and New Mexico in the early years but maintained friendly trading and visiting relationships with the villages. At times they even formed alliances with them against the Spanish. Ácoma Pueblo, for example, seems to have had Apache allies against the Spanish in 1583, 1598, and 1599 (Forbes 1960:91).

In 1599, although the Spanish saw the Apache as "a people who still haven't rendered obedience to His Majesty by public instruments" (Forbes 1960:91), the Apache had not acquired the image that later became their stereotype. Even at that early period, the Spanish had provided ample reason for hostile response. As the Count of Monterey observed in a letter to the King of Spain in 1598, "most of the people who go on new discoveries are troublesome" (Forbes 1960:76). Mass murder, rape, village burning, land theft, and repeated slave raids were thoroughly chronicled during this period in New Spain.

Vicente de Zaldívar was one adventurer who carried this pattern further than many. Foremost among his many exploits was the destruction of Acoma pueblo and the killing of its defenseless inhabitants in a slaughter that continued relentlessly for several days. Yet Zaldívar could travel unscathed among the Apache. In 1599 he wrote: "Traversing among many nations of warlike people, such as the Apaches, who are very numerous and extend for more than 200 leagues [about six hundred miles?] judging from what I have seen; . . . I went up the sierra with a lone companion . . . so that they could see we intended them no harm . . . they served as guides and gave us native blackberries" (quoted in Forbes 1960:92). Throughout these decades the relative amicability of the Apache is a consistent theme, despite a recognition of their potential, as Zaldívar notes, to be "warlike."

The historical impression often has been that the destruction of the Rio Grande Pueblo in the early 1600s was a result of "Apache depredations." In much of the literature from that time onward, the phrase "marauding Apaches" has become a cliché. But there is little doubt that Spanish exploitation and destruction was a far more significant cause of the Pueblo reductions. From the 1500s through the 1620s and beyond, the Apache trade relationships with Pueblo communities worked to the mutual benefit of both. These exchanges generally took the form of reciprocal gift giving between families who visited within the multiple dwellings of the pueblos. Cortés and others mention "trade fairs" (1989:61), although the system of transactions often was personalized and depended upon relationships that were peaceful, if not congenial.

During this period the Spanish were engaged in extending hegemony over the region, and the process frequently involved violent suppression of indigenous populations. Several pueblos along the Rio Grande were destroyed or abandoned during that time. After the Apache finally resorted to more energetic warfare against the Spanish, challenged the extension and stability of their control, and for a time occupied much of the area, however, there was no further reduction in the number of pueblos (Forbes 1960:175).

Apache and Pueblo

The Apache and the Pueblo villages shared some common interests in their encounter with the Spanish state, but their differing situations and the nature of their social organization entailed different vulnerabilities and affected their possible forms of reaction. The contrast between the Apache and Pueblo social systems is one example of such differences.

Although prehistoric political networks might have existed among Pueblo communities, in historic times each Pueblo village was a self-contained sociopolitical entity. Scattered along the Rio Grande and westward toward the Colorado Plateau, some of these communities at times developed alliances and interacted in significant ways, and they collaborated to an unusual degree in the Pueblo Revolt against the Spanish in 1680. But for the most part, their existence as independent units involved a separatism that tended to override or inhibit coalescence. The Pueblo communities spoke a variety of distinct languages. Each of these self-contained societies had its own farms, ceremonial calendar, and priestly government. Their masonry walls marked clear social boundaries between each community and the rest of the world.

Apache social organization, in contrast, was fluid. The Apache population amounted to a mass of individuals bonded only by networks of myriad kin ties and a sense of personal reciprocal obligations. These ties of descent and marriage were the basis for the clustering of extended families, which operated as small aggregates. These were largely self-sufficient, although they sometimes joined other similar clusters by extension of the same principles. Spanish writers referred to these groupings as *rancherías*. José Cortés in the late eighteenth century observed that "by chance it happens that sometimes many [Apache] *rancherías* come together at one place in search of certain fruits that abound in one given location or another" (1989:65). He also notes that "the *ranchería* can shrink in size, even though it may be very populous, the moment those who constitute it become discontented and form a separate rancho or join another *caudillo* or tribal captain" (1989:62).

The movements and coalescence of these groups depended on situational needs and opportunities. Immediate circumstances might bring people together in sizable groupings or lead to the dispersal of families, but this system of organization did not produce the sort of formally structured societies typical of the Pueblo.

The Apache concept of matrilineal descent and the matrilineal clans of the Western Apache and Navajo did not crystallize into highly structured political units like the clans of the western Pueblo. The western Pueblo clans were corporate entities in their own right. They were political groups that claimed an individual from birth and carried out ceremonial activities in which a person was obligated to participate. The Rio Grande Pueblo to the east, with dual organization, or moieties, rather than clans, also had sharply defined and complex social structures.

Western Apache and Navajo clans were abstract categories reflecting ties among persons, but these categories had little concrete political reality. In the nineteenth century Apache clan members did not all live together or normally, in fact, do anything together. They had no specific ceremonial functions, except perhaps in the female puberty ritual when clan members might gather for a few days. Even in that case, members of many other clans also would be present. The only significant social duties associated with clan membership among the Western Apache involved a sense of obligation to clan members if they needed assistance and a stipulation that members of the same clan should not marry. But there was no sense of collective enterprise pertaining to the clan as a whole.

In short, the Apache social system was far looser than that of the Pueblo—not less organized or less complicated, but arranged on a different basis. In contrast to the Pueblo's ancient heritage of agriculture in stable, compact communities, it was a social organization articulated to a mode of subsistence that grew from generations of hunting in mountainous regions.

Apache Differentiation

The Pueblo peoples, in achieving a stable livelihood in arid conditions, had concentrated their lives in communities near sources of water for their crops—particularly the Rio Grande and some natural springs. Between these communities and farms, vast areas of desert and mountains were essentially vacant. For thousands of square miles small groups of Apache could travel through the broken country of arroyos, mesas, and hills among the mesquite, creosote bushes, and cactus without encountering settled communities. There were wild foods in rich areas, but the food was of a sort that required mobility because of its thin dispersal, and it was sufficient only to maintain small numbers of people in any locality. The Apache established their ecological foothold in this rugged terrain and especially in the mountain ranges themselves. It was a setting in which their experience had prepared them to thrive.

The pueblo dwellers were not the only significant Native American populations the Apache encountered in the Southwest. A people known as the Suma appear in the Spanish records of the late sixteenth century in what was later to become Western Apache territory. Eventually they disappeared, as did other peoples of the area known as Janos, Jocomes, and Jumanos (see Forbes 1959). Some of them might have been Apache, but most of them probably were not (Naylor 1981). A few might have continued to exist under different names or merged with other populations. But by the early seventeenth century, a vast area in the region had come to be known as the territory of the Apache.

The Western Apache represent one of several local adaptations of the broader Apache population. This general population probably was far less differentiated when they reached the threshold of the Southwest than they later became, although there does seem to have been some cultural and linguistic difference between the eastern and western sections. The sound /t/ in the dialects of Navajo, Western Apache, Chiricahua, and Mescalero in the west becomes a /k/ in the Jicarilla, Lipan, and Kiowa Apache dialects of the east (see Hoijer 1971:4; Hockett 1977).

José Cortés in 1799 wrote: "The language spoken by all the nations called Apache is one and the same. It varies only in accent and in an occasional regional term, without this difference creating any problem in understanding one another, although the lands where they were born might be very far apart" (1989:56). Differences in the kinship systems of these eastern and western groups also suggest that there had been some regional differentiation in the past, but most of the characteristics that distinguish the historic Apache groups from one another apparently are recent.

Of the seven major Apache divisions, the Kiowa Apache probably had departed from the others before they reached the Southwest. There is an early reference to the Kiowa Apache near the Black Hills of South Dakota (Gunnerson and Gunnerson 1971:14). They allied themselves politically with the Kiowa, whose language is not Athapaskan, and became committed to an existence on the Plains. The Lipan Apache also spent a good deal of time on the southern Plains (see Sjoberg 1953). In the eighteenth century they were beset by the Comanche moving into the area from the north, and the surviving Lipan eventually joined the Jicarilla.

The Jicarilla Apache probably include descendants of various Apache groups who occupied the northeastern part of New Mexico and ventured from their mountain camps into the Plains to hunt buffalo (Opler 1936, 1938; D. Gunnerson 1974; Tiller 1983). In the seventeenth century they also practiced a significant amount of agriculture. The Mescalero Apache to the west are the descendants of Apache the Spanish referred to as Faraones, who in the eighteenth century exploited an area east of the Rio Grande (Schroeder 1974a).

The Navajo occupied the northern zone of Apachean territory. From the seventeenth century onward they came into much closer and more prolonged contact with Pueblo groups than most of the other Apache divisions did. The Navajo sheltered Pueblo refugees during the rebellion of 1680 and intermarried extensively with Pueblo peoples. Consequently, they were more heavily influenced than the other Apache by these cultures. In the nineteenth century, some of the Navajo moved from New Mexico into a region north of the Western Apache area.

The Chiricahua, who during the later eighteenth and most of the nineteenth centuries occupied what is now the southeastern region of Arizona near the mountains that bear their name, probably migrated into that area from the Mimbres Mountains of New Mexico. During most of this period they relied more heavily on raiding than the other Apache divisions and practiced little or no agriculture. They might have chosen their location because of its strategic position as a base for raids on the villages of Mexico (Schroeder 1974b). All of the Apache populations practiced raiding at one time or another, and eventually it became a major aspect of their subsistence for most of them.

The Western Apache dialect is most similar to the dialects of the Navajo and Chiricahua (see Dyen and Aberle 1974:210). Some of the similarity to Navajo might date to the 1860s, when the Western Apache spent some time living in close contact with Navajo who were moving into northern Arizona (Schroeder 1974b:478–482). The Western Apache also had a good deal of contact with the Chiricahua because they often passed through Chiricahua territory on the way into Mexico.

The Western Apache probably entered their own territory from the northeast, coming south over the Mogollon Rim that juts across in east-central Arizona (Goodwin 1969:34). On the southern side of the rim, many of them established small farm plots that came to be reflected in their clan system. Particular clans became associated with these farming localities (see map inside covers, Goodwin 1969). But this was an embellishment of a more ancient principle of matrilineal descent.

After a couple of centuries in the Southwest, the Apache had incorporated several innovations into their earlier mode of subsistence, including trade with other populations, but they remained self-sufficient. They produced and acquired resources for their own consumption. They retained possession of their territory and all but exclusive use of it, and unlike many other native peoples of the Southwest, they had not been incorporated into the Spanish state.

Apache and Spanish Interaction

The Spanish subjugated most of the Pueblo peoples and the village agriculturists to the south and west through force. A few of these peoples had acquiesced without much struggle, but most had resisted in various ways, either through confrontation or strategic accommodation. In the end, none could rid themselves of the invaders for more than a few brief respites. Spanish military garrisons occupied some villages. Others were within striking distance of Spanish forts, or presidios. Many had resident missionaries.

Missionizing was a major endeavor for the Spanish, and usually this process involved more than instruction in religious doctrine. In 1538, the Spanish Viceroy Antonio de Mendoza instructed Fray Marcos de Niza that "you must explain to the natives of the land that there is only one god in heaven, and the emperor on earth to rule and govern it, whose subjects they must all become and whom they must serve" (Forbes 1960:6).

At times the methods for effecting this conversion involved public hangings and the burning of recalcitrant converts at the stake, which were familiar measures for dealing with religious delinquents in Europe at the time as well.

Outside the Pueblo area, another policy associated with missions was to concentrate the region's inhabitants in administered villages. This not only collected the people for more effective tutelage, but it freed the lands they had occupied for Spanish confiscation (see Spicer 1962:281–306). In some areas the *encomienda* system, which involved the establishment of large plantation-like holdings, was more common during the early period of colonization, although they were abolished subsequently by the Spanish Crown. *Encomiendas* were labor-intensive operations, though not usually with Spanish labor. A wry Spanish missionary noted in 1608 that "no one comes to the Indies to plow and sow, but only to eat and loaf" (Forbes 1960:112). Indigenous peoples did the physical work, and for the work in mines to the south, slave raids were a major source of the labor. As we noted earlier, in some instances the Spanish raided the Apache for this purpose.

Gold and silver had long been the premium attraction, but other mineral resources received some attention as well. Minerals in the Southwest have continued to be of great interest to Euro-Americans for at least 450 years, and throughout those centuries, mineral exploitation has been a continuous theme.

The overall thrust of Spanish policies was to extend the hegemony of the state and establish it firmly among the native populations or, failing that, to eliminate the inhabitants and occupy their former territories. Various interest groups within the Spanish state, including rival missionary orders, often were at odds over policies. As the instructions of Viceroy Mendoza quoted above indicate, one motive of missionaries beyond saving souls was to incorporate native peoples into Spanish society—if not as slaves, generally as peons. No doubt this is one reason why a stress on discipline, agricultural and other forms of labor, and personal comportment ranging from sexual propriety to the wearing of proper clothing accompanied holy writ (see Spicer 1962:6).

Many of the Pueblo villages at the northern fringe of Spanish territory withstood centuries of this pressure and were able to remain culturally distinct despite the attempts to impose hegemony through violence. Even so, the lengthy exertion of power forced them to make accommodations. Village people in Mexico, deeper within the Spanish domain, underwent still more intense and prolonged pressure. Throughout the Southwest, village dwellers, because of their fixed existence, were hard-pressed to escape incorporation into the Spanish state. Their dependence on agriculture in a region of scarce water often left them with nowhere else to go, and ultimately they were unable to resist force through confrontation.

The Apache, on the other hand, were more elusive. Their mode of subsistence required free movement, and once they defined the relationship as hostile, they were in a position either to elude confrontation or take the initiative on their own terms. José Cortés observed in 1799: "The *rancherías* always occupy the steepest canyons in the mountains, surrounded by the most difficult passes for approaching the site where they are located. That site is chosen, as a general rule, adjacent to the greatest heights in order to command the surrounding valleys and plains" (1989:65). For the most part the Apache retained the options of avoiding the Spanish or raiding them, depending on their assessment of the advantages.

The Spanish eventually gave up hope of quickly subjugating the Apache, and the alternative of genocide turned out to be impractical. Unable to extend their hegemony throughout *Apachería* by force, they chose to consolidate their gains and contain the Apache beyond the state's frontier. Across northern Mexico they set up a line of presidios garrisoned with troops to intercept parties of Apache venturing south to raid villages, and they dispatched "flying squadrons" of cavalry to pursue raiders fleeing north with stolen livestock (Moorhead 1968: 15–16).

This did not prove to be very effective. Small parties of Apache raiders had little trouble slipping quietly between the presidios and returning to their mountain camps with livestock. Spanish flying squadrons were no match for the Apache on foot who eluded them among the crags and arroyos of the sierra. When the Spanish did venture into what they thought was Apache territory, they sometimes attacked any Native Americans they came across. Often these were the wrong target.

In at least one case the victims of Spanish retaliation turned out to be Sobaipuri Pima who had suffered from Apache raids themselves (Spicer 1962:214). Relationships between the Pimans and Apache in the late 1500s and beyond had not been particularly hostile, but the Spanish pursued a policy of promoting conflict among Native American populations in order to weaken them and prevent their uniting in common cause (Spicer 1962:240).

The ineffectiveness of Spanish military actions against the Apache during the seventeenth and eighteenth centuries was a result to some extent of a lack of sufficient information about them. For a century or more the Spanish had no clear sense of the range of Apache territory. Eventually it would become apparent that the home bases of many of the Apache who raided in Mexico lay far to the north among the mountains drained by the Gila and Salt rivers.

The situation also reflected differences between Spanish and Apache social organization and ecological adaptations. The Spanish represented the leading edge of a ponderous, cumbersome imperial state attempting to establish political control over a vast region by incorporating or eliminating the previous inhabitants. The Apache, on the other hand, were unhampered by any particular policy or by any incentives for territorial conquest. Such a concept would have seemed pointless, and perhaps even incomprehensible, among these free-ranging groups of kin.

The Spanish also tended to project some of their own political realities onto the Apache by attempting to deal with them as political entities rather than recognizing the fluid, individualistic nature of Apache life. Other European-based peoples over the centuries tended to do the same. This was to have many implications, but it often led to assumptions that one Apache group somehow represented others when, in fact, they had little or nothing to do with one another. For their part, the Apache did much the same thing. They were not particularly impressed by the idea that the various villages in northern Mexico were part of a larger political entity, and generally they dealt with villages in terms of their own political experience, treating them as independent, autonomous aggregates.

The advantage at the time lay with the Apache. They were able to tap the resources of regions far from their home bases but had no interest in claiming, conquering, occupying, or defending the regions they raided. During the early period they had no need to worry about maintaining or guarding territory, since their homeland was far from the scene of conflict. Even in later times, their main concerns were to protect their encampments rather than to maintain borders. They

The San Xavier del Bac Mission, founded by the Spanish in the late 1600s at the southern edge of Apachería

could control their territorial base while exploiting the products of others. It would be several centuries before Apache sovereignty was seriously challenged within their own territory.

In the eighteenth century, Spanish policy toward the Apache shifted. It had become clear that the most compelling motivation for Apache raids, aside from the occasional aspect of revenge for the deaths of relatives, was subsistence. For generations Apache raiders had herded Spanish livestock hundreds of miles northward into *Apachería*. Although they occasionally sold animals in the markets of Santa Fe, the Apache ate most of them. Raiding had become a major means to provide themselves with food.

Under the reforms that Bernardo de Gálvez, Governor of the Interior Provinces, instituted in 1786, the Spanish altered their policies in order to nullify that incentive. To dissuade the Apache from raiding, the Spanish decided to give them what they had raided to obtain. They invited Apache bands to camp under the presidio walls and receive issues of food from the troops. Tentatively, at first, many

Apache accepted this apparent largess. Their response suggests that, as Cortés and others argued, many Apache were receptive to peaceful overtures.

By this time the Spanish had a better understanding of the scattered, fluid nature of Apache social organization. Rather than attempting to deal with such an illusory political entity as an Apache nation, they exploited the Apache's lack of unity. The Spanish were aware that the various local Apache groupings sometimes were at odds with one another, and they tried to use this to weaken the Apache as a threat by encouraging disputes. To exacerbate the situation, they freely dispensed alcohol to the people in order to dull restraints, inflame quarrels, and induce as much social disintegration among the population as possible (Spicer 1962). As William Griffen points out, however, alcohol created so much disruption that the Spanish soon tried to prohibit it (1988:16). By that time, however, the local populace had begun supplying alcohol to the Apache, and the trade proved impossible to stop.

Apache who accepted the food and hospitality soon found themselves in a different relationship with the Spanish. Although the source of food ultimately was the same, control of the situation shifted. These Apache no longer raided or moved extensively throughout their own territory in seasonal rounds to gather wild foods or to garden. Those activities in the past had required free mobility and a thin dispersal of the population. Curtailment of that mobility led to an erosion of the social relationships that supported it, including the egalitarian distribution of food and the mode of interaction associated with it.

At the presidios, Apache who normally would not often have encountered one another now spent day after day in close contact. In the past, disputes had been avoided or defused by the capacity of offended parties to go their separate ways. An important means of resolving conflict among free-ranging peoples is simply to part company. This is easy when both groups have vast territories available to them. To hamper or discourage this movement through the concentration of people not only undermines an important means of controlling conflict but also increases its frequency. In a society without a formal overall governmental structure, disputes may result in violence because the people directly involved are left to settle the matter themselves. Kinship ties provided mediating mechanisms, but many of these Apache were not closely linked by kin ties and therefore lacked this mechanism to resolve frictions.

For a time this policy of distributing food and alcohol to the Apache was quite successful from the Spanish perspective. Many of the southernmost Apache who had been closest to the presidios were among the first to be drawn into this relationship. A few of them eventually became incorporated into the hegemony of the Spanish state. Some of these became known as *Apaches mansos*, or "tame Apache." The Spanish regarded them with some contempt, and other Apache came to see them as enemy people (*inda*). As late as 1848, long after Mexican independence from Spain, the census showed two hundred Apache, most of whom apparently spoke Spanish, living at the old Tubac presidio (Officer 1987:214). Others, particularly those farther to the north who were more remote from Spanish influence, were less involved in this pattern, and many of those groups who did frequent the presidios retained some of their autonomy.

To assess what the outcome of this process might have been if the Spanish policy had continued is difficult. As it happened, other historical circumstances intervened. Mexican independence unseated the Spanish government early in the nineteenth century, and with its departure, the resources for continuing the program dwindled. Unlike the Spanish Crown, the new Mexican government did not have sufficient funds to provide free food and alcohol to the Apache. As a result, Apache drifted away from the presidios and eventually resumed their former patterns.

Repercussions of the Interactive Process

The episode of the presidio ration program suggests an important aspect of the Apache experience in the Southwest. For more than two centuries, the power of the Spanish empire had failed to defeat the Apache in direct confrontation. The hegemony of the Spanish state had stopped short at the frontier of Apache territory. The vulnerable point, finally, was the Apache's subsistence base. By luring at least some of them to relinquish the former patterns of their food quest in favor of what appeared to be a much easier and preferable alternative, the Spanish posed the first serious threat to Apache autonomy.

The concept of state hegemony has long been a subject of discussion. Antonio Gramsci stressed the aspect of consent in the extension and maintenance of hegemony (1971). This does not seem applicable to the earlier Spanish conquests of Pueblo and other sedentary peoples during the sixteenth and seventeenth centuries, since that process involved a good deal of raw force and violence over unwilling populations who had virtually no escape. The Apache were able to resist this force more successfully. But the Gálvez reforms created a different situation in which Gramsci's insights may be more appropriate. The events of history which brought an end to this episode, however, leave the issue somewhat unresolved.

We might wonder why many of the Apache resisted the temptation to accept Spanish offers. Perhaps some perceived the implied
dangers. But up to that time they had risked their lives and expended
tremendous effort traveling on foot through the mountain ranges for
hundreds of miles to capture livestock. They had stalked sleeping villages deep in Mexico and led their cattle and horses away in silence,
trying to distance themselves without raising the alarm. They had
suffered hot pursuit, and in some cases, they had been killed in the
process.

The Apache had trained their children to harden them for such a
life. Grandfathers roused young boys before dawn to make them run
up mountain sides holding water in their mouths. Elders taught children to break through the ice to swim in frigid rivers at daybreak and
hold snowballs under their arms until they melted. José Cortés wrote
in 1799 that "they are so agile and quick that they rival horses for
endurance, outrunning them on rugged or hilly terrain" (1989:57).
Even so, the Apache had suffered innumerable hardships. Recurring
accounts over the centuries reveal a consistent willingness of Apache
to seek a peaceful coexistence with surrounding peoples.

The Spanish program introduced a new and somewhat bizarre element into the Apache universe. Resources that the Apache had won
only at the cost of great hazard and extreme physical endurance they
now could acquire without such entailments. The implications and
possible repercussions of this could not have been very obvious to
more than a few. Perhaps the most surprising aspect of the period is
not that some Apache took the bait but that many resisted it.

Raiding had been only one aspect of Apache subsistence, one of
two major innovations that marked their adaptations to the Southwest. Agriculture also became important to many of them. The contrast between the two, and the repercussions that both would eventually have for the people, are worth considering. In adopting the
technique of planting gardens as well as raiding, the Apache added
to their existing subsistence pattern without replacing it. They still
inhabited mountain areas, hunting game and gathering a range of
wild plants, and throughout the centuries many Apache chose not to
grow crops.

Among populations in various parts of the world, the adoption of
agriculture has had profound implications for social organization.
When people invest time and effort to prepare soil and plant, tend
their fields, and harvest crops, concepts of personal or group ownership often develop. Because the labor of the farmer transforms the
land, the land itself can become property. If people depend on their
crops, they may have to defend them. Agriculture can stimulate con-

cepts of private or restricted ownership rights, and if it produces a surplus it can bring about a situation in which some people have more and others have less. It brings new problems of distribution and resource allocation. Agriculture often leads to social differentiation and sometimes to clear distinctions among social classes.

This did not happen in the Apache case. The Apache's reliance on wild foods remained important enough to perpetuate the kind of social organization best suited to that pursuit. Wild-food gathering continued to predominate over agriculture in influencing the social organization.

Wild foods usually are not stable or concentrated enough to allow claims of exclusive access in one locality. Sooner or later the food source is bound to become depleted in any limited area. Animals move, and plants bear at different times of the year. This means that people who depend on these resources must also be able to move and to be in the right places at crucial times. In such a circumstance, collective access to resources, which entails egalitarian distribution, mobility, and sharing, works better than a system of individual property holdings that might inhibit people's movement from one region to another. The Apache were not swayed toward a sedentary existence by a commitment to agriculture because agriculture never was important enough to overpower these other considerations. Apache groups varied a great deal in that regard. The White Mountain Apache did a great deal of farming, and the Chiricahua did almost none. But for most, it remained little more than a useful option.

Ancient Athapaskan beliefs also militated against the establishment of property ownership through inheritance. When a death occurred, the survivors destroyed the dwelling and abandoned the site. People never mentioned the name of the deceased, especially close relatives. They buried the personal property of the dead person or left it, damaged, at the grave. Such practices and patterns of belief and the emotional force that they carried inhibited the establishment of propertied kin groups which in other populations have developed into hierarchical, or stratified, systems based on the unequal control of property. The trajectory of Apache historical experience was not congenial to the development of such patterns. It tended instead to reinforce and perpetuate an egalitarian, fluid social system.

Apache social organization could achieve this balance among multiple subsistence activities because, for the time being, they were in control of their lives and territory. They could make choices that worked best for them because there was little to interfere with those options. Apache agricultural enterprises were secondary in the sense that their pursuit did not have significant repercussions or induce the need for radical adjustments in social organization. This was not the case, ultimately, with subsistence raiding.

Like agriculture, raiding during the Spanish period supplemented older modes of subsistence. In some ways it was more compatible with existing patterns than was agriculture. In a sense the older pattern was preadapted to raiding as a means of getting food. The Apache's mountain orientation had accustomed them to mobility and the need to travel significant distances to tap a variety of resources. It afforded them effective means of retreat, a domain that was relatively safe from pursuit. The villagers who produced or defended the livestock they had stolen generally were far less mobile and were at a disadvantage in unfamiliar mountainous terrain. José Cortés writes that Apache escaping with stolen livestock "scale nearly inaccessible mountains, they cross arid deserts in order to exhaust their pursuers, and they employ endless stratagems to elude the attacks of their victims" (1989:72).

The older Athapaskan pattern was compatible with raiding in another sense as well. The kinship system that provided the ground rules for interaction among Apache also defined those to whom one had no obligations whatsoever: people who were not kin. Among the scattered Apache population, kinship ties through women, whether based on descent or marriage, were the main criteria for defining relationships. Beyond these ties that pervaded the local clusters of people operating together on a day-to-day basis, broader categories of descent—the matrilineal clans—provided a more extensive basis for affiliation among the free-ranging, mobile groups of the Western Apache.

Together these networks and categories linked every individual to a large number of people. Cortés noted in 1799: "Despite the continual movement in which these nations live, and the great deserts in their lands, the *rancherías* can easily find one another when they wish to communicate, even when they have not seen or had any news of one another for a long time. They all know with unmistakable certainty in which areas the surrounding *rancherías* should be living, according to their well-known familiarity with the mountains, valleys, and water holes that they possess" (1989:74).

But the role of kin ties in providing a basis for interpersonal reciprocity, mutual obligations, and predictable behavior had an obverse side. Where no kin ties existed, the obligations that would have provided a basis for peaceful interaction also were absent. Kinship specifies modes of interaction, but encounters with strangers and non-kin were devoid of this "social script." There were few formal rules to guide mutual behavior.

The Apache did recognize cultural similarities with other Apache, including those with no apparent kin ties, but interactions with such people were tentative. The Western Apache term for "people," *nde*, essentially means "Apache people." Its counterpart, *inda*, meaning non-Apache people, is usually translated as "enemy" and was applied to most other peoples, often with descriptive qualifiers. Such a pattern made village dwellers, as well as other populations in the Southwest, potentially fair game.

This does not mean that anyone who was not kin was necessarily subject to attack. The Apache traded and interacted on a friendly basis with many other groups in the Southwest, but such relationships tended to be uncertain. To be outside the range of kinship was to be beyond the hearth of social expectations and reciprocal obligations based on a consensus of ground rules.

Finally, raiding, unlike agriculture, was not simply a matter of harvesting or creating a resource. Livestock was produced by other populations whose intentions in doing so did not include feeding the Apache. For the Apache to acquire this resource meant that, inevitably, they placed themselves in conflict with the interests of other peoples of the region.

During the Spanish era the Apache could raid or plant gardens at will. The major criteria were the needs of the people themselves, but this situation was inherently unstable. It could go on unhampered as long as the people retained possession of their territory, but when the numerical advantage shifted overwhelmingly from the Apache to their adversaries, raiding came to have far greater repercussions for the Apache themselves.

The manner in which each of these populations viewed the other is also a significant factor in the relationship. Just as the Apache tended to see the scattered communities of northern Mexico as autonomous groupings comparable to their own, the Spanish, the Mexicans, and the Anglo-Americans who later confronted the Apache tended to view them as a political collectivity. In 1636 the Spanish chronicler Alonso de Benavides referred to "the huge Apache nation." In the usage of the period this term did not necessarily have the implication of a nation state but generally referred to any foreign population—the "natives" of the region. Benavides was aware of differences among the Apache and continued that, "although, being one nation, it is all one language, since it is so extensive it does not fail to vary somewhat in some bands" (Bolton 1916).

More important than the accuracy of the perception, however, is what difference it made in the mode of interaction between the Apache and these populations. To consider the Apache a collective entity implied dealing with them as if they were. This involved expectations of appropriate actions or responses on their part and could justify certain reactions when they failed to act accordingly. As we shall see, this disjuncture of perception continued well into the nineteenth century and beyond.

These processes of change have many facets, and to over-emphasize any one or a few would be misleading. Most significantly, perhaps, with the development of subsistence raiding and during the brief episode of Spanish rations, the Apache departed from direct reliance on their own productivity to reliance on resources produced by others. This led them into relationships with neighboring populations that involved some degree of dependency, although it was far from pervasive. The balance between the Apache and the villages they raided was especially delicate because it meant that even though the Apache placed themselves in a conflict of interest with the village peoples, they could not drive them out without losing their source of food. Changes in the relative size, density, and political circumstances of these populations eventually led to a disruption of that balance.

Throughout the era of the Spanish presence in the Southwest, the Apache retained the fundamental structure of their older social organization. Men continued to do most of the hunting, and women formed a stable residential core in their mountain base camps. Even though groups moved throughout their territories to exploit resources at particular times of the year, the joint families in base camps continued to constitute the core of Apache life.

The garden plots were a part of this pattern. No rigid sexual division of labor relegated farming exclusively to women, but the bulk of such work fell to them because hunting and raiding took men away much of the time. Raiding perpetuated the old pattern of prolonged male absenteeism.

During this era some Apache continued to engage in market exchanges with other groups (see Hall 1989), and Apache visited Pueblo communities to trade tanned hide clothing or meat for woven cotton mantas or agricultural products. In many cases this took the form of gift exchanges to reinforce social ties. This exchange did not, however, become an indispensable source of subsistence for the Apache.

In such Spanish strongholds as Santa Fe, eastern Apache became more heavily involved in trade and sold in the Spanish markets some of the livestock they acquired on raids into Sonora and Chihuahua. This appearance of animals from one province in the markets of another came to be a chronic point of contention among the Spanish of different regions.

The Spanish also created and maintained a market for slaves. Some Apache, whose own people were captured and sold into slavery, sold enemy captives to the Spanish.

None of these exchange relationships ever seems to have become more than marginal to Apache subsistence, though. Generations later, the Apache still could have survived entirely on the resources of their own territory. The processes that had been put into motion, however, would not allow this subsistence to continue forever.

CHAPTER 4

The Apache in the Nineteenth Century

By the mid nineteenth century the Apache of Arizona included several regional populations who differed in dialect and minor customs, but these differences were slight compared to the similarities they derived from their common heritage. They encountered one another from time to time, and most of them continued to interact sporadically. The population who came to be known as Western Apache consisted of three major populations. The Coyotero territory included the mountains and relatively high altitudes north of the Black River in Arizona. The Pinal lived farther south among the broken country between the Gila and Salt rivers. The Arivaipa had extended their domain farther south toward the San Pedro River, after having displaced the Sobaipuri Pima who formerly lived there (Worcester 1979:33).

A strip of uninhabited territory to the north separated the Western Apache from the Navajo. In the 1860s the Navajo had spread westward into northern Arizona to escape military pressure in New Mexico, and in doing so, they encountered a few Western Apache (Schroeder 1974b:478–482; see also Kelley 1980:307–332). The relationship between these two populations was uneasy, punctuated by sporadic violence. Although they shared a common past and spoke dialects of the same language, they had been separated for several generations. Eventually they had become strangers to one another.

In the 1930s, Western Apache recalled the time when they had lived in the north near the Navajo and the Hopi, but the impression is one of ambivalence. According to the Western Apache account, an irksome Navajo woman precipitated a quarrel, and the two populations parted company (Goodwin 1969:71–72). Whether this account has any basis in fact, it reflects the attitude with which they regarded one another. Although they had a great deal in common, they considered themselves to be different peoples.

It seems to have been common among the Apache to leave territory between such distantly related populations unoccupied. Where kinship forms the fabric of the social organization, the atrophy of kin ties means a lack of the social mechanisms that regulate behavior and render it predictable. Interactions among people without such bonds become uncertain and somewhat dangerous. José Cortés in 1799 went so far as to assert that "although they may encounter their relatives they take the greatest precautions, which vary more or less according to how long it has been since they last saw one another, and they will not approach a brother without their weapons in hand" (1989:76).

John Cremony, with characteristic hyperbole, asserts that the Apache were "instructed to regard every other race as their natural enemies" (1969:85). But Cremony had been reared in a heterogeneous society in which broad social categories, "racial" or otherwise, were important criteria for defining the nature and degree of interaction among people. In projecting this view on the Apache, he distorted the situation. For them, distrust of people beyond the sphere of kinship was not based on "race" or a stress on cultural differences or similarities. It was founded on the sense that the actions of people who are not relatives are unpredictable and, therefore, unsafe. Where one's own territory abuts a region inhabited by people who are not kin, the frontier marks the edge of social rules.

Although the Navajo and Western Apache had long forgotten their past relationships by the time they met in northern Arizona in the 1860s, their linguistic and cultural similarities were apparent. There probably was some intermarriage in this period, which could have produced the social bonds needed for regular interaction. In the twentieth century some of the Western Apache matrilineal clans had Navajo names (Goodwin 1969:102), which could be a result of Navajo women marrying Apache men and transmitting their clan membership to their children. But this interaction was not enough to bring about a reunification of these groups, and their subsequent split allowed the process of differentiation to resume.

Another Apache population lived east of the Western Apache, toward the headwaters of the Gila River in the mountains of western New Mexico. They were referred to as Gila, Mimbres, Coppermine, and Warm Springs (*Ojo Caliente*). They, too, lived beyond an uninhabited strip of territory that separated them from the Western Apache, and they considered themselves to be different people. Still farther east toward the Rio Grande were the Faraones, later known as the Mescalero Apache (Schroeder 1974b:166). To the south of the Western Apache, the Chiricahua Apache occupied the mountains of southeastern Arizona. In the nineteenth century the Chiricahua had only recently separated from the Apache of the upper Gila drainage region of New Mexico, moving closer to the towns of Sonora and Chihuahua

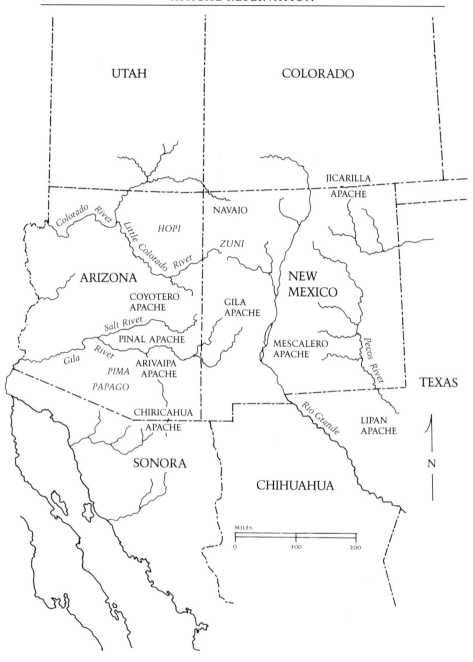

*Map 2. Distribution of Apache populations in the Southwest,
mid-nineteenth century*

(Schroeder 1974b:183). The Western Apache had good relations with them and often passed through their territory on raids to the south.

Together, these populations constituted the western segment of southern Athapaskans. By the nineteenth century the Western Apache probably were no longer aware of their eastern relatives who came to be known as the Jicarilla and Lipan Apache, in northern New Mexico and the Plains, and the departure of the Kiowa Apache was several centuries in the past (see Goodwin 1969:93).

Western Apache Subsistence

In the nineteenth century many of the Western Apache had gardens. Usually they would plant in low valleys and camp in the mountains, especially when they were threatened with possible attacks. Cortés wrote in 1799: "They always judge it more fitting—and choose with good reason—to locate their living sites among very rugged hills and mountains; and consider themselves better or worse situated according to the greater or lesser difficulty of access to their chosen sites. These must necessarily have water and firewood in abundance, the requisite wild fruits, and a natural layout of terrain such that they can barricade and defend themselves against their enemies" (1989:57).

They hunted throughout the year, but most plant foods were available only at certain seasons, and their subsistence pattern was far from random. Again, according to Cortés: "In the ravines of the same mountains the men seek large and small game, extending their hunts to the adjoining plains. When they have what they need, they carry it back to the *ranchería* and turn the spoils of the hunt over to their women" (1989).

In spring and early summer after they had planted their gardens and the crops had begun to sprout, they would gravitate toward the lower desert regions in search of saguaro fruit. By late summer, acorns were ripe, and families camped in higher elevations while they gathered them. People could eat the acorns from the shell, but they also pulverized the flesh and mixed it into a mush to be eaten with meat or other foods. Some people would bring green corn up from the gardens and use it to make *tulpai*, a milky, mildly alcoholic beer-like beverage. The Western Apache had learned to how make *tulpai* from the Chiricahua, who in turn had learned it from peoples in Mexico. In early fall, mesquite beans ripened in the desert areas, and juniper berries and pine nuts were available later in the season. This was the prime season for raiding (Goodwin 1969:156–160).

Throughout the year the Apache also used a variety of other foods. They hunted deer and trapped wood rats and other small game, and they cooked mescal, the tuber of the agave plant, in pit ovens. The process took a couple of days and produced a sweet, starchy substance whose flavor has been compared to sweet potatoes or winter squash. Generally, they shared among themselves whatever they produced in sufficient quantities in their gardens or through these other pursuits (Cortés 1989:58; Buskirk 1986:38).

The Apache considered certain potential food sources unacceptable to eat, for a variety of reasons. They associated owls with death. Bears had a special power that was dangerous to humans. Dog-like animals also held potentially dangerous power. They were not eaten, and the people viewed them with ambivalence. The Apache distaste for fish is widely shared among various peoples of the Southwest. Cortés writes that "these nations have not the slightest interest in fishing, despite the great abundance available in their rivers" (1989: 68). But even with these restrictions, the Apache food supply was diverse (Jorgensen 1983). As it happened, the versatility that characterized most aspects of Apache life, including the food quest, allowed them to retain their independence and control of their territory as long as they did. Eventually, though, this was not enough.

Western Apache Social Organization

Throughout this period Apache social organization had retained many of its earlier characteristics. When a couple married, the husband usually moved to live near his wife's relatives, and people continued to define relationships through women. A Western Apache cluster of relatives typically consisted of an older couple with their unmarried children, their married daughters and sons-in-law, and the children of these couples. If the group were larger, two or three older sisters and their children and grandchildren might live together. The adult couples with their young children would have their own dwellings—conical or dome-shaped structures covered with brush in the summer or hides in the winter. Later in the nineteenth century they often used tarpaulins instead of hides. Usually the dwellings were within easy shouting distance of one another. Women built the dwellings, which belonged to them.

The structure of these simple units was the basis for much of the dynamic nature of Apache social organization. The variability of their size reflects the fundamental flexibility in Apache life, accommodating the need to respond to threat as well as opportunity. In theory there was no practical limit to the number of people who could gather and camp together, but in most circumstances the local food sources would not support large groups for very long. Smaller groups, or even single households, might sometimes have to operate on their own.

Children who grew up in this social system lived in the midst of their mother's relatives. A child's playmates were the children of the mother's sisters. The kinship terms for these cousins were the same as the terms for brothers and sisters. The mother's brothers' children, on the other hand, usually lived off in some other group with their own mothers' close kin. A child referred to them by different kinship terms from those of the mother's sisters' children.

The mother's mother usually was one of the child's most important teachers. *Shiwoye* was the term by which grandmothers and grandchildren addressed one another, and it expressed a warm, jocular, informal bond. The most vivid concept of "close relatives" in Western Apache thought was nurtured within the joint family setting, where almost all of the most intimate and significant figures in a person's early life were maternal relatives.

This principle extended beyond the joint family to the clan system. With the Apache's range of mobility, members of the same clan might be scattered far and wide, but they retained a sense of relationship. Clan members of the same generation used brother/sister terms. People belonged to the clans and joint families of their mothers and, with regard to married men, to the joint families of their wives.

Since married men of a joint family had moved in from elsewhere, their status as outsiders imposed a degree of ambiguity on their situation. A man might be a valued and well-liked member of the cluster, but this was something he had to achieve. Often, his wife's family would have assessed his qualities before the marriage. Generally he had no prior bonds of kinship that automatically gave him a status in the group.

There were inherent uncertainties in the relationship between a man and his wife's mother. Each had a different claim on the same woman, either as wife or daughter, and often the bond between mother and daughter was very close. Since the mother and her daughter continued to live in the same small cluster of people, the older woman's influence could be especially strong. At the same time, the wife's parents had the right to expect their son-in-law to work for them and contribute to the group. Their relationship with him clearly had a hierarchical aspect to it, and it contained a potential basis for friction.

While this potential for internal conflict might pose a threat to the well-being of the entire cluster of people, the social convention of mother-in-law avoidance alleviated the problem. The social strategy for preventing conflict was to keep interaction to a minimum, and it

Apache household, late nineteenth century, Arizona Territory (National Anthropological Archives, Smithsonian Institution, 2580-B-1)

was expressed as a matter of etiquette. Avoidance did not take the form of mutual hostility but of respect. A man who thought highly of his wife's mother treated her with courtesy by staying away from her. For a man to treat his mother-in-law with casual familiarity showed disrespect and constituted an affront. A man could not easily avoid his wife's father, since their duties as adult males often required them to collaborate in subsistence and raiding activities, but the relationship did entail deference and respect on the part of the younger man.

The joint family structure had some other sensitive points as well. Generally, the men who had married into the group were not kin to the unmarried men who had been born into the joint family, nor were they necessarily related to the other in-marrying husbands. Yet normally they would have to cooperate effectively with them. In accordance with the gender-based division of labor, they would have roughly the same allocation of responsibilities and expectations. For the same reason, any conflict among them would be detrimental to the entire group.

Their shared social roles meant that they could not very well avoid one another. Tensions or conflicts that might arise among them would have to be dealt with in a different way. In some cases, men in this situation could adopt a "joking relationship" if they had certain kinds of clan ties with one another. This might be the case because of marriage practices. This meant that they observed a pattern of heavy-handed, mutual pranks and jocularity. Probably this helped to defuse any low-level friction that might otherwise have built up and become disruptive. In the absence of clan relationships, brothers-in-law were often expected to be respectful toward one another, even though avoidance might not be feasible. Joking might sometimes be an element of the relationship between brothers-in-law who were not clan relatives, but they avoided physical horseplay. A pattern of respect in a man's behavior toward his wife's father was still more pronounced.

This array of avoidance, respect, and joking patterns of behavior probably involved a spectrum of psychological causes and effects, but collectively these explicit, prescribed expectations served to quell and control some of the flash points of interpersonal friction. They made it more feasible for small groups of people to operate successfully under stressful conditions. Survival in many cases hinged on the effectiveness of these patterns.

People of the same clan did not marry, and brother/sister kinship terms extended to all clan members of the appropriate generation. The marriage prohibition also extended to members of different clans that were considered closely related to one another. Western Apache sibling terms designate gender with respect to that of the speaker rather than designating sex in an absolute sense, as do the English terms "brother" and "sister." The Apache terms distinguish siblings of the same sex, whose children are potentially members of the same clan, from siblings of the opposite sex, whose children can never be in the same clan.

In all, the Western Apache had over sixty clans whose tales of origin were associated with particular farm plots (see Kaut 1956, 1957, 1974). Their social organization reflected changes in the mode of subsistence that occurred when some of the Apache took up farming. But the principle of matrilineal descent, and probably the clan system itself in its general form, were much older than the Apache presence in the Southwest. Dyen and Aberle (1974) argue that Proto-Athapaskan social organization was matrilineal. Contact with other groups with matrilineal clan systems in the area, such as the Hopi and Zuni, also may have had some influence on the system of Western Apache clans.

Authority and the Distribution of Resources

Clan relationships and other kin ties connected the scattered population and provided a basis for interaction in complex, far-flung networks. The sets of relationships enmeshing every individual specified obligations and expectations, but it did nothing to hamper Apache mobility or alter the fundamentally egalitarian nature of the society. Clans were not ranked in any way. At any particular time certain clans had more members than others and, consequently, may have had more influence in certain respects, but clans had no means of accumulating and retaining an excess of property or political power. Social expectations continued to stress the wide distribution of resources.

It might be possible to see deer hunting as a proprietary activity because it was restricted to a certain segment of the population. Deer were a valuable resource, and only adult men had effective access to this game (Buskirk 1986:118). Young boys were discouraged from hunting deer before they were married because deer power was considered too strong for them to cope with. Women, and femaleness as a general force, were incompatible with deer hunting (Buskirk 1986:213). Like northern Athapaskans, the Apache believed that contact with women could spoil a hunter's luck.

But a successful hunter might end up with none of the meat from his kill. The hunting companion of a man who had killed a deer had the right to claim it, and even he normally would distribute the meat to a range of people. His wife's sisters had special priority in the distribution. By the end of this process, any game large enough to have a significant impact on the food supply would have found its way to a wide range of recipients. As Grenville Goodwin observed, "To remark of a man, 'He always gives away meat,' or of a woman, 'She always gives away food,' is the same as saying that he or she is generous, wealthy, successful, and influential" (1969:543). Only the desperate or impoverished would try to hide meat. Social "leveling mechanisms" worked to ensure that the more successful, prominent, or fortunate a person was, the greater were the social pressures to distribute resources.

A very good hunter might be able to take two wives, but typically these would be sisters. In the context of the joint family pattern, this might enhance the efficient use of resources. With matrilocal residence, the wives would remain together in their mother's group, and the husband would move in from elsewhere to help provide for the well-being of the group as a whole. Even so, by some accounts this pattern appeared in the nineteenth century as a response to a shortage of men after intensive warfare had taken a serious toll on the population. Some older Apache leaders in the early 1850s explained to John Cremony that, although their present situation called for polygamy, they felt uneasy about it and did not quite consider it proper

Apache hunters, late nineteenth century. The man on the left is thought to be the Chiricahua leader Chato. (National Anthropological Archives, Smithsonian Institution, 2491 A)

(Cremony 1969:249). Cortés, on the other hand, wrote in 1799 that polygamy was "widespread" (1989:54).

The raiding pattern, which, like hunting, was primarily a matter of meeting subsistence needs, also remained consistent with the egalitarian tendencies of Apache social organization. Raiding did, of course, entail a unique element of danger. Certain men achieved great respect for their courage and success in raiding, but this did not lead to authoritarian leadership. There is little evidence of any pattern approaching the sort of adulation and accolades that some of the buffalo-hunting Plains peoples accorded heroic warriors. The Apache seemed consistently skeptical of authority, and Apache leadership tended to be fleeting and to require constant validation. It was based on the willingness of people to agree with a leader's persuasions and to respect his opinions. Cortés asserts that "this authority does not instill any particular subordination or dependency on the rest, because each one is free to leave, remain, or disapprove of the plans of the chief" (1989:65).

The role of raid leader was institutionalized only to the extent that it was given a title meaning "he destroys dew" (Goodwin and Basso 1971:254). The term referred to expectations that a leader would show exemplary courage, walking ahead of the party as they entered dangerous territory. Apache expressed disdain for American military officers who commanded their troops from behind the lines and observed the action through binoculars (Ball 1980:45). During a raid the Apache leader had complete authority, but this did not carry over into other aspects of life. After the return home, his role dissipated, and he became "just a common man" (Goodwin and Basso 1971:254).

This is consistent with the general individualism and autonomy that pervaded Apache social organization and values. As early as 1778, the Spanish commissioner Teodoro de Croix expressed frustration in reaching a treaty with the Gila Apache because of "the difficulty of coming to an agreement with a nation so dispersed in which every Indian was a free republican" (quoted in Schroeder 1974b:87). In the mid nineteenth century, Agent Michael Steck reported: "[the Apache] have no civil regulations that give their chiefs power to act for and controll [sic] their people. At their councils the old men or chiefs talk for the tribes, but as soon as they separate every one acts as an independent agent, and refuses to be controlled and the chief has not the influence with others to compell [sic] him to obey as they seem to fear each other" (Schroeder 1974b:172). Cremony wrote of the famous and respected Apache leader Mangas Coloradas: "[He] could assume no authority not granted to him by his people. He never presumed to speak for them as one having authority but invariably said he would use his influence to perform certain promises and engagements" (1969:47).

Among some of the White Mountain Apache, to whom gardening was relatively important, there is some hint of a tentative drift toward hereditary chiefs associated with farmlands. But despite a possible tendency toward father-to-son succession, local leaders still achieved their recognition through personal qualities and actions rather than inheritance (Goodwin 1935:154). In any case, the role was more a matter of coordinating access to resources by initiating activity, overseeing distribution, and mediating conflicts rather than authoritarian coercion. Given the shifting nature of individual farm plot use within the collective group, it was desirable that someone coordinate access or adjudicate possible disputes.

Where farming was significant, land use patterns were compatible with this shifting nature of authority. There was some feeling that the matrilineal kin groups collectively had special rights to particular farming areas, but individuals did not own garden plots in a permanent sense or pass on ownership to their heirs, although the use of some plots passed from mother to daughter. A local cluster tended to involve a core of people who were members of the same clan, and leadership within such a group tended to fall on the most qualified of the senior men of the most numerous kin group—if only because such a person normally would have kin ties to the greatest number of people. If other considerations arose, people would look to someone else as leader.

Beliefs and the Structure of Relations

Nineteenth-century Apache beliefs involved ancient concepts, embellished by influences from other peoples of the Southwest and molded by their experiences since leaving the North. For the Apache the universe was a living entity, as it had been for their ancestors. It continued to hold myriad capricious powers that could be benevolent or harmful. Bears, snakes, lightning, and other creatures and phenomena had powers beyond their apparent physical characteristics. The yellow pollen of the cattail was charged with the benevolent power of the universe, and people took care to keep some with them whenever they could (Goodwin 1938:26; Opler 1941a:154).

Practices associated with death—the destruction of property and avoidance of the dead person's name—continued to inhibit whatever tendency might have arisen for power to become entrenched along kinship lines or for wealth to accumulate unevenly among the population. But many of the problems the people faced in the Southwest were different from those in the Subarctic. How did Apache culture reflect this?

Some of the influences of other cultures of the Southwest are fairly obvious. To their ancient cosmology of spiritual powers, the Apache added the concept of a unifying deity whose name *yosn* substantiates the resemblance to the Spanish *Dios*, but this belief seems to have been little more than a rather inconsequential addition to their cosmology. Cortés writes of the being he calls the Chief of Heaven but states that "they render him no worship or veneration whatsoever" (1989:53). Cremony characterizes the Apache as "a people not overburdened with reverential ideas, or prone to self-humiliation" (1969: 285).

Perhaps a more fundamental change had to do with the treatment of femaleness. The fundamental Athapaskan concern with femaleness as an abstract, powerful quality remained central to the Apache, but in the Southwest the emphasis on different aspects of this power shifted. Apache beliefs downplayed the potential threat to men associated with femaleness that appears in many northern Athapaskan cultures. Men still avoided contact with menstrual blood and childbirth, both of which could cause aching, swollen joints (see for a Chiricahua example Opler 1941a:154). People also believed that a man should avoid sexual intercourse before hunting deer, since this would cause the animals to avoid him (Goodwin 1969:332). But young women no longer underwent prolonged seclusion during menstruation, and many of the restrictions associated with this among other Athapaskan peoples either were dropped or relegated to token observances.

Instead, the Apache celebrated female puberty in a major public ceremony that became a central ritual among the various groups. There was no comparable male puberty ceremony, although young boys on their first raiding parties underwent a variety of ritual restrictions (Goodwin and Basso 1971:288–298). John Bourke does, however, refer to a nineteenth-century Chiricahua practice in which boys made "pilgrimages to secluded spots, during which periods they will not put their lips to water, but suck up all they need through a quill or cane" (1886:64).

The female ceremony incorporated many identifiable Southwestern influences. Masked dancers representing spirits called *gaan* played an important role among many of the Western Apache groups. These figures, with black hoods over their faces and elaborate wooden crowns, superficially resembled the *katcina* of the Hopi. Like the *katcina*, the *gaan* were benevolent figures, although they seem to have been associated more with mountains than with rainfall as *katcina* were (Goodwin 1969:64; Greenfeld, personal communication, 1989).

In the course of the ritual, a young woman performed a range of tasks associated with women's economic roles and responsibilities. She gathered wood to show her strength, for example, and carried water. An older woman massaged her to ensure her health, strength, and beauty. The young woman and a female companion also danced under a frame of poles that might have been symbolic of the ancient seclusion hut. She used the age-old scratching sticks and drinking tube, as women in the North had for centuries. She was supposed to keep her eyes downcast for fear of provoking excessive rainfall.

In this ritual the young woman personified a benevolent female deity. She not only received the personal blessings of the deity but conveyed good fortune, strength, and health to others. She could bless babies and old people and benefit the sick. The details of this ceremony are far better documented for later periods, but its general outlines reveal something about continuities in Western Apache culture from the Subarctic.

Certain aspects of Apache life manifest in this ceremony remained consistent with their Athapaskan heritage. The association with mountains, the reliance on wild foods, and the concerns with femaleness as a central theme all have ancient roots. Beyond that, such aspects as the masked dancers or the ritual corn grinding young women performed in some puberty ceremonies suggest the influences of other peoples in the Southwest. Aside from the Pueblo origins of their costuming, though, the *gaan* were a personification of more abstract, positive associations with mountains as a refuge and source of subsistence. Even in the twentieth century they are often referred to in English as "mountain spirits."

The puberty ceremony itself manifests a similar process through which complex, abstract concepts had become personified. The array of connotations associated with femaleness were transformed and shifted in the Southwest, and the abstraction became reified in the deity Changing Woman (see Basso 1966:26). Like other powers in Athapaskan thought, femaleness was capable of ebbing and flowing, imbuing people to varying degrees as well as endangering males' luck in hunting. But this concept now was distilled in the figure of a supernatural female figure whose characteristic aspect was overwhelmingly benevolent.

The antiquity of Changing Woman is difficult to assess, but a curious incident in 1627 or 1628 suggests that it is at least several centuries old. The Spanish in Santa Fe noted that a visiting band of Apache became extraordinarily interested in a statue of the Virgin Mary (Forbes 1960:120). The Spanish were intrigued by this, apparently interpreting it as a receptivity to Christian theology. More likely, though, the statue may have coincidentally struck a responsive chord in the Apache's own beliefs.

The positive shift in the connotations of femaleness and the decreased emphasis on its dangers might have been linked with some of the changes in Apache subsistence. Women in the Subarctic had been excluded from hunting, but in that environment there was very little plant food to gather. As a result, even though matrilocal residence had allowed women a pivotal role in the definition of interpersonal relationships and despite the range of essential tasks women performed, they were not able to contribute a great deal directly to the food supply. They did not possess or control access to the primary means of subsistence. Even though they received, prepared, and physically distributed meat, they did so according to established procedures and customs that precluded their having much discretionary control over the resource.

The division of labor in the Southwest remained essentially the same, but the resources were different. Wild plant food was much more abundant, and women's contributions to subsistence were far greater in proportion to the total food supply than they had been in the North (see Perry 1977).

Some writers have argued that agriculture also had an effect on women's status in the Southwest. There was a general sense that women were "more interested" in gardening, or that they tended to be better at it than men (Buskirk 1986:47). But differences among individuals of either sex in that regard were far greater than any categorical contrast between males and females. Many men worked gardens with no discernible social stigma. There was no particular feeling that gardening was "woman's work" (Buskirk 1986:47; see also Goodwin 1969:334; Opler 1972).

In most Apache groups, moreover, the gardens themselves were not a significant enough aspect of overall subsistence to have made much of a difference. Wild plant foods were more important. Grenville Goodwin writes: "Agriculture among some of the Western Apache was almost considered a luxury; that is, agriculture was not an integral part of their culture, and they could easily get along without it if they had to, as in all parts of the W.A. territory there were a sufficient variety of wild plants growing and game on which they could sustain themselves alone. Thus there were local groups living continuous to each other, some of which planted, some of which didn't. This was true in almost all the different bands" (quoted in Opler 1973:53). In the early years of the reservation, Lieutenant Britton Davis wrote that "the mountains in which [the White Mountain Apache] lived were a game paradise abounding in deer, turkeys (which they did not eat), bear, and an occasional elk" (1951:67).

The linkage of cause and effect is far from clear, but in the Subarctic, where women's role in subsistence was less contributory, femaleness itself was viewed with some ambivalence despite the key position of women in the social organization. In the Southwest, where women's role in subsistence became greater and more crucial, femaleness itself became a far more benevolent concept.

These are some of the things we can glimpse about Western Apache society in the mid nineteenth century, when the final decades of intensive warfare were underway. As fighting escalated and the interaction became increasingly brutalized, the victory ceremony came to be a major social event. Despite the increasing pressures on them, the Apache retained their sovereignty. When they finally lost control and possession of most of their territory, this would change.

Apache Raiding and Trade

Apache raiding poses some interesting theoretical problems. José Cortés wrote in 1799 that "the foods with which they sustain themselves include meats, provided by their constant hunting and cattle stealing carried out in the territory of their enemies" (1989:58). We might consider raiding production for consumption, since the thrust of it was to acquire animals for food. But this depends upon whether it is valid to perceive raiding as production. Perhaps *acquisition* for consumption would be more accurate. Whatever the case, though, the major purpose of Apache raiding was to get food for their own use.

In 1871, Lieutenant Colonel John Green wrote that he asked the Apache at Camp Goodwin: "'Why are you so poor?' and the answer invariably is, 'How can we be otherwise: We had not much originally, and now we can get nothing; we do not steal. We cannot go to the mescal country, as we are liable to be met and killed by scouting parties.' I know myself this to be the case, hence they have either to starve or steal or we must feed them until they can raise enough for themselves" (Colyer 1971:48). In 1857, Agent Michael Steck observed that "brave men with arms in their hands will not starve, nor see their children starve around them, while the means of subsistence is within their reach" (Colyer 1971:4).

The raiders distributed the stock they gained from raids to others—women, children, and other kin—who did not participate in acquiring it. This collective use of resources was consistent with their egalitarian social organization and the system of values that emphasized sharing. But the Apache did not eat all of their livestock. From the seventeenth through the nineteenth centuries, they carried out a small-scale but consistent trade and exchanged some of the livestock they had stolen from one region in the markets of another. Occasionally they even returned livestock for rewards offered by the aggrieved owners (Cremony 1969:81). The Apache stole horses in Sonora, for example, and sold them in the markets of Santa Fe or Chihuahua. General George Crook referred to this pattern as stealing on one side of the mountains and selling on the other, and he believed that the practice continued at least until 1886. "They steal stock from this side and sell it in Mexico; they do the same on this side, vice versa. This is the trade that built up Nacori. In two years that the Indians were on the reservation this town was nearly deserted, while now it is booming" (Crook 1946:181).

What was all this about? Why did the Apache sell livestock, and what did they get for it? Was this an incipient sort of commercial enterprise that might have had other repercussions in their social system?

Despite the long-standing existence of this practice, there is no evidence that any Apache became wealthy as a result of it. The profits, if any, did not seem to accumulate in any discernible place. Apache society continued to be egalitarian, and even prominent leaders who might have been in a position to control a major portion of these resources apparently did not do so. Mangas Coloradas of the Mimbres Apache, as one example, commanded enough respect to bring about a massive cooperative alliance among scattered Apache bands, but he operated on the basis of consensus and had neither authoritarian power nor great wealth. What, then, was the impact of this trade in stolen livestock?

From one perspective, the trade involved a transition in the value of these animals from their intrinsic use as food to their value as a commodity for exchange. But the Apache do not seem to have acted as entrepreneurs in these transactions. They did seize valuable livestock, produced by the labor of others, and sell it in the market. But at this point the potential profit seems to have dissipated. The reason, apparently, is that the Apache converted their surplus cattle into something else that had comparable use value. Since the Apache were mobile hunting people in mountainous regions, they could not support extra grazing animals for very long. Surplus horses and cattle had little use to them except in trade. Any livestock they could not eat within a fairly short period of time either had to be converted into something else or wasted.

Much of what they acquired from livestock trading was ammunition and firearms. Unlike livestock, ammunition could be held indefinitely, but it was not likely to be accumulated as a surplus or kept for long either because, like the animals, its value lay in its use. And in being used, it was used up. The Apache used some ammunition in hunting, but often it was depleted in the very process of raiding that resulted in more livestock.

Apache use of guns and their need for ammunition grew in the nineteenth century, as more firearms became available, their quality improved, and the intensity of conflict increased. They do not seem to have abandoned the bow and arrow as an alternative weapon until the reservation period, possibly because unlike the bow and arrow, guns put them in need of supplies they could not produce for themselves and which sooner or later they had to replenish. José Cortés wrote in 1799 that "we can be sure that the reason why the Indians have not thrown away their bows and arrows when they manage to acquire a rifle is their frequent lack of ammunition and the total lack of means to repair them when they break down" (1989:71).

Just as the Apache acquired livestock primarily to eat, they traded their excess stock for ammunition to shoot, and the value of guns and ammunition for the Apache was in their use rather than in their value as commodities. They also obtained guns and had them repaired in exchange for jerked meat and hides in towns on both sides of the border during this period, just as the eastern Apache had traded buffalo robes with Pueblo peoples for cotton mantas and other goods during the Spanish era.

From the viewpoint of merchants in the markets of Santa Fe who dealt with the Apache in these transactions, the livestock and the ammunition were indeed commodities for exchange. For them, the value of these goods lay in what they could bring in further trade. But the Apache's emphasis on use rather than exchange value buffered them, in a sense, from the implications of commodity exchange. For the Apache, the system of transaction was inherently stable and not likely to generate social inequities within their population. The ammunition they acquired in their livestock sales was a tool to obtain more stock for consumption rather than storable wealth. Other potential items of wealth—jewelry, blankets, and so on—were fairly incidental in Apache life, and the demands of mobility would have prevented them from amassing more possessions even if they had been inclined to do so.

On balance, Apache trading appears to have been little more than a marginal flirtation with the market system. The constraints inherent in their way of life essentially immunized them from being drawn into dependency on the market since there was no practical way for them to amass profit beyond the limits of their own consumption or incentive for them to do so. Raiding and peripheral trading did bring about subsistence linkages with other populations, but they helped the Apache maintain a formidable resistance to assaults from outside rather than imposing a dependency on a wider system. Eventually, though, the broader base of Apache life was to be undermined by other processes.

The Course of Events in the Nineteenth Century

In their first few centuries in the Southwest, the Apache had confronted the leading edge of the world's first modern imperial state. They did a good deal to stall the northward extension of Spanish hegemony. Despite the threat of ingestion, the Apache turned out to be largely indigestible and resistant to the processes by which the state broke down and absorbed native populations. Repeatedly they accepted offers of trade and peaceful interaction and initiated many themselves, but they balked at the acceptance of Spanish sovereignty. They could neither be incorporated nor eliminated from their territory, and by the time Mexico expelled the Spanish Crown from the region, this standoff had prevailed for many generations.

The initial effectiveness of the Spanish rations policy the Gálvez reforms brought about might have continued, but the Mexican government was unable to pursue it. Instead, the newly independent Mexican state, whose leadership was inspired by ideas of the European Enlightenment, embraced a political philosophy of equal status under the law for all peoples (see Spicer 1962:334–336). This presented some problems for Native American peoples within the territory effectively under Mexican control because, in precluding official recognition of their cultural identities, it also challenged their territorial claims, at least by implication. This gave rise to considerable agitation. But as far as *Apachería* to the Mexican north was concerned, Mexico's sovereignty had never been more than a legal fiction. As the Apache drifted away from the old presidios and returned to their former ways of hunting, gathering, and gardening in mountain camps and venturing south to raid for livestock, they became a growing problem which the Mexican state was unable to resolve.

Eventually the northern provinces of Mexico addressed the problem in an extreme reversal of the earlier stance. Ideals of equality gave way to a policy intended to eliminate the Apache, and governors of Sonora and Chihuahua offered cash bounties for Apache scalps. No doubt this measure reflected the frustration, and perhaps even desperation, that followed more than two centuries of persistent Apache raids. But the policies had explosive consequences.

The Anglo-American Presence

By the early years of the nineteenth century, still another population became a factor in the region. A small but growing number of Anglo-Americans had appeared on the periphery of *Apachería*. Initially the Apache seemed willing to accommodate these people in their territory, although relations soon deteriorated. The bounty on Apache scalps proved to be an attraction for some of these newcomers. A few Anglo-Americans who were willing to participate in the process of genocide quickly found their way into the Southwest. During the 1830s and 1840s, parties of scalp hunters roamed *Apachería* in the hope of collecting Sonora's bounties of one hundred pesos for the scalps of Apache men. Chihuahua offered a more precise breakdown of one hundred pesos for "warriors," fifty for women, and twenty-five for children.

One man named Santiago Kirker claimed to have killed hundreds of Apache while suffering the loss of only a few of his men. The murder of the Apache leader Juan José in 1837 by an Anglo trader he believed to be his friend led to a retaliatory killing of twenty-two trappers by aggrieved Apache. One J. H. Lyman, who spent a year trapping beaver in Apache territory in 1840 and 1841, described the incident.

Lyman maintained that the Apache at the time had "treated the Americans with the most cordial hospitality" (Colyer 1971:5). According to Lyman:

> The Indians were then, as now, hostile to the Mexicans of Sonora, and they were constantly making raids into that State, and driving off the cattle . . . At that time American trappers found the beaver very abundant about the headwaters of the Gila river, among those rich mountain vales where the Apaches had, and still have, their secure retreats. At the time I speak of there were two companies of trappers in that region. One of the companies, about seventeen men, was under a captain named Johnson. The other company consisted of thirty men, I think. I was trapping on another head of the Gila, several miles north. The valleys were full of Apaches, but all peaceful toward the white men, both Indians and whites visiting each other's camps constantly and fearlessly, with no thought of treachery or evil. Besides the Mexicans, the only enemies of the Apaches were the Pi-Utes and Navajoes on the northwest. But here in their fastness, they felt themselves safe from all foes.

One day Johnson concluded to go down into Sonora on a spree, as was occasionally the way with mountain men. He there saw the governor of the department, who, knowing that he had the confidence of the Indians, offered him an ounce of gold for every Apache scalp he would bring him. The bargain was struck. Johnson procured a small mountain howitzer, and then, with supplies for his party, returned to his camp. Previous to entering it, he loaded his howitzer with a quantity of bullets. On approaching the valley, he was met by the Indians, who joyfully welcomed him back, and proceeded at once to prepare the usual feast. While they were boiling and roasting their venison and bear meat, and were gathered in a dense group around the fire, laughing and chatting in anticipation of the pleasure they expected in entertaining their guests, Johnson told those of the party who had remained behind trapping of the offer of the governor, and with such details of temptation as easily overcame any scruples such men might have. As they were all armed with rifles which were always in hand, day and night, together with pistols in belt, they needed no preparation. The howitzer, which the Indians might have supposed to be a small keg of whisky, was placed on the ground and pointed at the group of warriers, squaws, and little children around the fire, watching the roasting meat. While thus engaged, with hearts full of kindly feelings toward their white friends, Johnson gave the signal. The howitzer was discharged, sending its load of bullets scattering and tearing through the mass of innocent human beings, and nearly all who were not stricken down were shot by the rifles of the white men. A very few succeeded in escaping into the ravine and fled over the dividing ridge into the northern valleys, where they met others of their tribe, to whom they told the horrible story.

The Apaches at once showed that they could imitate their more civilized brothers. Immediately a band of them went in search of the other company of trappers, who, of course, were utterly unconscious of Johnson's infernal work. They were attacked unprepared and nearly all killed, and the story that 'the Apaches were treacherous and cruel' went forth into all the land, but nothing of the wrongs they had received. (Colyer 1971:5–6)

If such people constituted a threat to the Apache, they were not much more congenial company among themselves. Army officer John Cremony, who traveled through the region in the 1850s, offered some observations on the subject. "Arizona and New Mexico were cursed by the presence of two or three hundred of the most infamous scoundrels it is possible to conceive. Innocent and unoffending men were shot down or bowie-knived merely for the pleasure of witnessing their death agonies. Men walked the streets and public squares with double-barreled shot guns, and hunted each other as sportsmen hunt for game. In the graveyard of Tucson there were forty-seven graves of white men in 1860 . . . and of that number only two had died natural deaths, all the rest being murdered in broils and barroom quarrels" (1969:117).

Before long, scalps brought in for payment exhausted the government funds. The origins of these scalps were difficult to determine. Many people in the Southwest besides the Apache happened to have straight black hair, and bounty hunters no doubt obtained many of their scalps from victims who were easier than Apache to kill. One scalp-hunting entrepreneur named John Gallatin was particularly notorious. Once again we can turn to Cremony's comments. "Determined to make money out of the [Chihuahua] Governor's terms, he commenced killing Papago, Opatah and Yaqui Indians, whose scalps he sold in considerable numbers at thirty dollars each, declaring that they had been taken from the heads of Apaches . . . he was actually caught taking the scalps from the heads of several Mexicans murdered by his people in cold blood" (1969:116).

To distinguish the scalps of grown men from those of women and children was also difficult, but for the purposes of the bounty, all were acceptable. Even though not all of the scalps brought in were Apache, certainly many of them were. Bounty hunters often entered Apache territory hoping to strike unsuspecting encampments. The Apache pattern of male absenteeism meant that often the camps would contain only women, children, and old people. In this era the bitterness of Apache relationships with peoples to the south reached a new intensity.

In the earlier period, the acquisition of livestock had been the predominant motive for Apache raids. Generally the small parties of Apache who wended their way south along the ridges of the Sierra Madre had been cautious to avoid contact with the inhabitants of the region. But as the violence of the bounty hunting escalated, many Apache lost relatives to scalp hunters, and more often, raiders began to seek revenge on the people of northern Mexico. There was a greater tendency to kill people as well as take their livestock, and more captives were taken from Mexico back to *Apachería.*

The Apache sometimes killed these captives, but they adopted others. After hostilities were over, many continued to live with the Apache. They became absorbed into Apache social organization, and frequently they became beloved members of Apache families.

In the mid nineteenth century the U.S. Boundary Commission took captive children away from a group of Apache they encountered. The Apache leaders objected vehemently on behalf of a man who had captured and kept one of the children, arguing: "He has had one of these boys six years. He grew up under him. He is as a son to his old age. He speaks our language, and he cannot sell him. Money cannot buy affection. His heart cannot be sold. He taught him to string the bow and wield the lance. He loves the boy and cannot sell him" (Cremony 1969:65).

But these years marked a bloody episode in the Southwest during which the Apache came to consider themselves bitter enemies of the people of Mexico. The historian Herbert Bancroft notes that, as a result of Apache attacks in northern Mexico between 1820 and 1835, "no less than 5000 lives had been lost . . . at least 100 ranches, haciendas, mining camps, and other settlements had been destroyed; . . . from 3,000 to 4,000 settlers had been obliged to quit the northern frontier; . . . in the extreme north absolutely nothing was left but the demoralized garrisons of worthless soldiers" (quoted in Schroeder 1974b:365).

In some beleaguered parts of Mexico during that period, the rumor that even a single Apache had been seen in the vicinity was sufficient to cause panic among the populace. Many small towns were all but defenseless against Apache raiders, and in the absence of firearms, local Mexican militias often had to use bows and arrows. The military governor of Sonora told Cremony: "Our territory is enormous, and our Government is weak. It cannot extend its protecting arms throughout all portions of the country. Whole provinces are left for years to themselves, except in the matter of taxation, and things run to ruin" (Cremony 1969:39).

Despite the occasional hiatus in active conflict, the turmoil did not fully end until late in the nineteenth century. In the meantime, the Apache, despite their losses, retained control of their territory.

Outside the immediate sphere of Apache territory, other political processes were unfolding that eventually would affect them profoundly. Battles far from *Apachería* had decided Mexico's defeat in a war with the United States. As part of the settlement, the Treaty of Guadalupe Hidalgo in 1848 gave Apache territory, which Spain and Mexico had claimed as their own but had never been able to occupy, to the United States. The treaty stipulated that the United States accept responsibility for order within the territory and prevent Apache raids into Mexico.

The Apache learned of this rather late in the process. In the mid nineteenth century a small delegation of Anglo-Americans traveled through Western Apache territory and conferred with the leaders of several local groups. The Apache met the emissaries, no doubt with some alert wariness as well as curiosity, but for the most part they accepted the outsiders as people who were different from Mexicans, and apparently they deferred judgment. It is possible that during the

Mexican War agents of the United States had provided guns to the Apache to encourage their raids into Mexico (Dobyns 1971:20). Whatever the reasons for the Apache's tolerance, their initial reaction to the foreigners was marked by cautious forbearance and even hospitality, in the absence of any clear reason for hostility.

The Apache were pleased with the news that these Anglos had defeated Mexico in a war, and apparently they interpreted this as a basis for an amicable relationship, since they shared a common enemy. But the assertion that the Mexicans had given their territory to the United States made little sense to the Apache, since they themselves had maintained control of it for centuries. The idea that they should cease their raids into Mexico at the request of these strangers was equally unintelligible.

The Apache did not accept the idea that peace between the United States and Mexico had much relevance to their own affairs. Among the Apache, small groups of people were entirely independent of others in their actions, and collaborative efforts were voluntary. No individual could speak for any other. In the 1860s, Cremony observed that "Apaches are pure democrats, each warrior being his own master, and submitting only to the temporary control of a chief elected for the occasion" (1969:21–22).

The idea that the various Mexican towns were politically linked within a broader political structure was not a compelling argument for the Apache. The extension of state authority in northern Mexico had, in fact, always been weak, and in one sense the Apache assessment was not entirely inaccurate. The concept of a large state system was foreign to their own experience of human affairs, and the assertion that they should conform to an agreement reached elsewhere by two nation states must have seemed absurd. Whether or not they comprehended the argument, there was no particular incentive for them to honor these alien concepts—particularly since they not only belied their own first-hand observations but also offered them no particular advantage.

Despite these points of disagreement, though, relationships between Apache and Anglo-Americans began on a fairly peaceful note. Michael Steck, who was placed in charge of an early New Mexico reservation, wrote in 1858 that "the White Mountain Coyoteros have occasionally visited the agency during the year, have remained quiet, and faithfully kept their promise that 'no depredations should be committed on the California road as far west as their country extended'" (Colyer 1971:4).

The Apache had many reasons to feel confident in their control of the region, notwithstanding the legal abstractions that were so significant to these outsiders that the Apache had allowed into their territory. Anglo-Americans were few at that time and must have seemed to pose little threat. In 1859, Agent John Walker reported: "The Pinals, who visit me frequently, professing great love for the American people, and say they will not violate the treaty made last March with Agent M. Steck, which I am disposed to credit, as they have been visiting Tucson ever since, and I have no recollection of any animal being stolen which the Indians have been charged with . . . I had a long talk with them; they appeared very candid. As they tell the same consistent every time, I am compelled to give them credit; for they have frequently met Americans, and not interrupted them in any way, when there were but two or three together, and the number of Indians was large" (Colyer 1971:5).

In the course of this interaction, the Apache had allowed outsiders to settle in their territory and accepted gifts from them in return. The Apache might not have realized that they planned to stay. Many of the Anglo-Americans, who had entered the region in search of gold, did, in fact, hope to leave once they got rich.

Industrial Capitalism and the New Order

For the Apache, like many other peoples of the world, the exchange of gifts was more a social than an economic transaction. The gifts were a medium for expressing, affirming, or creating ties and for defining relationships between parties. Hospitality was a matter of pride and a social expectation. A stranger who was not an enemy should be given some accommodation. To the Apache, who exploited thousands of square miles of territory on a collective basis, the idea of selling rights of exclusive, permanent ownership of a parcel of land in exchange for money or some other item was a bizarre concept. But what the Apache considered gifts, the Anglo-Americans in some cases considered payments.

Such misunderstandings are often a basis of conflict among peoples whose contrasting cultural systems lead each to mistake the significance of the other's actions. As it turned out, the Anglo-Americans and the Apache were operating by different rules. The outsiders were engaged in a game that led to consequences the Apache could not have fathomed.

Besides these transactions, though, Anglo-Americans often simply settled on land they considered unoccupied. Since the Apache exploited a vast region in their subsistence patterns, their encampments were widely scattered. José Cortés observed: "The number of persons constituting the tribe bears no relation to the territory which they hold as theirs, or seek to control. Thus one finds empty spaces in such vast lands, and each family father or *ranchería* captain is considered the sovereign of his district" (1989:57).

For this and many other reasons, the amicable relationships between Apache and Anglo-Americans were fragile, and they became increasingly so as more outsiders moved into the territory. The Apache could not have known that this was more momentous than the appearance of a few strangers. These people represented a different political phenomenon as well.

Even the incoming miners and settlers themselves probably were only dimly aware, at best, that they were the vanguard of an encroaching capitalist state. They were the first representatives of a social and economic order that operated according to principles quite different from those of the Spanish empire, different even from those of the Mexican state. The Anglo-Americans were the early spawn of an expanding economic system whose driving engine was the market, whose forces were manifest in aggressive growth, and whose sustenance lay in a ravenous hunger for raw materials.

The Spanish had sought gold, silver, and other minerals to feed the wealth of the Crown. But the Spanish treasure had dissipated throughout Europe toward the east, and their overextended holdings slipped from them (see Wallerstein 1974). By the mid nineteenth century, though, the Apache found themselves in the path of a state apparatus with more powerful global implications. Its growth rested in industrial capitalism rather than in the simple appropriation of wealth from conquered regions and the conversion of local populations to the status of peasants. The settlers who came into Arizona in the nineteenth century were not operating within the same framework as either the Apache or the Spanish nor, for the most part, did they employ the same strategies for subsistence.

Even in those years of the mid nineteenth century, the Apache continued to produce and acquire little more than they needed for their own direct consumption. They ate or otherwise used up most of the resources they obtained. They had neither the capability nor the inclination to amass surpluses. Not only would their social ethic with its requirements of generosity and the distribution of goods among relatives have inhibited such accumulation but also their mobile life would have prevented it.

The Spanish had operated according to a set of rules quite different from those that now drove the Anglo-Americans who staked claims in *Apachería*. The Spanish state had been more rigidly hierarchical, with little social mobility. Adventurers and priests had played out their ambitions in audacious maneuvers, intrigues, and strategies to gain advantage over their rivals, but this had taken place within the small arena of a privileged hereditary class.

In outlying reaches of the empire such as northern Mexico, agents of the Spanish state—military officers and priests—had drawn native peoples into the state by making them peasants. The object, however unsuccessful, had been to incorporate them as docile agricultural peons. The process of missionization that instilled the appropriate Christian values of hard work, humility, sacrifice, and frugality addressed the ideological aspect of this status. Native peoples who remained implacably hostile were to be humbled through severe military response. In the Apache case, neither incorporation nor pacification worked, and they remained a perennial anomaly, a bone in the throat of the empire.

But for the most part the Spanish state did not separate the native peoples from their resource base. It sought instead to appropriate the indigenous population's value by subjugation, utilizing their labor as a resource in itself. Soldiers were rewarded for service by small grants of land, but these *encomiendas* included indigenous populations to do the work. The people who represented the Spanish state held elite positions within their own system and had no particular incentive to work the land directly with their own hands. They were far more interested in creating a peasant class in the New World comparable to the peasants who supported that same elite in the Old. Immigrant Spaniards remained a small proportion of the population of northern Mexico.

The Anglo-Americans were neither an elite within their own system like the Spanish colonists nor merely self-sufficient producers for their own consumption like the Apache. Their milieu was a cash economy. They farmed for a market as well as for their own consumption, and they raised livestock to sell as well as to eat. Like the Spanish, they sought minerals for their monetary value, but they operated within a system that offered far more social mobility.

Just as the Spanish who confronted the Apache represented a far larger state apparatus with roots in Europe, the Anglo-American settlers in the Southwest were the outliers of a far larger entity, but in this case that entity was increasingly linked to a global system in which more complex, ponderous forces far beyond the local scene played upon the lives of the people.

Here was an immigrant population vastly more numerous and growing. Their background was not characterized by nobility but by marginal poverty. These were the disenfranchised, the spin-off of a population of immigrants who, by leaving from the cities of the East for the wilderness of the West, became more marginal still, even as they sought access to the benefits of their system. Although wide differences in wealth existed in the nineteenth-century United States, the ideology of the times conveyed a myth of potentially equal access to that wealth. This myth disguised the inequality that pervaded the social system and implied that such unequal distribution somehow represented a fair precipitation of the surplus. It implied that the success of a few was attainable by others as well. Unlike the Spanish empire, birthright was somewhat downplayed as a determinant of status in the ideology of the nineteenth-century United States.

The situation was rife with contradictions between ideology and social reality. The statistical distribution of wealth throughout American history amply demonstrates the importance of having been born into a wealthy family if one hoped to be rich. The squalor of nineteenth-century industrial America made the myth of equal access a bitter irony for many, but there were legendary cases of poor boys becoming tycoons. Philip Armour did, for example, travel to the West as one of eight children, find enough gold to stake a business, establish a meat-packing empire in Chicago, and die a multimillionaire.

The forces at work were not absolutely impersonal, directing the movements of human actors as if they were so many marionettes, but they did amount to collective phenomena that operated largely beyond the control of individuals. They resulted from preexisting conditions, but their dynamics generated new circumstances to which individual actors responded.

An array of diaries, journals, newspaper reports and even novels reflect the times, and we can discern individual actors more sharply than we could in earlier periods. We can see the expressions on their faces in old photographs. They are too immediate, too familiar, to seem like unwitting automatons reacting mindlessly to superorganic social forces. They were people who chose strategies and courses of action according to the insights and information at hand, who reacted to circumstances whose causes and implications they did not always fully understand. Apache and Anglo-Americans operated according to rules they perceived and in ways that made the most sense to them in the situations they faced. The circumstances they confronted made certain choices probable, and these choices often led to unforeseen outcomes. Eventually these processes and interactions led to the San Carlos Reservation.

The overriding thrust of these dynamics was to divest the Apache of their resource base—the land—which was to be appropriated by the state. The "state" in this sense includes missionaries, traders, even frontiersmen who often were anything but exemplars of their own society. They all, knowingly or not, were agents of a ponderous foreign sociopolitical system whose dynamics affected their choices and in whose interests they acted. They were the importers and imposers of a new set of rules and motivations.

Many of these frontiersmen were outlaws by the standards of their own society. For many of them, the weakness of formal law enforcement was an attractive aspect of the frontier. A few of the more notorious of these were escaped convicts. Two noted examples, Bill James and Sugarfoot Jack, were escaped convicts from Tasmania. But on the whole, their motives were the same as the motives that drove the capitalist state which spawned and marginalized them. They wanted to get rich.

While the Apache were embedded in networks of kin, many frontiersmen were people who had cut ties to their former social milieu or whose ties had been severed for them. Their actions and motivations were not constrained by the array of reciprocal bonds that governed Apache life.

The Apache entered this era with every reason to be sure of themselves and convinced of their superiority as a people. They had an ancient way of life developed over centuries of difficult existence, and their culture provided a coherent and satisfying system. Despite the many threats to their survival and the daunting odds against them, things had worked fairly well for them. Many of the outsiders who knew them, including military men who came to be their professional enemies, acknowledged the remarkable qualities that the Apache had forged in themselves through the centuries.

Whatever disdain the Apache may have held for other groups in the Southwest, it was not a concept of inherent "racial" superiority in the same sense in which Anglo-Americans held such beliefs about themselves. The Apache sometimes adopted and intermarried with people of different groups. Their ethnocentrism rested more on a conviction of the superiority of their own knowledge and skills, a confidence in their mode of life and the cultural system it entailed. But despite this élan, the Apache recognized value in some aspects of the cultures of the people around them. They had interacted peacefully with Pueblo societies, in particular, for centuries.

In 1858 Michael Steck reported on the Mimbres and Mogollon Apache: "[They] have confidence in the kind intentions of the government toward them. In their intercourse with the citizens they have suffered many impositions; have been made drunk; have been swindled out of their horses, and many of them stolen by the Mexicans, at or near the agency. They have also been murdered in cold blood, yet not a single instance is known of their having committed a murder, or even stolen a horse to retaliate for their wrongs" (Colyer

1971:4). He reported in 1867: "Many attempts have been made by interested and dishonest parties to create the impression the Pinals are stealing, with the hope of inducing the department commander to send more troops to their territory. I know, however, that the country has never been so safe as at present" (Colyer 1971:5).

The Anglo-Americans who confronted the Apache had a drastically different view of themselves and their relationship to the universe. The Judeo-Christian tradition assumed the distinctness of human beings from the rest of nature and placed the world at the disposal of humankind. In the context of a capitalist economy, this translated into extracting resources as commodities for exchange with the motive of accumulating profits. Given these ground rules, the profits ideally should be as great as possible in the short term and accumulate as much as possible in the long. As obvious as this wisdom might have been to Anglo-American seekers of fortune, for the Apache, to whom the accumulation of surplus was impractical and the value of objects lay in their use, it made little sense.

Competition was a central theme of the Anglo-American quest for wealth. The concept of a limited quantity of wealth, combined with open-ended possibilities of accumulation, implied that its seekers must vie with each other. In conventional Anglo-American wisdom, competition was a stimulus, a driving force promoting achievement and accumulation. Not only was competition the normal state of affairs among individuals, but it also seemed natural and inevitable that societies and populations compete among themselves as well.

Among intellectual circles this was associated with the popular idea of social evolution, sometimes expressed as social Darwinism (see Sumner 1906). It implied that human societies vary in the degree to which they have advanced. In a world visualized as a competitive arena, the inferior, or less advanced, must and should fall before the more progressive and highly developed.

All of this was part of the situation the Apache confronted in the nineteenth century. A huge and growing population to the east was spreading westward, not only impelled by the idea that anyone could get rich, but also buoyed by an ethnocentric ideology expressed in the aphorisms of social Darwinism and Manifest Destiny. Most of these migrants, if asked, probably would have agreed that their way of life and their "race" represented the epitome of human progress. Given these beliefs, the inclination to eliminate such indigenous, non-European populations as the Apache could be justified in humanitarian terms, and it often was.

Probably few of the prospectors who moved into Arizona Territory would have considered themselves social philosophers, but they were steeped in a milieu in which the idea of progress through competition was taken as an axiom. Anglo-American ideology differed from that of the Apache not so much in its assumptions of the superiority of the social system from which it sprang—the Apache had a compatible attitude—but it relegated the Apache and other Native American peoples to the status of anachronisms. However formidable the Apache might have been at the moment, they were seen as savages who posed an obstacle to human progress.

The extreme racism that continues to plague the United States was a part of this milieu. Arizona Territory saw some of the most vitriolic bigotry American society has ever produced, but it was a product of the social, political, and economic conditions that shaped Anglo-American society in the mid nineteenth century. It colored the tone of interpersonal relationships between the Apache and outsiders in the mountains and deserts of *Apachería*. We can see an ironic reflection of this aspect of the times in the surprise registered by the few Anglo-Americans who discovered that the Apache they encountered were intelligent, articulate, reflective, humorous, or vulnerable to sorrow—that, in effect, they were human beings.

The Apache, for their part, treated Anglo-Americans with the combined forbearance and close attention with which one might regard an unpredictable or insane person. Anglo-Americans generally treated the Apache with arrogance unless they felt themselves to be at a serious disadvantage. Perhaps one of the more revealing examples of the period is the case of prospectors who, intruding into the territory of the Mimbres Apache while searching for gold, encountered the prominent leader Mangas Coloradas and questioned him about gold deposits in the area. He told them that there were rich deposits far to the north. Accusing him of lying, they tied him to a tree and beat him severely.

John Cremony, who as a member of the Boundary Commission met Mangas Coloradas in 1850, states that he was "beyond all comparison the most famous warrior and statesman of this century" (1969:30). As astute as the Apache leader was, he probably shared the concerns of other Apache who told Cremony that they feared the discovery of gold would lead to intensified invasion of their territory by prospectors and more permanent settlement. Mangas Coloradas may well have been misleading this particular party of prospectors, hoping to get rid of them.

Such incidents increased tension in the Southwest to a critical point. When the explosion finally occurred, Mangas Coloradas, for one, exacted a heavy recompense for the indignities he suffered at the hands of the prospectors. But the incident that finally precipitated the outbreak of widespread violence involved one of the most prominent Chiricahua Apache leaders, Cochise.

Mangas Coloradas had come to agreements with army representatives in 1845 and 1852, and Cochise had agreed to allow the overland mail riders to pass through Chiricahua territory unmolested. Even though the Chiricahua had raided in Mexico for generations, Cochise had helped maintain peaceful relationships with the Anglo-Americans, even contracting to supply firewood for the Butterfield Stage line. Travelers generally were allowed to pass through the area without problems. Michael Steck reported in 1857: "With the bands west of the Rio Grande, since my last annual report, our relations have been of the most friendly character. During the year not a single depredation has been committed on the California road east of the Chilihuihui [sic] Mountains, and parties of from two to five men are constantly traveling that road from the Rio Grande to Fort Buchanan undisturbed" (Colyer 1971:4).

But at last, in 1861, an army lieutenant blundered into a new era of Apache wars in the Southwest. There are several versions of the incident. Considering its pivotal importance, the record is surprisingly unclear. Perhaps the confusion has something to do with the uproar that ensued, but most versions agree on the essential events.

Lieutenant George Bascom learned that the Chiricahua had a Mexican captive, and he invited Cochise and other leaders to discuss the matter. When they arrived he had them arrested. Cochise and some of the others escaped, but after a series of negotiations, Bascom hanged the remaining captives (see Spicer 1962:247; Thrapp 1968: 16–18). In the wake of this episode, the Chiricahua lost patience with the foreigners. Throughout *Apachería* the Pinal, Arivaipa, Coyotero, Mimbres, and other Apache groups joined them.

By this time, scattered Anglo-American settlements had appeared throughout Apache territory, but before long most of them were abandoned or destroyed because of Apache hostilities. When the Civil War broke out in 1860, most of the troops stationed in Arizona left for the campaigns in the east, and once again the Apache held control of *Apachería*. Except for a small settlement in Tucson, the outsiders appeared to be in retreat.

In retrospect, the Apache were engaged even then in their final struggle as a sovereign people. During the early part of that decade, their main opposition had been in the form of irregular groups of volunteers and vigilantes bent on genocide. Sometimes these parties succeeded in killing Apache. One of the most famous such incidents was the expedition led by one King Woolsey whose members invited a group of Apache to negotiate and then opened fire on them. Dan

Thrapp cites a book by Daniel Ellis Conner: "[Conner] tells how miners often banded together, when they had little else to do, and went a'hunting Indians. When they could trap them, they killed them to the last man and, sometimes, to the last woman and child" (1968:32).

But often these citizens' groups wandered the countryside for weeks or months and returned disheveled and unshaven with their ammunition supplies intact, unless they had happened upon some unfortunate women and children. Despite the ferocity of their intentions, on the whole these volunteers posed little serious threat to Apache control of the territory.

Much of the fighting between Apache and settlers throughout the nineteenth century had involved the Apache's defense of their camps that fell under attack. Many of these camps were joint families consisting of women and children, attacked when most of the men were away hunting. Other clashes involved Apache vengeance in the aftermath of such bloody encounters. Subsistence raids to acquire livestock for food continued throughout this period as well. Most of these raids were directed toward Mexico, but with the increased number of settlers in Arizona, the availability of local stock and the pitch of the animosity encouraged raids within Arizona. As one Chiricahua leader put it, outsiders had come into the region, hunted and depleted the game, and grazed their stock in the Apache domain. The Apache saw little reason to refrain from taking what they needed, and, in fact, they may not have taken the distinction between wild game and range stock very seriously (Ball 1980:40).

With the opening of the Civil War, the Confederacy claimed the Territory of New Mexico, which included what later became Arizona. Most of the local population were in sympathy with the South, and the administration in Washington decided that a Union military presence in the region was advisable. In 1862, General James Carleton with his California Volunteers entered Arizona from the west near Yuma and advanced eastward toward the Rio Grande.

This show of force was an affront to the Apache and a challenge to their control of the region. Up to that time most outsiders had come from the east. Now they were invading from the opposite direction. Cochise and Mangas Coloradas combined their fighting force to attack Carleton's column as it made its way through the mountains of southeastern Arizona at Apache Pass. They might have succeeded in stopping the column had it not been for an element they had never encountered before. Attacking from behind crags and boulders, the Apache began to pick off the troops below. After the initial volley, Carleton's troops were able to set up artillery pieces and began to return fire. Amid blasts of splintering rock and dust, the Apache fell back with their rifles and bows, and the column continued on through the pass (Thrapp 1968:21–23).

In many ways this was a turning point for the Apache. As yet they were nowhere near losing their territory, but the exchange at Apache Pass demonstrated the staggering resources that lay behind the invasion. Two centuries earlier, Spanish officers often had begged their superiors for forces of up to a hundred men. But in the 1860s masses of Union and Confederate troops in the East were slaughtering each other by the tens of thousands. Soon the war would end, and the full force of an industrializing state would provide the supply base to direct more concerted violence in Arizona. The few thousand Apache living off the land would be hard-pressed to withstand that power.

Cochise and other Apache leaders comprehended their situation, although they could not have realized the full magnitude of the force that was about to bear upon them. In the early 1860s several of them concluded that they could not possibly win (Ball 1980:20). Their combined attempt to stop Carleton's column in 1862 exposed them to some of the firepower they could expect to confront in the future. It also impressed upon them the seemingly inexhaustible sources of provisions and reinforcements that supported these invaders. As a Chiricahua man said many years later, the Apache "had known for a long time that the *Indah* [enemies] outnumbered them by tremendous odds, that they had better weapons, and that they seemed to have unlimited supplies of necessities furnished them, while the Indians were compelled to rustle everything they obtained" (Ball 1980:252). In the 1940s the aged son of Juh, a leader who died without acquiescing, stated that "all of us knew we were doomed, but some preferred death to slavery and imprisonment" (Ball 1980:40). Yet despite that conclusion, they continued to resist for almost three more decades. For the most part, their battle was defensive, a struggle for existence.

After the Civil War ended and the troops returned to Arizona, the Apache faced more sustained pressure. Their skills in guerrilla warfare made them formidable opponents in their own territory. They were at home in the mountains. For successive generations they had instilled physical toughness in their children. They eluded confrontation with conventional troops unless they had an overwhelming advantage. Cremony, who had considerable experience with Apache combat methods in the mid nineteenth century, wrote that "in no case will they incur the risk of losing life, unless the plunder be most enticing and their numbers overpowering, and even then they will track a small party for days, waiting an opportunity to establish a secure ambush or effect a surprise" (1969:87).

When pursued, they would scatter in all directions. If they were driving stock, one or a few would drop back and fight holding actions from a series of sheltered points until the rest could escape. They were masters of the technique of fake retreat to draw their pursuers into ambush. When attacked, according to José Cortés: "They never lose their composure, even when they are surprised and have no defense at hand. They fight to the last breath, and members of several groups prefer death to surrender" (1989:74).

The Apache adopted rifles in very early times and used them with great skill, although their bows and arrows continued to be effective. They innovated and adapted, using whatever resources became available to them. Writing in the 1860s, Cremony contrasted the "modern" Apache warrior of his day with the older stereotype, chiding those readers who would assume "that the Apache of to-day is like his ancestor of half a century ago; that he fights with bow and stone-headed arrows; . . . the Apache of to-day is armed with the best kind of rifle, with Colt's six-shooters and with knives, and . . . in addition to these, he is never without his silent, death-dealing bow and quiver full of iron-headed arrows" (1969:188).

As to the continued use of older weapons: "The bow and arrow in the hands of skillful warriors proves very deadly; it makes no noise, and for night attacks or the taking off of sentinels, is far superior to the gun. Secondly, it is the best weapon that can be used in the chase, or, more properly, on the hunt, as half a dozen animals may be slain in a herd before their comrades are made aware of the fact. Thirdly, they are so light that they can be worn without the slightest sense of encumbrance. Fourthly, they can always be relied on, at close quarters, when other weapons fail, or ammunition, of which they possess limited supplies, gives out" (1969:188–189).

Often their raids were carried out by a handful of men—usually fewer than a dozen—which allowed them to escape more easily. Cortés writes that "for this purpose they always make their approach over rugged and rocky mountains, from which they descend to the vicinity of the villages and haciendas, make their raid with the utmost swiftness, and retreat hastily to the same rugged terrain . . . it is nearly impossible to find them even when they are pursued with the greatest effort" (1989:74). They signaled each other across miles of territory from mountaintops and mesas with mirrors and smoke and kept each other constantly informed of enemy movements (Ogle 1970:15; Cortés 1989:74–75; Cremony 1969:183). They were able to travel forty miles or more a day on foot and could keep up the pace for weeks.

Adversaries who were not adapted to the rigors of Apache life and who did not share their minute acquaintance with the thousands of square miles of broken country were hard-pressed to confront them effectively. Eventually, though, the demise of the Apache came from factors other than military confrontation. If conventional troops could not out-track, outmaneuver, or outsmart them, the tactic of interfering with their subsistence activities finally undermined the Apache's ability to persist.

The Erosion of Apache Sovereignty

The process by which the Western Apache came to lose control over their territorial base amounted to a loss of access to an adequate supply of food. In the aftermath, their survival in the reservation period was subject to the decisions of others and largely beyond their control.

How did some of the most fiercely independent peoples in the world find themselves in that situation in the course of a couple of generations? The process involved a long and sporadic series of violent confrontations, but the military record of this period emphasizes only one factor. Through this history of battles and campaigns, administrative maneuvering, political infighting among high-ranking officers over policy and power, and the lobbying of special interest groups, the Apache's progressive loss of their resource base occurred in several phases.

During the first phase, the Apache held control over their domain. Although intruders harassed them, these incidents constituted little threat to their possession of the territory. The opening crack occurred with the end of the Mexican War in the mid nineteenth century, when Apache hostilities with Mexicans had led them—with some ambivalence—to perceive Anglo-Americans as allies. Many of the bounty hunters for Apache scalps had been Anglo-Americans, but this did not prevent the Apache from allowing an increased Anglo-American presence in their territory. No doubt the Apache's confidence in their own ability to maintain their grip on the territory was a contributing factor. Their misperception of Anglo-American concepts of ownership and economic motivations may have played a role. The Apache also tended to view the foreigners on an individual basis rather than as a collective category.

Yet the arena in which this took place was rapidly changing. In 1860, according to the United States Census, the "non-Indian" population in *Apacheria* was only 2,421, and it was almost entirely Hispanic (Thrapp 1967:79). The Apache still vastly outnumbered Anglo-Americans in their own territory. Ten years later the number of outsiders had grown to 9,658, including army troops (Thrapp 1967:79).

Of this population, 686 were immigrants from the United Kingdom and 379 from Germany. There is some evidence, too, that by this time the Apache had suffered some major losses from *viruelas*, smallpox (see Dobyns 1971:10).

The Bascom Affair of 1861, in which the army lieutenant touched off warfare with the Chiricahua, is often cited as a cause of the Apache wars. But when we observe the broader trends of the times, including the shifts in relative populations and the changes in their origins, it seems clear that the processes unfolding in the region ensured that there would be conflict eventually, regardless of the incident that touched it off. From that period onward, sporadic violence increased as the invading population wrested *Apachería* from the Apache.

The vanguard of this new population were prospectors and miners who were entrenched in Arizona well before the establishment of formal government. In 1863 President Lincoln created the Arizona Territory by separating it from New Mexico, and when the Arizona Legislature convened for the first time in 1864, half of the representatives were miners. One of their first items of business was to call for a war of extermination against the Apache and to appeal for volunteers (Wagoner 1970:22).

Minerals continued to play a major role in both drawing people into the territory and setting the tone of their relations with the Apache. In his 1864 book, *Adventures in Apache Country,* J. Ross Browne wrote "I believe it to be a Territory wonderfully rich in minerals, but subject to greater drawbacks than any of our Territorial possessions. It will be many years before its mineral resources can be fully and fairly developed. Emigration must be encouraged by increased military protection" (1864:34). Territory Governor John N. Goodwin took a petulant tone in referring to the Apache, stating that, "but for them, mines would be worked, innumerable sheep and cattle would cover these plains" (Wagoner 1970:34).

When conflict escalated in the latter half of the nineteenth century, much of the fighting took the form of escapades by parties of civilian volunteers who took to the field hoping to kill as many Apache as they could. Apache retaliation, attacks on ranches, and theft of stock kept the Anglo anti-Indian sentiment at a high pitch. In 1871 the Arizona Legislature published a pamphlet entitled *Outrages Perpetrated by the Apache Indians, in the Territory of Arizona, during the Years 1869 and 1870.* It listed ninety-seven affidavits complaining of Apache attacks and demanded that the Federal government provide assistance. In the same year citizens at a public meeting in Mimbres, New Mexico, passed a series of resolutions expressing their intention to "follow their stock wherever it may be, and take it by force wherever found, even if it be at the sacrifice of every Indian man, women [*sic*], and child, in the tribe." They passed another resolution declaring "that if opposed by Indians or their accomplices, be they Indian agents, Indian traders, or Army officers, let them be looked upon as our worst enemies and the common enemies of New Mexico, and be dealt with accordingly" (Colyer 1971:8).

Many of the hostile encounters involved treachery. Apache killed in the infamous massacre carried out by the Woolsey party in 1864 were shot during negotiations (Thrapp 1968:28–30). In numerous instances Apache were given poisoned food or whiskey. Thrapp described King Woolsey, who later became an Arizona legislator: "[He] had an undying hatred for Indians, in common with many pioneers. On one occasion, while prospecting in the Bradshaw Mountains, he mixed pinole with strychnine and saw to it that some savages obtained the lethal concoction with disastrous results" (1968:27). The *Arizona Miner* of January 12, 1867, ran an editorial stating: "We are glad to know that our Yavapai [County] Rangers do not think it worth their trouble to make prisoners of the murderous red skins. The custom heretofore adopted, even by our regular army, of making prisoners of women and children, and in many cases of the full grown bucks, seems to be dying out" (quoted in Thrapp 1968:38). Apache sometimes took children captive and raised them, while Anglos, in many cases, deliberately killed Apache babies.

Eventually the brutalization of fighting affected the Apache's approach to warfare as well. Only after revenge and hatred came to dominate the conflict did they begin mutilating the dead and removing scalps, a practice that had been repugnant to them. Even so, they rarely kept the scalps. Lieutenant John Bourke, describing a recently attacked wagon train in 1870, wrote: "There were the hot embers of the new wagons, the scattered fragments of broken boxes, barrels, and packages of all sorts; copper shells, arrows, bows, one or two broken rifles, torn and burned clothing. There lay all that was mortal of poor Israel, stripped of clothing, a small piece cut from the crown of the head, but thrown back up on the corpse—the Apaches do not care much for scalping" (Bourke 1971:25).

The death of the Mimbres leader Mangas Coloradas became a pivotal point in the Apache's treatment of their victims. Although Mangas Coloradas and Cochise had well-established warring credentials, both had worked on several occasions to bring about peaceful relationships between their people and the Anglo-Americans. This willingness, finally, led Mangas Coloradas into a trap. Carleton's troops invited him to discuss peace at their camp near the Santa Rita mines in southwestern New Mexico. His followers urged him not to risk capture. He entered the trap fully aware of the possible consequences, hoping that the troops would keep their word. They took him prisoner.

While his people waited for him in the hills overlooking the military camp that night, he lay bound by a campfire. Troopers taunted him, heating their bayonets in the fire and placing them against his feet. He responded angrily that he was no child to be played with, but he was tied and unable to move freely. One of the troopers fired point blank and killed him. According to reports, he was "shot while trying to escape" (Thrapp 1968:21–23).

His people were devastated. But the next day their sorrow and anger turned to horror when, as they watched, troopers boiled Mangas Coloradas' severed head in a cauldron to prepare the skull for "scientific study."

In that age of scientific racism, there was great interest among the scientific community in brain size, skull shape, and other features thought to be associated with intelligence, character, "racial characteristics," and so on. Mangas Coloradas had been a large, powerfully built man with extraordinary abilities. The skull of this leader of the "savage Apaches" was quite a specimen indeed.

To the Apache who watched, the mutilation was a barbarity that exceeded the murder itself. The treatment of Mangas Coloradas incensed and disgusted them and served to intensify the brutality of conflict (Ball 1980:20). In subsequent years, Apache mutilation of enemies they had killed became more common.

This escalation manifested itself in many ways on both sides. General Crook, eventual victor over the Apache, was an eminently successful military professional, but eventually his sense of military discipline eroded to the point at which he called for head hunting by his troops. He ordered them to bring in the heads of particularly notorious Apache and Yavapai leaders (Crook 1946:181).

Crook's lieutenant John G. Bourke offers some insight into the ways in which these experiences changed their participants. Bourke's career shows a growing sensitivity to the Apache and increasing disgust with the atrocities committed against them. As a young officer posted in Arizona after his graduation from West Point, Bourke had no apparent qualms about participating in the "battle" of the Salt River Cave, when troops annihilated a camp of over forty Apache trapped in a rock shelter. But Bourke later recounted an incident that made him realize the extent to which the Apache conflict had affected his perceptions.

One of his men had given him a dried Apache scalp with the ears attached as a souvenir. Bourke used it as a lampshade on his desk until a friend visiting from the East spied it and almost fainted (Porter 1986:10–11). The man's reaction caused Bourke to reflect on the impact his Southwest experience had on his sensibilities. Eventually, he was to spend his last years in anger and frustration, fighting unsuccessfully for humane government policies toward the Apache he had helped to defeat.

This phase through the 1860s was one of escalating but largely chaotic conflict. Anglo-Americans had genocidal intentions, but for the most part they were incapable of carrying them out. Although the Apache suffered many losses, there seemed to be little likelihood at that time that they were about to be driven off their land.

With the close of the Civil War, the United States government resumed its attempts to impose control over the territory. The military at first was no more successful in subduing and eliminating the Apache than the local irregular volunteers had been. This began to change when the army began to employ Native American scouts. The scouts were able to track Apache groups and locate many of their encampments.

These military strategies did not always lead to victories, but they did constitute to a growing harassment of Apache in their own home bases. The troops forced the people to move more often than they otherwise would have yet kept them from moving as freely as they had before. The expeditions hampered their seasonal round of food gathering, and troops destroyed their gardens whenever they could. Usually the Apache could avoid military confrontation and outright defeat, but increasingly they were hard-pressed to get enough food. Eventually this, as much as anything else, led Apache groups to come to terms with the government. When they did, they relinquished a great deal of control over their lives.

Military Policies and the Escalation of Force

Apache scouts were indispensable to the army in their campaigns against other Apache. There seems to be no reason to doubt General Crook's assertion that "during the entire [1886] campaign, from first to last, without any exception, every successful encounter with the hostiles was due exclusively to the exertions of Indian scouts, and it is the unanimous testimony of officers commanding scout companies, that the Chiricahuas were the most subordinate, energetic, untiring and, by odds, the most efficient of their command" (quoted in Thrapp 1968:364). How did the army manage to persuade Apache to serve as scouts? Apparently several crucial factors were involved.

Apache social organization did not lend itself to a sense of over-all political unity. The essential bonds, couched in the medium of kinship and marriage, were the ties that linked individuals. Al-though the people recognized their cultural and linguistic similarities to other Apache, there was no particular sense of loyalty on that ba-sis to people who were not kin. Ironically, perhaps, the Apache seem to have harbored little or none of the racism that allowed Anglo-Americans to see themselves as "whites" having something sig-nificant in common in opposition to "Indians." Consequently, the Apache did not necessarily perceive the situation as a categorical struggle between two "races."

Local groups of Apache who were not linked by close kin ties often were at odds with one another. There was no strong sense of group affiliation that could automatically be brought into play. The achieve-ment of Mangas Coloradas, who brought a range of groups into con-certed action in the 1860s through his personal influence and who used judicious marriages to invoke the principle of kinship, was re-markable, but this was unusual in the Apache context. After his death, even that coalition fell apart.

Some of the northern groups of Western Apache suffered early de-feats to the army, particularly the Coyotero. They relied more on farming than the Pinal and Arivaipa did, and their planted fields made them more vulnerable. The Arivaipa leader Eskiminzin de-scribed an attack on a White Mountain encampment in the mid 1860s that took place, as usual, when most of the men were away. It was just prior to harvest, when roughly a hundred men on horseback sur-prised the camp at dawn. Learning that the men were gone, they broke the Apache water jars, trampled the fields, and destroyed as much of the food as they could find. Eskiminzin claimed that many of those Coyotero died of starvation during the following winter be-cause their food supply had been destroyed (Clum 1936:83).

Eventually such attacks led many of the Coyotero to seek a truce with the invading forces and try to maintain peaceful relationships in the hope of survival. Working as scouts provided some compensation for those who signed on. It provided at least a means of subsistence, and it was compatible in many ways with existing Apache patterns. Scouting conformed to the age-old pattern of men leaving on sporadic forays for hunting and raiding while women remained the more stable core of the residential groups. The army did not use Apache scouts against other Apache until the later phase of this period.

There was a good deal of ambivalence among Apache about scouts. According to one Chiricahua man, in the 1870s "the Apache scouts had not been used by the army against their own people, but even then those who wore the red headband (the insignia of the scout) were regarded with suspicion by many Apaches" (Ball 1980:31).

That Crook also used coercion to recruit Apache as scouts seems clear. Vincent Colyer reported in 1871 that his Mexican scout "said that the Mexicans employed by General Crook, whom he met at his camp, were among the worst villains in Mexico, and the Indians were part of Miguel's band of peaceable Apaches from the White Mountain reservation, who said they had to enlist in the service or be considered enemies" (Colyer 1971:10–11). Colyer also commended Crook for "abandoning the practice of taking peaceable Indians from the corn-fields and compelling them to go on the war-path against their brethren" (Colyer 1971:11).

Hiring scouts and co-opting the Apache to help defeat one another was more than a simple military expedient. It was also part of the process of incorporating these people into the state through "individualizing" them. Lieutenant Bourke was explicit about this. "By the Crook method of dealing with the Savage he was, at the outset, detribalized without knowing it; he was individualized and made the better able to enter the civilization of the Caucasian, which is an individual civilization . . . As a result, the Apache was enlisted as an individual; he was made responsible for all that he did or did not" (Porter 1986:143). Crook hoped that weaning the individual away from identification with kin and, more broadly, from a sense of ethnic identity would erode the sense of common interest among Apache.

But this strategy was not entirely effective. Clan affiliation remained strong among the Western Apache scouts. Generally they were formed into companies on the basis of clan membership, since the army recognized that they worked most effectively that way. As to winning the hearts and minds of the Apache over to the state, in one case when Apache scouts helped the army track down some Mescalero Apache, they deliberately led the troops past two they knew were hiding in a ditch.

More often, though, many Apache leaders became convinced that the only hope for the physical survival of their people was peaceful submission to reservation life. For years many of them had witnessed the slaughter of their children and relatives. They had seen their numbers depleted and had lost control of their territorial base. Some, such as the Arivaipa leader Eskiminzin and the Chiricahua Loco, decided that to continue resistance would mean the complete destruction of their people. Helping the army to locate the few bands who remained off the reservation was, to them, a matter of helping their people go on living.

But the tales of fighting, slaughter, and destruction are manifestations of other processes that acted to shape events. From one perspective we might be tempted to view the process as an inevitable outcome of Apache raiding. When the Apache began depending on the production of other groups, they placed themselves in conflict with the interests of these peoples. This brought about increasing assaults on their own population. One might argue that if the Apache had stuck to hunting, gathering, and gardening within their own territory this might have been avoided.

But such a scenario has its flaws. We have only to look at the scores of peaceful, stable Native American populations elsewhere whose territories were overrun long before the Apache lost theirs. Many of those peoples were all but eliminated. The Apache, on the other hand, managed to hold off the concerted assaults of three different states for centuries before they finally succumbed.

In 1871 the Arizona Territorial Legislature complained that Apache depredations constituted an obstacle to "immigration and capital" necessary to develop the region. They went on to assert:

> Probably, but few countries on the face of the globe presents greater natural resources inviting to immigration and capital than the Territory of Arizona. Nearly every mountain is threaded with veins of gold, silver, copper, and lead. Large deposits of coal and salt of an excellent quality are found. Nearly every foot of the Territory is covered with nutritious grasses, and stock thrives the year round without shelter or prepared forage. Nearly every product that grows in the temperate or torrid zone can be grown here to perfection and in abundance. There are vast forests of excellent timber; the mountains and valleys are amply supplied with pure water; the climate is warm, genial, and healthful, equal to any on the American continent. (Arizona Territorial Legislature 1871:3)

The Legislature urged that the federal government lend them assistance "in subduing our hostile foe, and thereby reclaim from the savage one of the most valuable portions of our public domain" (Arizona Territorial Legislature 1871:4).

The escalation of military conflict and the increase in troops operating in Arizona provided an additional economic resource. By 1870, the economy of Arizona was dependent on selling supplies to the army, and peaceful relations with the Apache would have been financially disastrous to many citizens of the territory. General George Stoneman, commander of the Department of Arizona, recommended in 1871 that two of the existing army posts be abandoned because they were too expensive. He asserted that they would be no loss "except to those people in the immediate vicinity who were disposing of their hay and grain to the government at exorbitant prices" (Wagoner 1970:125–126).

That many of the proposals for seeking peaceful relationships with the Apache came from the military is noteworthy. General William T. Sherman, in a letter to W. W. Belknap on January 7, 1870, wrote, "The best advice I can offer is to notify the settlers to withdraw and then to withdraw the troops and leave the country to the aboriginal inhabitants" (quoted in Ogle 1970:73). As it was, the relentlessness of Anglo-American settlement all but ensured that fighting would continue until the Apache had lost almost all of the territory. Whenever peace negotiations began, some citizens' group usually would perpetrate an outrage and ignite hostilities once more. Many of the poisonings and treacherous negotiations with Apache groups took place in this context.

Perhaps the most notorious atrocity in this period took place at Camp Grant, north of Tucson. Early in 1871, a young lieutenant named Royal E. Whitman who recently had been placed in command of the small outpost at Camp Grant found to his surprise that Arivaipa Apache were drifting into the post, a few at a time. They asked his permission to quit the fighting and camp peacefully near the protection of the military. Realizing the implications of this in the wake of long years of bloodshed, Whitman gave them temporary permission to stay under his protection and hastily wrote his superiors for confirming orders. According to Whitman's report on the incident, a young Apache leader had told him that his people wanted to "make a final peace and never break it." "I told him I had no authority to make any treaty with him or to promise him that he could be allowed a permanent home here, but that he could bring in his band and I would feed them, and report his wishes to the department commander," Whitman reported (Colyer 1971:31).

He continued: "I wrote a detailed account of the whole matter, and sent it by express to Sacaton, to department headquarters, asking for instructions, having only the general policy of the Government in such cases for my guidance. After waiting more than six weeks my letter was returned to me without comment, except calling my attention to the fact that it was not briefed properly" (Colyer 1971:31). It was unopened, apparently because he had neglected to follow the procedure of specifying its contents on the outside of the envelope (Thrapp 1968:84).

Whitman allowed the Apache to remain near Camp Grant. He reported: "The ranchmen in the vicinity were friendly and kind to them and felt perfectly secure, and had agreed with me to employ them at a fair rate of pay to harvest their barley. The Indians seem to have lost their characteristic anxiety to purchase ammunition, and had, in many instances, sold their best bows and arrows" (Colyer 1971:32). The young officer wrote "I had come to feel respect for men who, ignorant and naked, were still ashamed to lie or steal, and for women who would work cheerfully like slaves to clothe themselves and children, but, untaught, held their virtue above price. Aware of the lies and hints industriously circulated by the puerile press of the Territory, I was content to *know* I had positive proof they were so" (Colyer 1971:32) [emphasis in the original].

In the meantime, citizens of nearby Tucson became agitated over the idea that hundreds of Apache were living peacefully within forty miles or so of the town. The Apache had been working as hired hands, cutting hay for neighboring ranchers, but this did little to enhance their reputation in Tucson. One night in April a "Committee of Public Safety" gathered a group of about 140 Papago, Mexicans, and Anglo-Americans. They made their way to the camp of sleeping Arivaipa. Attacking them by surprise, they clubbed to death as many as they could.

Whitman reported:

On the morning of April —, I was at breakfast at 7:30 o'clock, when a dispatch was brought to me by a sergeant of Company P, Twenty-first Infantry, from Captain Penn, commanding Camp Lowell, informing me that a large party had left Tucson on the 28th with the avowed purpose of killing all the Indians at this post. I immediately sent the two interpreters, mounted, to the Indian camp, with orders to tell the chiefs the exact state of things, and for them to bring their entire party inside the post. As I had no cavalry, and but about fifty infantry, (all recruits,) and no other officer, I could not leave the post to go to their defense. My messengers returned in about an hour, with intelligence that they could find no living Indians. (Colyer 1971:32)

As Whitman learned: "Their camp was surrounded and attacked at daybreak. So sudden and unexpected was it, that no one was awake to give the alarm, and I found quite a number of women shot while asleep beside their bundles of hay which they had collected to bring in on that morning. The wounded who were unable to get away had their brains beaten out with clubs or stones, while some were shot full of arrows after having been mortally wounded by gunshot. The bodies were all stripped. Of the whole number buried, one was an old man and one was a well-grown boy—all the rest women and children" (Colyer 1971:33).

The leader of the expedition, William S. Oury, estimated that they had killed 144 Apache, but only about eight of these were adult men

(Thrapp 1968:89–90). Many Arivaipa children were taken alive. Thrapp writes that "less fortunate than the slain were almost all of the 27 children taken prisoner, who were sold by the Papagos into Sonoran slavery." An Apache leader appealed to Whitman: "Get them back for us; our little boys will grow up slaves, and our girls, as soon as they are large enough, will be diseased prostitutes to get money for whoever owns them. Our women work hard and are good women, and they and our children have no diseases. Our dead you cannot bring to life, but those that are living we gave to you, and we look to you, who can write and talk and have soldiers, to get them back" (Colyer 1971:33).

In the following October, R. A. Wilbur, agent for the Papago, sent Whitman the names of local citizens who were holding eight of the children captive. By that time the government was taking measures to prosecute the attackers. Wilbur wrote, "I would suggest that immediate action be taken in this matter, as the indictment for murder found by the late United States grand jury against a portion of their citizens has brought the people of this to such a pitch of excitement that any unnecessary delay would result in the disappearance of all trace of the identity of these captives, if not in their death" (Colyer 1971:50).

George Crook claimed in his autobiography: "A good many children were carried off into Tucson and vicinity. These children had been taken into many of the families, and in the year that had elapsed became more or less identified with their new associates." Crook maintained that the children did not wish to return to the Apache (1946:171). General O. O. Howard, who engineered the return of the children, gave a different version and described the reunion of the children with their relatives as a joyous occasion (Howard 1978:162).

The perpetrators of the massacre appeared to be unabashed, and in the aftermath, they basked in some glory. Colyer reported later that year, "That the massacre at Camp Grant fairly illustrates the sentiment of a large portion of the people of Arizona and New Mexico on the Indian question, is painfully confirmed by the fact that nearly every newspaper here has, either justified or apologized for the act" (Colyer 1971:19). The story of the massacre did not play as well in the East, and President Ulysses S. Grant threatened to impose martial law on Arizona unless the murderers were brought to trial (Thrapp 1968:92). Accordingly, the Arizona legal system dealt with the issue.

At the hearing, several witnesses substantiated the argument that the Apache had been living peacefully at Camp Grant. Oscar Hutton, post guide, testified under oath that, since 1850, "I have been constantly on the frontier and in Indian country . . . and have perhaps seen as much active service against the Indians as any man living in Arizona . . . and I further state that I have never seen Indians on a reservation, or at peace about a military post, under so good subjection, so well satisfied and happy, or more teachable and obedient than were these, up to the time I left the post five days previous to the massacre." Hutton stated: "I was repeatedly requested to watch every indication of anything like treachery on their part, and I will give it as my deliberate judgment, that no raiding party was ever made up from the Indians fed at this post. I have every reason to believe that, had they been unmolested, they would have remained, and would have gradually increased in numbers, as they constantly had been doing up to the time I left the post" (Colyer 1971:35). Other witnesses corroborated these points.

After fifteen minutes' deliberation, the jury acquitted all defendants. As historian Dan Thrapp observes: "You couldn't convict a man in Arizona for killing an Apache, whatever the circumstances. At least not before a jury of Arizonans" (1968:92).

Lieutenant Whitman, in the meantime, became one of the most reviled public figures in Arizona because of his sympathetic stand toward the Apache. He testified against the Camp Grant murderers and continued to provide a place for Apache at the military post. Surprisingly, perhaps, the survivors of the massacre continued to live there. Whitman was court-martialed three times for a series of accusations, including such charges as "conduct unbecoming an officer and a gentleman" and having become drunk while playing cards. In September 1871 Lieutenant W. W. Robinson wrote to Colyer: "Attempts have been made, principally through the columns of the Arizona Citizen, a journal published in Tucson, Arizona Territory, to make it appear that this officer was a debauched scoundrel and a slave to vice. Among other things, he has been accused of associating with Indian women, and of being a confirmed drunkard. I know little of this officer's history previous to his assuming command of this post, December last, but from the time the Indians came in up to the 11th of April, and from May 21 to the time they left, to the best of my knowledge he touched not a drop of liquor" (Colyer 1971:38). Whitman finally retired in Washington on a colonel's pension (Thrapp 1968:111n).

The Pacification Process

Against the backdrop of this era, the observations of Eric Williams seem appropriate: "An outworn interest whose bankruptcy smells to heaven in historical perspective, can exercise an obstructionist and

disruptive effect which can only be explained by the powerful services it had previously rendered and the entrenchment previously
gained" (1944:211).

In 1871 the Indian Peace Commission, with the endorsement of
President Ulysses S. Grant, sent Vincent Colyer to tour through
Apache territory. Colyer's mission was to persuade the various
Apache groups to retire peacefully to five designated reservations.
Colyer was a man of considerable personal courage and social con-
science. His sympathy for the plight of the Apache made him immensely unpopular in Arizona. His earlier record as a vocal opponent
of slavery did little to make him welcome among Arizona's numerous
disappointed proponents of the Confederacy. During the course of
his tour, he observed beleaguered Apache living on reservations in
chronic danger of attacks by the surrounding population.

Colyer opened his report to the President by stating that "this report shows plainly that, according to the records of the Indian Department, the Apache Indians were the friends of the Americans
when they first knew them; that they have always desired peace with
them, and when placed upon reservations in 1858 and 1859 were in-
dustrious, intelligent, and made rapid progress in the arts of civilization" (Colyer 1971:3).

Colyer toured the area visiting various Apache bands. In September 1871, a few months after the Camp Grant massacre, he ventured
through what later would become the San Carlos Reservation.

> Our route lay across the mountains to Black River, over to the head-
> waters of the San Carlos, down the San Carlos to the Gila River, across
> the Gila to Mount Trumbull [Turnbull], over that mountain to and
> down the Arivapa [Arivaipa] Valley to Camp Grant. Our march
> through this portion of the heart of the Apache country was very en-
> couraging. Our Indian guides, improvising white flags and signaling
> their friends of our approach by lighting fires and making smokes,
> brought them out by scores. They met us on the trail, bearing white
> flags made of white buckskin, and came from the most inaccessible
> places and from where you would least expect them. At night our camp
> was surrounded with them, and the soldiers soon got so used to their
> presence that we all slept soundly though they frequently outnum-
> bered us five to one. During the whole march, though we were thus
> surrounded, not an animal was disturbed nor an article stolen. (Colyer
> 1971:13)

Colyer's tour provoked outrage among the citizens of the Territory
and withering disdain among some of the prominent military leaders,
particularly General Crook. In August 1871, Arizona Governor

A. P. K. Safford issued a proclamation announcing his temporary absence. He instructed the citizens that if Colyer's party "come among you entertaining erroneous opinions upon the Indian question and the condition of affairs in the Territory, then by kindly treatment and fair, truthful representation you will be enabled to convince them of their errors" (Colyer 1971:51).

Colyer reported that:

> The Arizona Citizen, a professedly republican paper, published at Tucson, and the Arizona Miner, democratic paper from Prescott, have been excessive in their abuse of Lieutenant Whitman, Colonel Green, and all other officers of the Army who have shown the least sympathy for the Apaches, charging them with many crimes. The editors seem to fear the damaging effect produced on the public mind by the statements made officially by these Army officers of the general good conduct of the Apaches whenever they have been allowed an opportunity to display it, and of the horrible brutalities committed by the people of Arizona upon them at the Camp Grant massacre. Their statements that the Indians left that reservation and went on raiding parties against the citizens is denied by every officer and citizen at the post. (Colyer 1971:17)

The *Arizona Miner* expressed its views of Colyer by editorializing: "[People] ought, in justice to our murdered dead, dump the old devil into the shaft of some mine and pile rocks on him until he is dead. A rascal who comes here to thwart the attempts of military and citizens to conquer a peace from our savage foe, deserves to be stoned to death, like the treacherous black-hearted dog that he is" (quoted in Wagoner 1970:133). Colyer reported that "Mr. Merriam, the editor of the 'Arizona Miner,' and several other gentlemen, called to invite me to address in public meeting the citizens of Prescott on the Indian question" (1971:28). Colyer reminded Merriam of his recent hostile editorial. "The gentlemen assured me that they would protect me with their rifles and revolvers; but as my official duties were wholly with the Indians, and the officers of the Government having them in charge, and I was unable to see sufficient reasons for addressing a public meeting in which I should have to be protected with rifles and revolvers, I respectfully declined" (Colyer 1971:29).

When Colyer visited Camp Grant a few months after the massacre, he found Lieutenant Whitman a congenial host. Soon after Colyer's arrival, an armed mob of up to two hundred people from Tucson and another large party from another direction led by Governor Safford approached the settlement. "As the reservation is within a valley and

surrounded with mountains, without a road or trail through it leading anywhere, and as the Indians had only just come in after much
persuasion, and were under evident fears of another attack, the im-
propriety of allowing these armed bands of citizens to rendezvous
upon the reservation was apparent" (Colyer 1971:14).

Captain William Nelson, the post commander, ordered the party
not to approach closer than ten miles from the reservation.

[Nelson] then directed Lieutenant Whitman to ride out and meet the
party and inform them that he was prepared to enforce his order, and
had his guns in position, and would open fire upon them on their appearance at the mouth of the cañon opposite the post. Captain Nelson
loading up the water-wagon belonging to the post and sending it out to
them, that they might not suffer in case they should conclude to go
back, which the report of Captain Nelson says they very reluctantly
consented to do. They left with the declaration that they could use the
white flag as well as we, and if that would bring in the Indians they
would bring them in and put them on a reservation where it would not
cost much to feed them. (Colyer 1971:14)

General Crook reprimanded Nelson for his protection of the
Apache. "Your action in this matter was unwarrantable," he wrote,
"as you transcended the limits of your authority." Crook warned Nelson that such actions threatened to "unnecessarily provoke the hostilities of the citizens toward the military and the Indians under their
protection" (Colyer 1971:53).

Shortly after Colyer had completed his humanitarian odyssey,
the volatile relationships between Apache and settlers erupted once
again. In November a stagecoach near Wickenburg was attacked, and
six people were killed. Brevet Colonel N. A. M. Dudley wrote in November 1871: "The robbery of the mail-stage, and the killing of five
citizens, a week ago, by an unknown party, near Wickenburgh [sic],
of course is laid to the Indians. At first even the Prescott papers par-
tially admitted that it was a party of Mexican bandits from Sonora.
Indians, when they attack a stage, are not apt to leave the horses,
blankets, and curtains of the coach behind; in this case they did.
I do not believe there was an Apache near the scene of the murder.
All honest men have the same opinion, if they dared to express it"
(Colyer 1971:27). Colyer, however, who had been referred to in the
Arizona press as a "cold-blooded scoundrel," was further reviled
and returned to Washington "followed by the curses of Arizonans"
(Wagoner 1970:125–126).

After Colyer's departure, General Crook, with some personal

satisfaction and the approbation of Arizona citizens, mounted his winter campaign. A military order stated that "all roving bands of Indians . . . will be required to go at once upon their reservations, and not to leave them again upon any pretext whatever." The order stated further that "every Indian found off his reservation without permission, after a time to be fixed by the department commander, will be regarded and treated as hostile" (Colyer 1971:56–57). General William T. Sherman wrote to General J. M. Schofield, commander of the Military Division of the Pacific: "[if the Apache] wander outside they at once become objects of suspicion liable to be attacked by the troops as hostile. The three reservations . . . seem far enough removed from the white settlements to avoid the dangers of collision of interest" (Colyer 1971:55).

Crook surrounded the Tonto Basin, driving Apache before him and killing those who would not surrender. The Western Apache suffered severe losses and intense harassment, and many of them agreed to settle on the San Carlos Reservation because it offered the one remaining hope of staying alive. They had fought doggedly to retain their sovereignty over several centuries with brilliance, courage, and self-sacrifice, but at last, physical survival ultimately became the only option left for them. A few remained at large to the south.

The process of ending the Apache's control of their territory had many facets and phases. Individual actors in the process played a variety of roles, some of them in conflict. Many of the participants who tried to deflect the course of events were frustrated, embittered, and subject to considerable abuse. In the end, the macrocosmic social and economic forces that eventually swept the Apache from their territory and relegated them to reservations rewarded some of the actors and thwarted many who had tried to move in opposition. Those who sought to bring about peaceful coexistence between the invading Anglo-American population and the Apache were subject to special excoriation.

Many of these incidents were fueled by the raw racism that characterized the nineteenth-century American frontier. But this racism had economic underpinnings also. Numerous people profited from the perpetuation of war. Many of the military were convinced that a policy of genocide could never be carried out, but its espousal in the region kept hostilities intense enough to assure that the Apache wars would continue to feed the economy.

The major shift took place, finally, when Arizona's copper deposits became a significant resource in the national economy. Gold and silver had been sought and found for generations, but in many parts of

Apache prisoners, late nineteenth century (National Anthropological Archives, Smithsonian Institution, 56208)

the broken country of *Apachería*, copper, which was of use to industry, could be had in abundance. But there was no way to profit from
this fact unless the copper could be mined, and this could not occur
if the territory remained in the hands of hostile Apache. Since genocidal efforts to get rid of them had not succeeded, the only alternative
was to make them less hostile. With the inception of powerful economic incentives to pursue a serious effort for peace, the Apache wars
wound down to an end from the early 1870s toward the end of the
century.

CHAPTER 5

The Apache and the
American State

By repression should be understood first and foremost organized physical violence in the most material sense of the term: *violence to the body*. One essential condition of the establishment of power is the coercion of bodies through the threat of violence or death. (Poulantzas 1980:29).

As early as 1857, Colonel James L. Collins had advised that in lieu of a policy of "total extermination," Apache bands should be concentrated near a military post, given supplies, and kept peaceful (Ogle 1970:39). In 1870 a large reservation was proposed for the Apache, its lines drawn by Engineer Major H. M. Robert (Dobyns 1971:34). The northern edge coincided with the Arizona–New Mexico border from the south rim of Black Mesa to the mountains just north of the Gila River. The western edge was a line from Sombrero Butte at the crest of the Apache Mountains to Pinal Creek (Dobyns 1971:34). The military post in the northern part of this area, in the territory of the Coyotero Apache, was Camp Ord, eventually to become Fort Apache. Additional lands fifteen miles south of the Gila were added in December, 1872.

General O. O. Howard formally delineated the San Carlos Reservation. It was located within established Apache territory, but whatever reasons Howard may have had for selecting this site, apparently they did not include a concern for finding prime land for the Apache. Decades later, a Chiricahua man in retrospect exclaimed: "San Carlos! That was the worst place in all the great territory stolen from the Apaches. If anybody had ever lived there permanently, no Apache knew of it . . . Nearly all of the vegetation was cacti; and though in season a little cactus fruit was produced, the rest of the year food was lacking. The heat was terrible. The insects were terrible. The water was terrible . . . Insects and rattlesnakes seemed to thrive there . . . There were also tarantulas, Gila monsters, and centipedes . . . At times, it was so hot that I am sure a thermometer would have registered well above 120 degrees" (Ball 1980:37).

The Chiricahua were not alone in their feelings about San Carlos. Lieutenant Britton Davis, who was assigned to San Carlos in 1882, referred to it as Hell's Forty Acres. "Scrawny, dejected lines of scattered cottonwoods, shrunken, almost leafless, marked the course of streams. Rain was so infrequent that it took on the semblance of a phenomenon when it came at all. Almost continuously, dry, hot, dust- and gravel- laden winds swept the plain, denuding it of every vestige of vegetation. In summer a temperature of 110 in the shade was cool weather" (Davis 1951:48).

The San Carlos Agency, established in the early 1870s, reflected a distinction between the Fort Apache and San Carlos areas, but a formal boundary between the reservations was not established by Congress until 1897. Populations of Apache were moved about within these areas many times in the intervening years. In the meantime, the external borders continued to be altered.

In 1874 President Grant restored the eastern corridor of the reservation, which contained copper-bearing lands, to the public domain. A series of executive orders removed additional tracts of land from the reservation until 1912. Much later, in the late 1920s, Coolidge Dam flooded the Apache farmlands around the old San Carlos Agency to provide irrigation water for southern Arizona.

For a time the Chiricahua were able to remain with minimal supervision on a reservation near the border of Mexico, but a government decision in the 1870s called for their relocation to San Carlos. The Chiricahua leader Cochise had agreed to their original reservation on the basis of his friendship with a man named Tom Jeffords. Although the Chiricahua numbered only a few hundred, their reputation was formidable. The prospect of containing them within their old territory near the Mexican border seemed acceptable until the 1870s, but eventually, the apparent sovereignty of this population of Apache became a volatile issue. The growing population of settlers in Arizona became increasingly agitated about their presence. In 1876 the *Arizona Citizen* expressed the tone of local feeling, advocating the "slaying of every Apache man, woman, and child, until every fastness should send to high heaven the grateful incense of festering and rotting Chiricahuas" (quoted in Wagoner 1970:122).

By this time Cochise had died. His eldest son Tazeh had earned some respect as a leader, but he lacked the experience of his father. Tazeh agreed to relocate to San Carlos, and many of the Chiricahua decided to accompany him. Others, in keeping with the longstanding tradition of Apache autonomy, fled into Mexico or hid in the surrounding mountains. Some of those who allowed the troops to escort them northward bolted later. The government policy of consolidation also brought other people from the Camp Verde Reservation to the northwest, mostly Yavapai, removing them from the farms they had established.

In many ways the reservation was an alternative to genocide as a method of getting rid of the Apache. But some of the Arizona citizens opposed the reservation policy. Selling supplies to the army during the height of conflict had become even more lucrative than selling goods and services to prospectors, and the maintenance of hostilities was essential to those who depended on government contracts for an income.

The pall of peace was especially irksome when such agents and military officials as Lieutenant Whitman encouraged Apache to grow crops and then bought supplies from them rather than from Anglo-American contractors, who in the past often had struck comfortable deals with purchasing agents. Many citizens of Arizona had a vital interest in the Apache's remaining a threat, and in many cases the Apache were portrayed as ravaging the countryside even when they were not.

Why did the government in the early 1870s escalate its aggressive pursuit of peace with Apache and carry out pacification programs with such vigor? The dual strategies of Vincent Colyer and General George Crook represented drastic alternatives of persuasion by the offer of friendship and the threat of military punishment. Certainly these two men would have balked at the idea that they were acting in concert, but ultimately their approaches worked to the same end.

Crook was almost churlishly disdainful of the policies of "Vincent the Good," as he called Colyer (Thrapp 1968:105). And Colyer was politically "decapitated," as Crook put it, when his peaceful overtures were unsuccessful. No sooner had Colyer left the region after his peace mission than the attack on the Wickenburg stagecoach put to rest the idea that the Apache would acquiesce to peaceful overtures, if such an idea had been seriously entertained in Arizona in the first place. Questions as to whether Apache had attacked the stage became irrelevant. Many Arizonans would not tolerate peaceful Apache in any case, and many did all they could to eliminate them altogether. As one newspaper put it, the Apache should either be "out of Arizona or under it" (quoted in Porter 1986:152).

Crook was convinced that the Apache had to be beaten severely before they would agree to life on reservations, and the failure of Colyer's efforts gave him the free hand that he awaited. But if Crook was gleeful at the political decapitation of Colyer, we might recall that he resorted to that atrocity in a more literal sense in his own campaign. In the mid 1870s his scouts or troops cut off the heads of some "renegade" Apache leaders, and in one order, Crook himself called for the head of a man named Chunz. When a new Apache agent named John Clum arrived at the San Carlos Agency in 1874, scouts dumped a head from a gunny sack onto his office floor (Clum 1936:131).

The Economics of the Apache Wars

Most of the earliest Anglo-American settlers in Arizona had sought fortunes from the resources of the area. Some were attracted by the bounty on Apache scalps, others by fur trapping. Gold and silver attracted still more. Prospectors and miners eventually formed the economic basis upon which towns developed, creating a demand for troops to protect them and the need for ranches to feed the troops. But at this stage the basic resources of the region continued to be commodities that individuals, with luck and perseverance, could obtain and sell.

A heightened interest in Arizona by the federal government and the government's increasing tendency toward intervention coincided with an interest in the deposits of copper that lay beneath the rocky terrain of *Apachería*. What good is copper? It was not worth much to the individual prospector. Copper has never been considered a precious metal. A tremendous amount of copper ore would be necessary to equal the value of only a small amount of gold. Copper was not the sort of resource that could make an individual prospector rich through his own physical efforts. It was of interest mainly to industry.

In the wake of the Civil War, American industry had plenty of uses for copper and its alloy, brass. Exploiting copper resources required large-scale operations. Open-pit mines with a large labor force, smelters, and other means of production demanded massive capital investment. The copper potential of Arizona did not become important until a time of expanding industrial capitalism, but when it did, large-scale capitalist enterprise was to eclipse the small-scale individual fortune seeker. To this day, prospectors still wander the mountains of Arizona looking for semiprecious gems and lost mines, but economically they have become marginal in the age of corporations. Industrial interest in Arizona was already significant in the 1870s, but the economic potential of the region could not be realized until the Apache were removed. The interests of expanding capitalism drove the policies of the state, and the army was the most direct instrument for meeting the needs of these powerful interests.

While the army under General Crook readied itself for a major push to resolve the Apache problem, President Grant had sent Colyer to attempt a cheaper solution. Perhaps the President was influenced by his awareness that in the decade between 1861 and 1871, the government had expended 38 million dollars fighting a few thousand Apache at a cost of one thousand deaths (Dobyns 1971:35). This massive effort had netted only one hundred or so Apache killed, very few of whom had been men in their prime. But neither the Apache nor the citizens of Arizona would bow so easily to capitalism's sudden need for peace.

Throughout the history of conflict in the nineteenth century, the military produced many advocates for the Apache. Certainly not all military personnel were sympathetic to the Apache's plight; but in the diaries and memoirs of such men as John Gregory Bourke, Britton Davis, and others there is a common pattern of growing respect, admiration, and even affection for their adversaries. Part of this may be due to their closer exposure to Apache as individuals who worked with them as scouts, fought by their side, and ate with them over campfires. For most of the citizens of Arizona such close interaction with Apache was not a part of their experience and, in fact, would have been repugnant.

The army troops and officers were functionaries of the government, but for the most part their homes were not in Arizona. Most of them did not have the same personal stake in appropriating Apache territory, even though they eventually became instrumental in doing so. Their mission of enforcing the peace through defeating the Apache did not necessarily imply genocide. Perhaps this is one reason why some of the military were advocates of large reservations where the Apache could meet their subsistence needs. General Sherman's statement that the only hope of peace in Arizona was to relinquish the entire territory to the Apache may not have been entirely in jest. But in its role as enforcer of the will of the state, the army also became the device that eventually made Arizona safe for corporate capitalism.

In doing so, it also had to contend with continual sporadic attacks by citizens on peaceful Apache. President Grant's outrage at the Camp Grant massacre early in 1871 may have involved moral repugnance at the slaughter, but Ulysses S. Grant was no pacifist. A good deal of his exasperation probably had to do with the domestic disorder and disruption that could only set back economic development in the region. Grant's threat to impose martial law in Arizona Territory speaks to that concern. By 1871 he was very much aware of the copper potential in Arizona. In 1874 he signed an executive order approving the removal of copper-bearing lands from the new Apache reservation and placing them in the public domain.

One Man's View of the Apache: John Gregory Bourke

In the 1870s and 1880s, as the Apache found themselves increasingly enmeshed in the expanding American state, John Gregory Bourke participated in the process. His papers offer a vivid sense of the era. When he participated in Crook's winter campaign of 1871, apparently he fully accepted the rightness of the forces he represented. Bourke clearly was a man of his times. He had graduated from West Point and was conversant with the thrust of nineteenth-century American social thought. An aspect of this thought was the idea that progress was an inevitable law of nature, and that some human societies had progressed more than others. In the late 1880s he wrote a scholarly treatise discussing Apache practices in terms of cultural evolutionary stages (1892). There was little question in Bourke's mind that the United States and western Europe represented the epitome of human progress up to that time.

From this perspective, populations like the Apache were different—not because they represented alternative, equivalent varieties of human experience, but because they had not progressed beyond the stages of "savagery" or "barbarism." In many ways, according to this view, the Apache were something like what Europeans had been in the past. Human progress for the good of all, even for the good of the Apache, required that higher levels of social and cultural development replace savagery. To young John Bourke and other Anglo-Americans of his time, there was no apparent reason to question the idea that the Apache were an anachronistic obstacle to progress whose time had almost ended. Their fierce resistance to a civilized population's invasion of their territory did little to dispel these assumptions.

But Bourke also had a good deal of intellectual curiosity. As he became more familiar with Apache as individuals and perceived some of the complexities and intricacies of their lives, his respect for them grew. Moreover, he became conscious of a certain irony. The Apache of his acquaintance seemed to fulfill, far more rigorously than most of his own more "advanced" compatriots, many of the ideals that happened to be central to the ideology of his own culture. The Apache did not steal from one another. They scrupulously observed their own complex rules of etiquette, ethics, and religious strictures. They placed great importance on extramarital chastity. They demonstrated their physical courage time and again, and their self-control

The Chiricahua leader Naiche and Apache leader Geronimo (left) on horseback, with Chiricahuas Perico and Fun wearing face paint, 1886 (National Anthropological Archives, Smithsonian Institution, 43003-B)

and endurance were extraordinary. In many ways, Bourke could see some of the highest aspirations of the Victorian character in the qualities of the Apache (see Porter 1986:148).

Bourke also came to perceive many of the local Arizona citizenry as a scurrilous, unsavory lot who stood in the way of humane Indian policies. Perhaps the most tragic and poignant phase of the role Bourke played in the unfolding of this chapter in American history had to do with the eventual disposal of the Chiricahua Apache.

Many of the Chiricahua were unhappy at San Carlos, and in 1885 some of them—Geronimo among them—fled the reservation, beginning the last major army campaign against the Apache in the region. Most of the Chiricahua at San Carlos did not join their flight and remained behind. Lieutenant Britton Davis, who had reported to San Carlos in 1882 and participated in the resulting campaign, summarizes it incisively. "In this campaign thirty-five men and eight half-grown or older boys, encumbered with the care and sustenance of 101 women and children, with no base of supplies and no means of waging war or of obtaining food or transportation other than what they could take from their enemies, maintained themselves for eighteen months, in a country two hundred by four hundred miles in extent, against five thousand troops, regulars and irregulars, five hundred Indian auxiliaries of these troops, and an unknown number of civilians" (Davis 1951:lxvii–lxviii).

Davis notes that the fleeing Apache during this period were known to have killed seventy-five Arizona and New Mexico citizens, twelve White Mountain Apache, two officers, and eight enlisted army troops, and as many as a hundred or more Mexicans. As for the fleeing Apache: "Their losses in killed were six men, two large boys, two women and one child, *not one of whom was killed by regular troops* [emphasis in the original]. Moreover, one of the boys and two of the men were not killed in open warfare, but were killed by the citizens of the town of Casas Grandes, where they had gone on a peace mission" (Davis 1951:lxvii–lxviii).

In late March, 1886, Crook finally was able to negotiate with Geronimo and the other Chiricahua leaders at a place called the Cañon de Los Embudos, about twenty-six miles south of the border. The Chiricahua agreed to come in on the condition that, after no more than two years imprisonment, they would be allowed to join their families at Turkey Creek north of San Carlos. Crook left for Fort Bowie at the close of the conference, and the Chiricahua were to follow the next day with the scouts.

That night a local citizen named Bob Tribolett approached the Chiricahua and scouts and sold them sizable quantities of mescal liquor. After getting them drunk, he told them that if they went into Fort Bowie the next day they would be killed. Finding the story plausible, the Chiricahua bolted once again into Mexico. They could not be persuaded to surrender for another couple of months (Davis 1951:302).

After Tribolett had gotten them drunk and had told them that the army intended to kill them once they were taken prisoner, Lieutenant Bourke encountered Geronimo and the others. Bourke wrote in his diary that "this incident so alarmed and disgusted me and was so pregnant with significance that I rode up to Genl. Crook and asked him to have Tribollet [*sic*] killed as a foe to human society, and, said I, if you don't Genl. Crook it'll be the biggest mistake of your life" (quoted in Porter 1986:177).

There is some reason to suspect that Tribolett was acting on behalf of the infamous Tucson Ring of contractors who profited from the Apache conflict. Several contemporary observers expressed this view, and certainly he served their purposes well. Eventually Tribolett was to die in jail awaiting trial for planning a stagecoach robbery, shot while "trying to escape" (Thrapp 1968:346–347).

When the Chiricahua finally agreed to return to San Carlos, they did so with the understanding that they would be allowed to live with their families near Turkey Creek. After General Crook reached this agreement, he learned that the terms would not be honored by the government. President Grover Cleveland insisted on an unconditional

General Crook (second from right) conferring with Geronimo, March 1886.
Captain Bourke is third from right. (National Anthropological Archives,
Smithsonian Institution, 43003-A)

surrender. Crook resigned in protest, and General Nelson Miles took over to receive credit, eventually, for "bringing in Geronimo."

While Geronimo negotiated, Miles already had arrested the peaceful Chiricahua at Fort Apache and sent them on their way to imprisonment in Florida. He promised the others that they could join their families if they surrendered. When they did so, he wrote a carefully worded letter to his superiors giving the impression that he had secured the unconditional surrender of the Chiricahua. All of the Chiricahua were arrested and sent to prison, including the peaceful contingent who never had left the reservation, the scouts who had assisted the army in achieving the surrender of Geronimo's group, and the two who had risked their lives to make contact with the others.

In 1885, just before their removal, the Indian Rights Association had reported on the Chiricahua who lived at Fort Apache: "[They were] a fine, manly looking set, and did not talk much, but expressed themselves as well pleased with what had been done for them. They said that they wanted to turn their faces in the same way as the whites, to work and make money. The Chiricahuas were kept at San Carlos until the middle of last May. It was a month later by the time they began farming. Since then they have got seventy-five acres under cultivation" (Frazer 1885:7).

After their arrest and removal to the East, the Chiricahua men were kept separate from their families for years. Bourke, who had been present at the negotiations between Crook and Geronimo, was outraged. "Never was there a more striking illustration of the ingratitude of Republics. Never a more cruel outrage perpetrated in the name of a nation affecting to love liberty, honor, and truth" (quoted in Porter 1986:42).

In the following years Bourke achieved some renown in eastern intellectual circles as an ethnographer and a student of Apache culture, and he worked strenuously for their humane treatment. He visited the Chiricahua in Florida and lobbied to acquire a more healthful situation for them.

In Florida the government took the Chiricahua children away and sent them to the Carlisle Indian School in Pennsylvania. Of the 107 who went there in 1886, twenty-seven had died within three years (Porter 1986:256). In writing about the situation, Bourke quoted Thomas B. McCaulay in describing the action as "the saddest of all human spectacles—the strength of a great nation exerted without its mercy" (quoted in Porter 1986:231). After several relocations, the Chiricahua eventually were moved to Oklahoma. In 1913, long after Bourke's death, they finally were given the option of moving to the Mescalero reservation in New Mexico. Over a hundred of them chose to do so.

Throughout his life, Bourke accepted the ideology of his own society. Just as he had embraced the idea that the Apache represented a stage of evolution doomed to be replaced by civilization, he felt that civilization entailed a responsibility to invoke humane and refined standards of behavior. To his dismay, he found that his own government and society wanted nothing more than to let the Apache die off and disappear as a problem.

The disparity between his state's ideals and its actions never ceased to plague him. This conflict was manifest late in his life when he led troops against workers in the Chicago Pullman strike of 1894. He was incensed that the striking rabble, many of whom spoke poor English, should challenge a social system in whose ideals he had a faith that apparently was unshakable. At the end of the summer he spent defending Mr. George Mortimer Pullman's interests against the workers, Bourke left Chicago on the train with his troops. They were required to pay full fare (Porter 1986:299).

Bourke died at the age of forty-nine, apparently from the cumulative effects of a life of physical stress. He had been unable, at last, to convince his government that the Apache he had fought as savages and had come to admire and respect as persons should be treated humanely. But Bourke lived during one of the most corrupt eras in

American history. It was a time when collusion between corporate interests and the government was especially brazen, and racism was as American as frock coats and picket fences. For a person who truly believed in the ideals that his culture espoused, such an era must have been intensely frustrating.

Early Reservation Policies

The reservations were intended to serve as repositories for the Apache in areas with little or no economic value and far from anticipated Anglo-American settlement. After earlier attempts at genocide had failed, the process involved getting rid of the Apache in a geographic sense. It cleared them from their territory and opened this territory for exploitation by others.

But the reservations also were intended to promote change. The military kept the Apache under surveillance during the early years, and a variety of policies and programs sought to render them fit for existence within the American state. Although civilian and military factions struggled over the administration of reservations, each represented the extension of state hegemony and aspects of the process of incorporating the Apache.

The military pattern of administration involved a "prisoner of war" model. The military restricted Apache movements and imposed daily roll calls to keep raiding parties from leaving the reservation. This approach emphasized order more than change. The immediate result of this policy was enforced idleness and dependence on rations, since the military did not allow the Apache to leave on food-gathering expeditions or to use the weapons they required for hunting. As a result, many people suffered from a lack of protein. They could no longer pursue their former means of obtaining nutrition, and the rations were insufficient and unreliable.

In 1874, a new agent from New York State named John Clum adopted a model of civilian administration at San Carlos that emphasized change more than supervision. His policies represented alternative means of incorporating the Apache into the state, and whenever possible, he used the Apache to assist in the process.

One of his first moves was to form an Apache police force to keep order within the reservation itself. This turned out to be very successful. The reservation was an uneasy place. In the wake of military defeat, the crowding together of Apache groups who were not particularly friendly to one another had produced a volatile situation. It was aggravated by the deaths of many of their relatives, inadequate food, and generally unhealthy conditions.

The history of the Apache offers considerable support to Poulantzas' view that, ultimately, the power of the state over the individual is the threat of physical violence. The use of Apache to exert force against their own people was a major step in the process. Perhaps one of the most effective aspects of Clum's strategy was to ask the various Apache groups to select their own police officers. As additional bands arrived later, they too had representation on the force. It is difficult to ascertain how the Apache perceived this, but for the most part the police did manage to keep order. One incident in particular is especially puzzling, but revealing.

At one point Clum was brash enough to object to the way in which a man named Desalin treated his wives. The man became violently angry and seemed about to kill Clum. Before he could do so, Clum's sergeant of police, Tauelclyee, fired at and killed Desalin. As it happened, Desalin had been the sergeant's brother (Clum 1936:166–169).

How can we interpret this incident? Was Tauelclyee's affection for Clum so great that it overrode his sense of kin ties? Perhaps to understand what happened, we must consider the Apache's circumstances at that time. The troops were never far from the San Carlos Agency in those days, and voices for genocide in Arizona had never been silent. The Apache had good reason to fear the repercussions that would follow the killing of an agent, particularly one whose policies had been to loosen their shackles. In killing his brother, Tauelclyee may have fired to save his own people rather than to save Clum.

To a great extent, Clum's success did rest on his treating the Apache with more respect and latitude than they generally had received at the hands of Anglo-Americans. With a Victorian distaste for idleness, he organized work parties to dig irrigation ditches, plant fields, and carry out construction projects. He paid them in chits they could use to buy goods from the agency, and he allowed them to check out guns and travel to other parts of the reservation to hunt. Clum also insisted that the troops leave the immediate vicinity of the agency.

Clum's policies and personality led him into a series of squabbles with the government, the military, and, most particularly, the local citizenry. His attempts to make the Apache self-sufficient by growing their own crops alarmed suppliers who had done well with their government contracts. The *Arizona Miner* in 1877 sputtered that "the brass and impudence of this young bombast is perfectly ridiculous" (quoted in Wagoner 1970:147). But Clum's short career at San Carlos probably was most remarkable for its interminable haggling over whether he or the military should have control over the administration of the Apache.

John Clum with Alchesay (left) and Eskiminizin (right).
(National Archives, 111-SC-94849)

At one point Clum traveled to Camp Apache to secure the release of some Apache prisoners and take them back to San Carlos. A military detachment pursued him and rearrested the bemused Apache. In 1875 the military at Camp Apache deposed a civilian agent named James E. Roberts and installed Reverend J. M. Mickly in his place. The Indian Commissioner in Washington, meanwhile, ordered Clum to take charge of Camp Apache, and he left San Carlos with fifty

Apache work crew digging an irrigation ditch at San Carlos, late nineteenth century
(National Archives, 111-SC-83712)

Apache to carry out the order. When Clum arrived, he arrested Mickly for opening Roberts' mail.

The military commander fumed at Clum's interference. When Clum insisted on conducting a roll call of Apache without the presence of troops, the post commander ordered a simultaneous roll call and threatened to attack any Apache who failed to appear. The officer of the day arrested Clum for riding his horse too fast across the parade ground. When Clum asserted that he was now in charge of all the Apache, the post commander opened the doors of the guardhouse and released the Apache prisoners (Ogle 1970:150; see also Clum 1936:159).

Part of the problem at San Carlos stemmed from the government's policy of consolidating the Apache population. Some people, mostly Yavapai, had settled peacefully at Camp Verde in central Arizona but were brought to San Carlos in 1875 "in the interests of efficiency and economy." Wagoner suggests that the Tucson Ring, who had an interest in selling supplies to the government, prevailed to get the Yavapai removed from Camp Verde (1970:144). The Camp Verde people had spent the previous few years developing irrigated farms with the assistance of the army troops, and in 1874 they had produced forty acres of vegetables. They did not welcome the sudden order to abandon their farms and move to San Carlos. When they arrived there under Clum's administration, they constituted an uneasy and potentially volatile presence.

Subsequently, the Indian Commissioner, in consultation with Clum, decided to bring the Coyotero from Camp Apache to San Carlos, taking them away from their well-watered, high-altitude White Mountain homeland. When Clum set out to bring them in, he discovered that many of them were families of men who were serving elsewhere as army scouts. These people were reluctant to leave before the scouts returned. Many of them also had crops in the field that were almost ready to harvest. Still more of the Coyotero probably had misgivings about the government's motivations for wanting to take them away from their home territory.

Clum granted permission for several hundred of them to stay at their farms until the crops were in, and he set off for San Carlos with the rest. As he left, he burned the agency buildings. This later became a contentious issue, since only a week or two after ordering Clum to bring the Coyotero from Camp Apache to San Carlos, the Commissioner in Washington appointed an agent for the Coyotero at Camp Apache.

According to the 1885 report of the Indian Rights Association: "In 1876, a settlement near Fort Apache was broken up and the Indians moved to San Carlos, losing a portion of their crop. Alchise said that they had a great deal of corn planted, but that Clum, then Agent, insisted on their leaving them, saying that they might come back for them. But their dwellings were burned, including two government buildings, their corn trodden down, and their blankets stolen and sold. Except Pedro and his band, who absolutely refused to go, they were all moved to San Carlos. Pedro said that they should not take him away alive. He gained his point, and from that day to this his band has been self-supporting" (Frazer 1885:9–10).

This bickering over control must have been rather puzzling to the Apache. A few years later, a frustrated Clum would resign and leave San Carlos. He went on to become the mayor of Tombstone and founded the *Tombstone Epitaph*. He died in Los Angeles in 1932, walking to the back door of his house for breakfast after potting roses (Clum 1936:ix).

Many of the things the Apache had begun to develop during Clum's administration would decline, but the Apache police remained a permanent institution in San Carlos. Similar policies eventually were adopted on many other reservations. The Clum years in San Carlos were followed by decades of mismanagement. A succession of agents, some of them notoriously crooked, entailed hard times for the Apache (see Ogle 1970), and the years of fighting in the Southwest were far from over.

The government policy of consolidation at San Carlos continued through the 1870s. The Chiricahua and Mimbres Apache, including such noted leaders as Geronimo, Juh, Loco, and Victorio, came to San Carlos. Victorio and Loco departed on September 1, 1877, with 310 of their people and fled east to their own country. Victorio vowed never to return to San Carlos, and Mexican troops killed him in 1881. Occasional outbreaks occurred until the late 1880s, and life continued to be uneasy for the Apache at San Carlos. The last and most spectacular incident was the departure of Geronimo that touched off the campaign ending in 1886, resulting in the removal of the Chiricahua from San Carlos to Florida.

Despite the Apache police, order within the reservation continued to be tentative. The Apache had many reasons to chafe under reservation conditions. In the words of Lieutenant Britton Davis, who won the respect and affection of many Apache, despite their giving him the nickname Fat Boy: "The well-nigh universal testimony of all observers ascribes the outbreak of 1882 and the subsequent warfare to the mismanagement and dishonesty of the Indian agents. In particular, the administration of J. C. Tiffany in 1880 and 1881 was marked by wholesale graft and corruption, which was characterized by the Federal grand jury at Tucson in October, 1882, as 'a disgrace to the civilization of the age and a blot on the national escutcheon' " (Davis 1951:48).

The use of neck tags to assign people to administrative bands also was irksome to many Apache. All males over fourteen were given brass military identification tags: "They were ordered always to keep [the tags] on their persons. On these tags were letters and numbers indicating the band to which the Indian belonged and his number in the band" (Davis 1951:62).

In 1881 a religious movement promising the return of renowned dead Apache leaders such as Cochise and Mangas Coloradas developed among the Coyotero and spread through San Carlos. To some extent the movement was a response to the Apache's desperation. It centered on a respected figure known as Noche-do-klinne. The movement was not particularly militant, but the military commander, Lieutenant Carr, became concerned. He was especially alarmed when some of the Apache scouts and police seemed to be intrigued by it. Carr ordered his troops to arrest Noche-do-klinne and bring him in to the agency.

A scout warned Noche-do-klinne before the troops arrived, but he chose not to flee or resist. When the troops came to arrest him, he had sent the others away and was waiting alone in his dwelling. Many Apache followed at a distance as the troops took him back toward the San Carlos Agency.

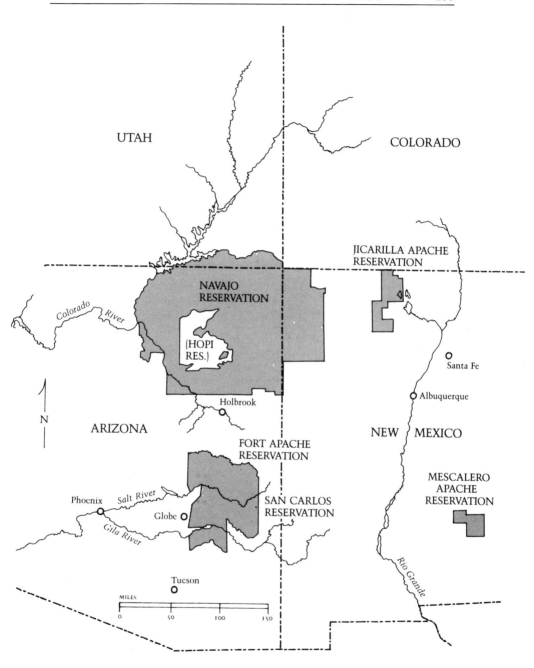

Map 3. Apache reservations in the Southwest

Carr was afraid that the religious leader would arouse the Apache to fight, but ironically, some of the more militant Apache leaders had been concerned that the movement would have a pacifying influence on the people. Whatever the case, Noche-do-klinne never made it back to the post. Firing broke out among the troops before they had gone very far, and one of them killed him.

In the next few days Apache attacked a couple of ranches, but the furor soon died down. After investigating the matter, General Crook concluded: "The Indians are firmly convinced that the affair . . . was an attack premeditated by the white soldiers . . . I am convinced any attempt to punish any of the Indian soldiers for participation in it would bring on war . . . I have no doubt from what I know of the Indians and the country in question, that if the Indians had been in earnest not one of our soldiers would have gotten away from there alive. Of course afterwards, it was perfectly natural for the Indians to commit the depredations which they did in the vicinity of Fort Apache" (quoted in Thrapp 1968:225–226).

By the end of the 1880s Apache fighting at last had almost ended in the Southwest. There were reports as late as the 1930s that a small group of Apache in the mountains of Mexico still managed to hold out. One of their little girls was captured by villagers and tethered to a tree, but she died before authorities could rescue her. By the end of the century the Apache had effectively lost possession and control of their territory. Local citizens continued to voice opinions about the Apache threat, but as time passed, the militancy of townspeople, ranchers, and miners moderated to a lower level of chronic animosity.

Eventually the government allowed the people from Camp Verde to leave San Carlos and return to their former lands. Most of the Coyotero were permitted to return north to the White Mountains on the Fort Apache Reservation. San Carlos was left mostly to the remaining Pinal and Arivaipa Apache and the few Coyotero who elected to stay.

The Western Apache in the Late Nineteenth Century

In the late nineteenth century the populations of the Western Apache reflected the general processes of local diversification that had gone on since their arrival in the Southwest. The so-called Tonto in the West were predominantly Yavapai who had closely interacted and intermarried with Apache. In later periods, many Anglo-Americans mistakenly considered them to be another band of Apache (Schroeder 1974b:395–441). The various relocations and placements on the reservations tended to produce other divisions, but overall, the Western Apache still shared close cultural similarities.

There were slight differences in speech and custom among the various aggregates, and Apache claimed that they could identify a person's local origins by subtle differences in appearance, even in photographs. According to Goodwin, writing in the late 1930s: "In the old days there was some variation in the mode of dress, and the Apache claim to be able to tell the group of a man or woman merely by scanning their features and mannerisms. When shown early photographs of Western Apache, they could not always correctly identify individuals but almost invariably and quite correctly could tell to what group they belonged by nothing more than an indefinable tilt of the headband" (1969:8–9). But beyond these distinctions, the Western Apache shared far more similarities than differences.

The individualized networks of kin remained strong and significant in Apache life, still allowing easy mobility within the structure of matrilineal clans. The association of these clans with farm plots in the past had done little to hinder the Apache's freedom of movement. Even on the reservation, the tendency to recognize senior kinsmen as local leaders did not develop into a rigid system of hereditary leadership. Individual qualities of judgment, personality, courage, and intelligence continued to be essential beyond the juristic claims of kinship. Many people who were influential de facto leaders were not drawn from any specified kin-based line of succession (Goodwin 1969:135).

In keeping with this ancient flexibility in their social organization and subsistence patterns, the Apache continued to prefer mountainous areas. The Coyotero's requests to return to their mountains north of San Carlos were chronic and insistent. They lived in the mountains and farmed in the lower river valleys (Buskirk 1986:22). Preference for mountains was equally strong among the Chiricahua. One man, referring to raids into Mexico, said: "When we traveled we followed the ridges, usually the high ones, and fortunately for us the mountains run generally north to south instead of east and west . . . we had a saying that the Indian follows the mountains and the white man the streams" (Ball 1980:32). Bourke's account of the statements of Chiricahua incarcerated in Florida also expresses this attachment to the mountains. They wanted to be placed in an area where there was snow, "mentioning that snow was often knee-deep in the mountains of *Apachería*, and they disliked living 'alongside the water,' saying they were a people who had been born and bred in the high mountains" (Porter 1986:256).

In the more stable life of the reservations, the Apache showed little tendency to develop wealth differentiation or concepts of privately owned land. Farm plots often had boundary markers, but usually people planted small areas that were large enough only for their own use. When they planted larger, irregular garden plots, people freely shared the crops they produced (Buskirk 1986:38). People who planted large gardens generally needed help at harvest time, and the volunteers received a part of the crop for their work. By some accounts, in fact, those who had planted gardens sometimes confronted an excessive amount of volunteered help from people who had not planted gardens of their own and, as a result, often ended up with a greatly diminished return for their efforts (Buskirk 1986:52).

It is difficult to find any basis here for a suggestion of farm "owners" exploiting the labor of their workers. "Ditch bosses" sometimes coordinated collective labor to maintain irrigation for farms, but they tended to be old men who were knowledgeable about irrigation and who took an interest in it but did not claim any particular privileges (Buskirk 1986:49). People generally assumed that women were likely to be more interested in gardening, and plots often passed from mother to daughter. Buskirk points out: "Both sons and daughters inherited farms from either the maternal or paternal side of the family. In the case of grown children, place of residence largely determined which of them inherited. Married daughters living at home were likely to receive the property, married sons living away from home relinquishing any claim in their favor" (1986:32).

Apache gardening and farming remained mostly a matter of production for direct consumption. Apache sold hay and firewood at the end of the nineteenth century, first to the army and later to people in nearby towns, but the lively commercial agricultural enterprises that John Clum had envisioned in the 1870s did not develop.

Incorporation into the State Economy

Acting Commissioner of Indian Affairs E. M. Marble wrote in his report of November 1, 1880: "That they are inclined to agriculture is shown by the persevering efforts to make and construct irrigation ditches and raise small fields of grain . . . In order to become owners of stock cattle, several families allowed their beef tickets to accumulate until they were entitled to one or more cows, and in that way obtained the nucleus of a herd." Nonetheless: "The subject of a water supply, which is an all-important one throughout Arizona, becomes a grave one whenever it concerns an Indian reservation, the prevailing opinion being that Indians have no water rights which white men are bound to respect. Although the San Carlos Reserve is comparatively well supplied with streams, and although scarcely a beginning in farming has been made, the water question is already assuming major proportions" (Washburn 1973).

On November 18, 1921, reservation superintendent Ernest Stecker wrote to the Commissioner of Indian Affairs: "Due to the amount of irrigable land available here, many Indians have no land assigned to them for farming purposes. This condition creates much dissatisfaction among them, especially when there is no work available, and food is scarce" (Hayden Coll. 622/8). The Apache did eventually come to sell their labor on a larger scale, but then they were not producing from their own garden plots. They labored on projects that other people owned and over which they had no control.

The projects of Clum and others after him were directed toward making the Apache a part of American society by linking them to the socioeconomic system and, in a sense, completing their capture by the state. People who promoted these programs usually expressed this as helping the Apache.

As the Apache's historical experience had demonstrated, the only practical alternative to acceptance of state hegemony was genocide. As late as the 1880s, the Governor of Arizona found it necessary to proclaim to his constituents: "The peaceful Indians occupy San Carlos by the authority of the law. The Federal Government will give protection to them and any unlawful attack on them would aggravate our present troubles and subject us to the just condemnation of the civilized world" (quoted in Wagoner 1970:232).

Whether through annihilation or incorporation, continued efforts sought to eliminate the Apache as an independent population. By becoming incorporated into the state, the Apache would become one of its constituencies rather than a sovereign population surrounded by it, in jeopardy of their physical existence. No longer could they retain control over their vast territory and remain independent of the state altogether.

The process of individualization that John Bourke had hoped would result from using Apache as scouts meant that, supposedly, the scouts would no longer see themselves embedded in networks of kin ties, subject to obligations and expectations passed on by ancient tradition. Nor, for that matter, would they see themselves as members of a small, beleaguered population struggling to keep their territorial base from being taken over by an inexorable invading force. Instead, as individuals equivalent to all other individuals within the state, their loyalties would be directed to the state itself rather than to smaller interest or ethnic groups, classes, or "tribes" within the broader system. Bourke was astute in recognizing the significance of kin ties to the Apache, but he underestimated the tenacity of these bonds. As it turned out, the Apache were not much more digestible to the American state than they had been to the Spanish state centuries before.

Certainly part of this persistent Apache distinctness was due to the racism that provided ideological rationalization for the capitalist state's expansion into *Apachería* in the first place. Racism denied the Apache full access to the fruits of the capitalist system. As the development of the West unfolded, more powerful interest groups and constituencies relegated the Apache to a role that would have precluded their blending into the broader population even if they had chosen to do so.

As late as the influenza epidemic of 1919, local citizens applauded the deaths of roughly 40 percent of the San Carlos Apache population as a "solution" to the Apache problem. In 1963, a middle-aged cowboy joked about his younger days when he and his friends sometimes raped young Apache women they encountered in remote areas. Yet by the turn of the century, the Apache had come to be more and more incorporated into the wider state as participants in the labor force.

Apache in the Labor Force

At first the Apache had merely been in the way of Anglos because they held contested resources. But by the end of the nineteenth century they were usable as labor and constituted a resource in themselves. Roads and railroads had to be built. Copper had to be dug from the ground. By 1900, the Apache had become the major unskilled work force in the Southwest.

How did this come to be? The programs of John Clum and other agents to help the Apache become good citizens were instrumental in creating a situation that prepared them to sell their labor. They had lost the means to subsist by producing for their own consumption, which would have allowed them to maintain some autonomy. Their government rations were inadequate. The meager commodities they could produce for sale, such as hay and firewood, did not bring in enough money to allow for survival. And even these efforts were severely challenged by outside contractors, who saw the Apache as competitors. Lieutenant Britton Davis notes that agents discouraged Apache from raising grain "in the interest of civilians who were selling supplies to the Agency at fabulous prices" (Davis 1951:67).

The government did provide some supplies, but the corruption associated with the ration program is notorious. In the 1880s a beef contractor at San Carlos kept his herds unwatered on the far side of

Issue Day at San Carlos, 1886 (National Anthropological Archives, Smithsonian Institution, 74-11687)

the Gila River until it was time to deliver them. Then he drove the scrawny herd across the wide, shallow river where the thirsty animals bloated themselves with water before being weighed on the hoof (Davis 1951:66).

Sometimes contractors and agents bypassed even these dishonest measures, and the government paid for a great deal of food that never reached starving Apache at all. Even when it did reach them, as reservation superintendent Ernest Stecker wrote in 1921: "This ration for single persons is in itself insufficient to properly subsist them. At the time this ration was established there was plenty of game to provide additional food- The game is gone, but the ration remains the same" (Hayden Coll. 622/8).

Resources on the Apache reservation that had significant value as commodities, such as copper, water, or timber, were extracted or expropriated by government action or by other parties with government support after their worth became apparent. Although incidents varied, the results were consistent. The Apache were enmeshed in a system in which the only way to survive was to have something to sell. Ultimately, all they had left to sell was their labor.

When the Apache ventured into the labor force, whether as scouts or construction workers, their old pattern of relationships persisted. Highway labor conformed to the pattern of periodic male absence that had been associated with hunting and raiding in the past. Women at home remained the center of interpersonal relationships. Matrilocal

Issue Day at San Carlos, 1886 (National Anthropological Archives,
Smithsonian Institution, 2575 T)

residence and the system of matrilineal clans continued without
much change.

A variety of other sources of employment developed around the
turn of the century. Seasonal harvest work became more common, as
farms and cotton fields grew up around the borders of the reservation. The work was sporadic and often involved women and children.
Apache became essential to the economy of southern Arizona partly
because they were willing to work hard for very little money. In one
case around 1920, Apache workers signed up for a job that the agent
told them would pay $2.50 per day. A truck arrived to take the work-
ers to the job site, and many brought their families with them. When
they arrived, they learned that the pay was only two dollars per day
and that the employer would take some deductions. These included
one dollar for board and five cents for a "hospital" fee. At the end of
the day the Apache workers were left with ninety-five cents apiece,
which was not enough to pay for their ride back to San Carlos (Institute for Government Research 1928:687).

As early as 1901, labor unions in Arizona were objecting to the use
of Apache workers because the Apache were willing to work at such
low wages (Adams 1971:119). As in other parts of the country where
the labor of one population had been systematically exploited by
another, the myth that Apache were physically better suited for
arduous, punishing tasks became conventional wisdom. Employers
claimed that severe working conditions such as field labor in the blaz-

ing Arizona sun, which "whites" would find intolerable, did not bother the Apache (Adams 1971:121).

Although use of Apache labor in Arizona around the turn of the century was highly exploitative and in some aspects was reminiscent of plantation labor in the Southeast, by then the historic processes had all but closed off alternative means of survival. The Apache had to work for wages, but although work at that time was available to them in abundance, it was restricted to the most grueling and low-paying jobs.

The Apache participated in great numbers. The Apache job market was so lively in this period that the government appointed an employment officer to expedite the hiring process. By 1901, so many Apache were working for wages that the government declared that further issuance of rations was unnecessary (Adams 1971:119–120). This did not turn out to be a permanent situation, however.

Throughout this period a complex process unfolded. The Apache were taking their place within the state at the low end of the labor force, but they were in no position to increase their power or wealth. They could not own the farms where they picked cotton or the mines where they dug copper ore. Their wages were at or below the minimal level of subsistence and had to be applied to consumption. Supplemental gardening, wild foods, and government assistance were necessary to get enough to eat.

In November 1921, reservation superintendent Ernest Stecker wrote to the Commissioner of Indian Affairs:

The San Carlos Indians taken as a whole are poor people. The great majority still live in grass huts. There is a shortage of warm clothing and bedding which forces many to sleep in the clothes they have worn all day, besides keeping up a fire throughout the night, in their efforts to protect themselves from the cold. Due to shortage of irrigable land there are insufficient crops to help out, which with a lack of employment, deprives these people of ample and nourishing food. It is simply a mystery how they do manage to survive. However, the lack of sufficient nourishing food, warmer winter clothing, and better shelter to meet the cold weather are the direct causes of so much sickness and death among them. (Hayden Coll. 622/8)

The reservation superintendent in 1921 was concerned about the excessive drinking of *tulpai*, the mild beer made of corn sprouts. "The present conditions depress these people, and this drink is used because it fills the stomach, temporarily relieving the pangs of hunger, while it stupefies their senses and drowns their worries, caused by constant poverty or non-employment" (Hayden Coll. 622/8). He closed his report to the Commissioner of Indian Affairs on a sad and rather ironic note: "Let us always remember that they are human beings, men, women, and children with souls, entrusted to our care and keeping, and we will not fail in our efforts to lead them into the paths of self-support with the aid and support of our generous government" (Hayden Coll. 622/8).

The Role of Education

Formal education became an important aspect of the Apache's lives during the first few decades of the reservation. For many Anglo-Americans, education is a means of attaining upward social mobility—a ticket into the system. But "Indian education" in the early twentieth century had a different thrust.

Much of this early education was conducted by missionaries, and even when it was not, there tended to be a heavy emphasis on behavior, comportment, and "attitude." The 1873 report of the Commissioner of Indian Affairs extolled the advantages of the boarding school for Native American children, which "take the youth under constant care, has him always at hand, and surrounds him by an English-speaking community, and, above all, gives him instruction in the first lessons of civilization, which can be found only in a well-ordered home" (quoted in Fletcher 1888:168). In 1886, the commissioner reported: "The greatest difficulty is experienced in freeing the children attending day schools from the language and habits of their untutored and oftentimes savage parents. When they return to their homes at night, and on Saturdays and Sundays, and are among their old surroundings, they relapse more or less into their former moral and mental stupor" (quoted in Fletcher 1888:170).

What this approach to education meant, essentially, was that children were to be de-Indianized—weaned away from an identification with their ethnic background and individualized in order to be integrated into the state. But for the Apache and other Native Americans, integration into the state was not intended to be in positions of power. It was to be in the labor force. In effect, this meant becoming a part of the reserve supply of labor. In this situation, young minds that were self-assured, critical, questioning, and imbued with a strong sense of ethnic validity were not appropriate. Acceptance of discipline, minimal instrumental skills, loyalty to the wider state system, and internalization of its ideology were more consistently the goals of Indian education.

This is one reason for the establishment of centralized Indian boarding schools. Centralization did have some logistic advantages in terms of efficiency. But in other parts of the United States, small local schools for white children seem to have been perfectly feasible. Centralized Indian schools had the effect of separating children from their families for long periods of time. The unhealthy influence of living among their traditional elders, it was thought by administrators, would interfere with the salubrious effects of education. Separating the children would make the process of "saving" them more effective.

This is one reason why children in Indian schools were beaten for speaking in their own languages. Even when such schools existed on reservations, discipline usually was very strict. A favorite punishment for children in San Carlos was to make them carry a ball and chain (Spicer 1962:257), and Apache children were taken to school in chains to keep them from escaping and running away. Even so, many did run away from boarding schools, and some died trying to find their way back to their people.

Despite this, many Apache perceived a value in education and tried to learn to read and write. But the directions of the education they received were almost inevitably toward preparation for low-paying labor.

The Expropriation of Resources

As outside interests came to recognize resources in the Apache's possession, these were systematically removed. Commissioner of Indian Affairs E. A. Hayt noted in his report of November 1, 1929: "The attention of this office has often been called to the encroachments of miners and other intruders on the Ute Reservation in Colorado and the San Carlos Reservation in Arizona. Numerous and extensive mines have been opened on both reservations, especially the latter, and every effort of this office to remove the miners has thus far proved ineffectual. The question of intrusion on the San Carlos Reservation must remain unsettled until the western boundary of the same is resurveyed, and an appropriation to cover the expense of such survey should be made without delay" (Washburn 1973: 278–279).

On July 21, 1874, President Grant had signed an official order that divested the Apache of the copper-bearing lands at the eastern end of the reservation, but many other people were involved as well. When those lands were placed in the public domain, the agent at San Carlos and the Commissioner of Indian Affairs in Washington had financial holdings in the copper enterprises that subsequently developed there. Governor Safford of Arizona was known for his alertness to mineral wealth and his political astuteness in using it to benefit the territory and its high officials.

After the presidential order, the towns of Clifton and Morenci grew up around the Phelps Dodge Corporation's open-pit mines on the former reservation lands to the east. In the western section, confiscated Apache lands are mined by the Inspiration Consolidated Copper Company, a subsidiary of Anaconda. These companies support the economies of Globe, Miami, and Superior. In 1974, Phelps Dodge, Anaconda, and Kennecott produced 55 percent of all copper mined in the United States (Mikesell 1979:7). Arizona lands contain some of the richest deposits of high-grade copper ever discovered in the history of mining (Joralemon 1973:203).

The historian Ira Joralemon notes: "Four major districts of this type were found at almost the same time, between 1870 and 1880. They came to full production just when their copper was needed toward the end of the nineteenth century. Clifton, Globe, Bisbee and Jerome, all in Arizona, were destined to produce as much copper per year as the whole country used at the time they were discovered. The apparent reason why they were developed at so nearly the same time was the opening up of Arizona by the Southern Pacific Railroad, following the pacification or extermination of the Apaches. A less obvious reason was the fact that the world needed the new copper and Fate supplied the need" (1973:203).

Few Apache now work at these mines. When labor unions became established during the Depression, employers replaced Apache labor with workers of European origin (Wagoner 1970:388). Apache lost their jobs, and during those years most of them returned to the reservation.

As they struggled to maintain a livelihood through wage work and saw their reservation boundaries altered to accommodate the appetites of developers, they also faced chronic usurpation of lands and resources within the boundaries of the reservation itself. This began early in the reservation period, when Anglo-Americans ran Arivaipa off their farms at gunpoint in the southern part of the reservation and occupied the land (Goodwin 1969:29). In the southeast, farmers near Safford diverted so much Gila River water to irrigate their farms that the Apache farms downstream dried up. The Acting Commissioner of Indian Affairs, in his report of 1880, quoted the San Carlos agent. "The water in the Gila is rapidly being depleted by large quantities being taken out by ditches in the vicinity of Pueblo Viejo, twenty miles above Camp Thomas, and a fifteen-foot ditch now being dug by

Apache on horseback, as photographed by Edward S. Curtis early in the twentieth century (National Anthropological Archives, Smithsonian Institution, 75-5945)

the Mormons in that vicinity will, in low water, seriously damage the water privileges on this reservation" (Washburn 1973:255). Settlers also encroached on the Fort Apache Reservation to the north.

The Bureau of Indian Affairs leased out most of the grazing land on the San Carlos Reservation to Anglo-American ranchers. In 1921, over 74 percent of reservation grazing land was used by non-Apache ranchers under grazing permits (Stecker to the Commissioner of Indian Affairs, November 18, 1921, Hayden Coll. 622/8). Eventually this led the Apache to a prolonged legal battle to regain the use of their grazing land for their own cattle herds.

The Apache experienced other prolonged struggles over land and resources as well. In 1896, the government persuaded the Apache to agree to subsurface mineral exploration on a 225,000-acre piece of the reservation known as the Mineral Strip. Ranchers settled in the area, and the Apache had to undertake a series of lawsuits lasting until the 1980s to regain possession. Also, in the 1920s, local interests proposed a dam across the San Carlos River that would flood the best Apache farmlands.

Coolidge Dam and the Mineral Strip

The decision to build Coolidge Dam on the San Carlos River became one of the bitterest experiences for the San Carlos Apache. The dam was planned to create a reservoir and provide irrigation water for non-Apache farms as far south as Tucson. In the early twentieth century, the needs of extensive commercial farms took clear precedence over a few acres of gardens where Apache grew vegetables for their own use.

The idea of building a dam in the deep canyon of the San Carlos River to impound water for irrigation had come up late in the nineteenth century, but a study by the Board of Reclamation Engineers in 1905 had concluded that the project was not feasible. In 1910, the Union Pacific Railroad requested right-of-way to lay track through the site. This would have precluded future flooding of the area. A law clerk in the Bureau of Indian Affairs named E. B. Meritt noted: "On the recommendation, in December 1905, of a Board of Reclamation Engineers, the Government abandoned the site as a proposed Government dam and reservoir. The Geological Survey, based on a report by Chief Hydrographer Leighton, dated February 10, 1910, recommend in favor of the rail way company, and against the private parties who propose to develop the dam and reservoir site" (Hayden Coll. 596/3).

Meritt, who was soon to become Acting Commissioner of Indian Affairs, lobbied for a reconsideration of the dam project. In 1914, an enthusiastic journalist estimated that the reservoir "would add approximately $22,500,000 to the wealth of Arizona." In a region where water was indispensable for commercial farming and was becoming an increasingly valuable commodity, the project produced a gleam in many an eye. The *Arizona Republican* proclaimed in 1924 that the project would help stimulate an "agricultural empire" in the region: "Supporters of the project even go so far as to assert without qualification that in considerable measure the future growth of Phoenix into one of the greatest cities of the Southwest depends in a measure upon the consummation of the San Carlos project or similar irrigation and development schemes which will provide a great territory of which Phoenix may be the wholesale and trade center" (*Arizona Republican*, Dec. 30, 1923).

There were a few problems. The "unusual fertility of the silty soil of the Gila River Valley" to the south of the proposed dam site stirred enthusiasm. With enough water, this soil could produce bumper crops. But a study concluded that when that water source was dammed, the silt would collect and settle and eventually fill any reservoir on the Gila or San Carlos rivers. According to the report, "the avergae [*sic*] quantity of silt brought into the reservoir each year is estimated to be about 4,500 acre-feet (par. 90) and it has been assumed that one-sixth of this will be carried through the reservoir, and that the remaining 3,750 acre feet, or about 6,000,000 cubic yards, will lodge in the reservoir, gradually decreasing its capacity" (Hayden Coll. 597/1). No matter. The silt could be dredged, or the dam could be built so high that it would take generations to fill.

The appropriation of Apache lands was another possible problem preventing dam construction, although for many regional interest groups this was no problem at all. But since the reservation was under federal rather than state jurisdiction, the confiscation of Apache lands required the approval of Congress. Some members of Congress were likely to balk at the prospect of flooding lands on an Indian reservation to enhance private commercial ventures. A scheme to help business interests at the expense of Indians was likely to seem a bit raw. But on the other hand, what if the project were presented as a scheme to help Indians?

To argue that the project would help the Apache would have taken some acrobatics in political logic. After all, they stood to lose their best farmlands. Nonetheless, San Carlos superintendent Stecker did write to the Commissioner of Indian Affairs in 1921 that "this construction would bring thousands of dollars to the Indians for labor and insure them employment for several years" (Hayden Coll. 622/8). And there was the more general sense that what helped the economy of the state would help everyone.

The rationale that the Apache could make a few dollars building a dam that would flood their farms was a bit weak. As it turned out, however, the Apache were not to be the main beneficiaries. For purposes of public consumption, the favored recipients of the dam's benefits were to be the Pima of the Gila River Reservation to the south.

On December 30, 1923, the *Arizona Republican* published an estimate that, of the 148,000 acres expected to be irrigated as a result of the project, forty thousand of these would be Pima lands. But despite the relatively minor portion of the water they were to receive, the project was widely touted as a government project to benefit the impoverished Pima.

We can probably assume that most of the members of Congress were not particularly familiar with the Pima. Representative Carl Hayden of Arizona took steps to correct that. He and his staff worked for months to collect a dossier of historical sources to portray the Pima as benevolent, peace-loving people who had been victimized by the

Apache and gone unrewarded for their loyalty to the United States. Hayden presented his Pima material to the House Committee on Indian Affairs in April, 1924. There is little evidence that the Pima themselves ever played a significant role in this campaign or that they were consulted in any meaningful way.

Reflecting the proreservoir view, the *Arizona Republican* declared that "a widespread demand for justice to the claims of these Indians [the Pima] has arisen, since it has been established that the record of loyalty of these Indians to White settlers and to the States is unmarred by any departure" (December 30, 1923). The article stated that the first Arizonan killed in World War I had been a Pima. Further: "[The Pima] constituted an invaluable aid in the repulsion of the attacks and marauding of the Apache Indians during the earlier pioneer period in Arizona . . . It is the boast of these Indians that they have never shed a white man's blood, and that without their aid the whites would have experienced inestimable difficulties in subduing the Apaches and settling Arizona, and perhaps a delay of many years would have occurred." If that were not enough to dispel any unease about appropriating Apache lands, the newspaper stated that "the San Carlos dam site is located in a box canyon of the Gila above Winkleman *near* the San Carlos Reservation" [emphasis supplied].

Suddenly, with the prospect of an agricultural empire at stake, the forgotten Pima found themselves an object of popular concern. They had a champion in Judge Otis J. Baughn. "The story of the Pima Indians, according to Judge Otis J. Baughn, president of the San Carlos association, perhaps the leading exponent of development of the Gila River, is one of neglect by the race whose cause they advanced materially in the Southwest . . . Where Apaches and other tribes bitterly hostile to white men and their occupation of the Southwest have received considerable treatment at the hands of the government, says Judge Baughn, the Pimas have received virtually nothing, but have at the same time been deprived of what may be their most valuable asset, water rights and supply" (*Arizona Republican*, December 30, 1923).

Who was Judge Baughn? According to the *Arizona Republican*, "Since 1917 the San Carlos association has been formed and is taking a leading part in the advancement of the project under the decisive and energetic leadership of Judge O. J. Baughn, formerly Superior Judge of Pinal County and now a practicing attorney in Phoenix."

Considering the extent to which the Pima were used to justify the project, it is interesting to glance ahead a couple of generations after the dam was built and see how they fared. A letter from Congressman Morris Udall to Representative Wayne Aspinall in 1967 provides a fairly vivid impression: "The Pima-Maricopa Indians of the Gila

River Reservation now live in deplorable housing conditions and have inadequate diets. Their income is derived from seasonal work such as cotton picking, supplemented by meager payments they receive from farming or leasing their land." What happened to the irrigation project? Congressman Udall elaborates. "Thanks largely to Senator Hayden, Coolidge Dam was authorized by Congress and constructed in 1926 to restore water to Indian lands. Waters from this dam, supplemented by wells, initiated the foundation of the San Carlos Irrigation Project. However, because of the inclusion of non-Indian lands in the project, there has never been enough water for the Indian lands. As a result, only 15,000 acres are usually farmed on the estimated 41,223 acres on the project" (Hayden Coll. 331/19).

Throughout all of this, the Apache could exercise little decision-making power. The government charged with representing their interests chose to act in the interests of far more powerful constituencies and to opt for capitalist development, or what would some day be called "agribusiness."

The dam did provide employment for Apache and others. As it turned out, there was some question about the workers being paid less than the normal local wage, but E. B. Meritt, now Acting Commissioner of Indian Affairs, clarified the issue in a letter to Arizona Congressman Carl Hayden. Meritt wrote that "as a matter of fact there are only five white persons employed on the present work and since the work now in progress will be completed at an early date, and in view of the fact that the workmen themselves are not dissatisfied with their wages, there seems to be no occasion for a readjustment of wages" (Hayden Coll. 597/1).

Coolidge Dam was the last major construction project in which large numbers of Apache participated. It was dedicated in 1923. After it was completed and the waters began to inch up over Apache farms, President Calvin Coolidge arrived by train for a dedication ceremony. In honor of the President, a band of Apache schoolchildren played a patriotic tune, their brassy music echoing feebly from the low hills and rock-faced mesas in the clear thin air. Without leaving the train, the President waved from the rear of the last car as it lurched away to disappear in the distance.

The San Carlos Mineral Strip affords another example of the Apache struggle to retain their resources. In the 1890s, entrepreneurs hatched a scheme to lure gullible eastern investors into a coal-mining project in the southern part of the reservation. Apparently someone seeded the area with coal, and "interested parties" prevailed upon the federal government to open 232,000 acres for mineral exploration.

As early as 1882, Commissioner of Indian Affairs Hiram Price had reported that "General Sherman, when on a recent visit to the San Carlos Reserve, expressed the opinion that the Indians could never be prevailed upon to move again, and it is exceedingly doubtful if they would be satisfied with any further reduction of their reservation, it having already been cut down no less than five times within the last ten years" (Washburn 1973:33). Nonetheless, the President submitted to Congress a draft proposing a joint resolution supporting coal leases, arguing that the government supposedly had spent $300,000 per year "for the support of the Apaches and other Indians in Arizona and New Mexico, and that this cost might be largely if not wholly reimbursed to the government without hardship to those who would be the natural purchasers and consumers thereof if coal were made available as an article of commerce." The draft suggests that "if any amount in excess of the sum required annually to maintain and care for said Indians shall be realized from the lease or leases that may be executed under the authority of this act, such amount shall be used to reimburse the government for any moneys that may hereafter be appropriated for the support and care of any of the other bands or tribes in the Southwest" (Washburn 1973:340).

In March, 1896, Federal Inspector Province McCormick examined the area and wrote: "I believe . . . that these lands will develop fine coal fields . . . Veins 16 feet in thickness have been and are now exposed" (Reynolds 1896). McCormick delineated a large tract of land, explaining: "[In addition to coal] on the lands segregated are many fine copper prospects. The agreement provides for coal and mineral lands, in order to cover any other minerals that may be located."

General Land Office commissioner S. W. Lamoreux, however, wrote to the Secretary of the Interior on March 21 of that year that "from the best information I have been able to obtain, it is evident that the coal lands in such ceded portion of the reservation are not of great value, and it is thought that the uniform price of $5 per acre for such coal is as much as the Government can reasonably expect to obtain" (Reynolds 1896).

Costs of surveying the land were to be charged against the Apache's account. Commissioner Lamoreux estimated this cost at about eighteen hundred dollars, comprising the expected sale price of about 360 acres of coal fields.

The government agents organized a meeting with the Apache to secure their agreement. The San Carlos Agency record showed "1083 adult male Indians residing on the San Carlos Reservation" at the time (Reynolds 1896). Despite the Apache matrilineal and matrilocal social organization, women were not invited to participate in the negotiations. By the end of the session, a slim majority of 603, including thirty-eight not present whose signatures were secured in absentia, apparently agreed to the transaction.

Who were these 1083 adult male Indians? At that time, the San Carlos Reservation included at least three regional Apache populations. The Pinal had formerly occupied a region overlapping the reservation lands. The Arivaipa territory had been farther south along the San Pedro River. The Coyotero lived in the mountains near Fort Apache, eighty miles or so to the north. There was also a contingent of Yavapai who were eager to depart for their own reservation as soon as possible.

With the help of translators, McCormick, this time acting as negotiator with the Apache, explained the government's proposal to the assemblage. He began by stating:

> Unlike most tribes of Indians you have not a treaty with the General Government. You are here, as it were, by the courtesy of the Government, and though you are here by courtesy, yet the Government proposes, in dealing with you on the business I am here for, to treat you as if you owned all of this land; it proposes to see that nothing is taken from you here without your full and free consent, and that every dollar realized shall go for your benefit alone.
>
> These coal fields, as you know, are utterly worthless to you; they have no timber or grass worth speaking of upon them. They are entirely valueless for agricultural purposes. Their value consists alone in what is under the ground in the shape of minerals. This coal land is worthless to you. Why? Because you can't work them. They are valuable to the white people because they understand how to utilize them. Now, in order to make them valuable to you, they should be worked by someone who can handle them.
>
> The Secretary of the Interior has, therefore, directed me to come here and say to you that if you are willing to relinquish these lands to the United States, the United States will take them and hold them in trust, as it were, and sell them for you; that the Government does not propose to make a dollar out of this transaction; it will act, as it were, as your agent, and that it will settle with you for every dollar realized from the sale of these lands, less the cost of handling and selling them. (Reynolds 1896)

Captain Albert L. Myer, acting Indian agent, then added his assurances that McCormick spoke in good faith. He reiterated the argument that the land was useless to the Apache and said, "I would advise that the money derived from these lands be used in the purchase of cattle and sheep for you, and in harness, and for such other purposes as the Secretary may decide upon later; some money may be paid, but that will rest with the Congress and the Secretary." McCormick affirmed this.

The first two people to respond were not Apache but Yavapai. One acknowledged that he had no claim to the lands in question but generally favored the agreement if it would benefit the Apache. The second agreed. The first Apache to speak was Alchesay, respected leader of the White Mountain people. According to the record, he said that "they did not want to sign the agreement as they had no interest in the land in question; that they lived at Fort Apache, in the northern part of the reservation, and wanted the reservation divided and an agent appointed for their half." Two other Apache men named Nosey and Cassador declined without comment. McCormick asked Cassador, "Does it make you any richer or better off to keep the coal under the ground?"

Chequito "spoke of his great love for these lands and opposed the agreement." Sabe Mucho said, "The Indians do not want cattle and mules, but money." Mose Gila opposed the agreement and noted that "their children, educated in Government schools, could develop these mines and sell the coal to the whites." Two Coyotero from the White Mountain population cited "their love for the land, and were opposed to having the whites any nearer to them." Ekilta said he would agree if money were paid. Others objected over the same issues.

The next morning McCormick announced that he had adjusted the boundary. Bylish, a Coyotero leader, stated: "The Government had its own way in respect to getting our children for schools, and in all instances the Government has had its way. Yesterday all the people objected to changing the line of the reservation and to give up their coal fields. The Government makes its promises, but where is the man who can say the Government has done what it has promised? We have been here three days talking about this matter and it should have been settled in one day. Let it be written down that it be paid in money."

Finally, the negotiators adjusted the offer to stipulate cash payments and secured the signatures or marks of over half the "male adult Indians over 18 years of age" living on the reservation. Alchesay stated that the Coyotero "would agree to the cession of the land, but desire none of the money derived therefrom, because they live north of the Black River and do not think they are entitled to it." The negotiators insisted, however, that the Coyotero were "considered to have an interest like the other Indians" (Reynolds 1896).

Was there much coal on the ceded land? Apparently not, nor was there evidence of other valuable minerals. From the time of the 1896 agreement until 1931, the Apache received $12,433—somewhat less than a dime per person per year (Exhibit A, March 31, 1973 Hearings, Dodge Coll. 2/13). In the meantime, though, other parties took an interest in the ceded lands. A handful of homesteaders began grazing cattle on what now had become known as the Mineral Strip.

In March 1931, the First Assistant Secretary of the Interior withdrew the lands in the Mineral Strip "from all forms of entry or disposition pending the enactment of legislation to authorize the restoration of that area to the tribe" (Exhibit A, Dodge Coll. 2/13). He cited insignificant financial returns. In 1933, reservation superintendent James B. Kitch wrote to the Commissioner of Indian Affairs that there was strong resistance to restoration of the Strip expressed by the Governor of Arizona, the State Land Board, Senator Ashurst of the Senate Commission on Indian Affairs, and others. Kitch urged instead that the land be sold at $1.25 per acre, with the proceeds, totalling about $300,000, credited to the San Carlos Apache.

Kitch also noted that "the Indians ceded this land for mineral purposes only whereas under later authority of the Secretary of the Interior it has been opened for every type of homestead and the best areas or water developments have been taken up by the White men for cattle or goat purposes." But the land was not sold, and in November 1936 the Secretary of the Interior placed the area "temporarily under range management in accordance with the provision of the Taylor Grazing Act." This opened the gates for more ranchers (Hayden Coll. 250/25).

In October, 1939, the San Carlos Tribal Council passed a formal resolution stating that, since ranchers had occupied all sources of water in the strip and the state had claimed a large portion and there appeared to be no minerals, they requested a payment of $1.25 per acre for the entire tract (Hayden Coll. 282/38). Reservation superintendent Ernest R. McCray elaborated in a letter to the Commissioner of Indian Affairs: "Without the land that has passed into white ownership, this area would be entirely useless to the Indians of this reservation. It would appear that the homesteaders and purchasers of this land are unwilling to sell unless, of course, they were paid a price far in excess of its actual value . . . A large part of this area has been used to graze goats and is practically denuded of all forage which would support cattle" (Hayden Coll. 622/10).

Nonetheless, in 1941 the Bureau of Land Management issued formal permits and leases to "various individuals who are present occupants of the mineral strip." (Exhibit A, Dodge Coll. 2/13). In August, 1951, the San Carlos Tribal Council filed a suit before the Indian

Claims Commission alleging that "200,000 acres known as the 'coal strip' and containing minerals has been used for grazing and other purposes, thus depriving plaintiffs of the use of the same and the income therefrom" and that the government "has failed to collect compensation for property sold and/or used, including grazing; has also permitted overgrazing, to plaintiff's damage, without recovering therefor" (Hayden Coll. 282/38).

By 1955 the Apache altered their strategy and requested that the 1931 withdrawal be lifted to allow for mineral exploration, and in 1958 they adopted a resolution asking for the restoration of the Mineral Strip. Attorneys for the ranchers filed an action to enjoin the restoration until the courts determined the Secretary of the Interior's authority to restore the lands. In 1963 the Apache modified their original request and asked only for subsurface rights, noting that "unreasonable and unjustified opposition has arisen to the restoration of the Mineral Strip, including the filing of an injunction suit against the Secretary of the Interior . . . which opposition threatens to cause the indefinite postponement of any action on the Tribe's petition." They withdrew their petition for restoration of the surface of the Mineral Strip, to be "held in abeyance by the Secretary until reactivated by the San Carlos Council" (Hayden Coll. 282/38).

Two months later, on June 11, 1963, Undersecretary James K. Carr wrote to Senator Hayden: "It now appears that the mineral deposits on the strip may be of considerable value. Consequently, I intend to act favorably on the Tribe's request for the restoration of the subsurface interests" (Hayden Coll. 282/38). He issued the order on June 17. The accompanying press release stated that "the Department said restoration to the tribe will allow development of this mineral potential and could add significantly to the economy of Arizona."

The ranchers' alarm was expressed in a June 20 telegram to Senator Carl Hayden, asking for "SOME ASSURANCE THAT NO FURTHER ACTION WILL BE TAKEN BY SECRETARY UDALL OR HIS OFFICE TO RESTORE SURFACE RIGHTS TO INDIANS" (Hayden Coll. 282/38). On September 12, 1968, the San Carlos Tribal Council adopted a resolution requesting the Secretary of the Interior to restore surface rights, and on January 16, 1969, Secretary Udall signed an order restoring them.

On February 20, 1973, Congressman John B. Conlan introduced a resolution to "allow the Secretary of the Interior to purchase all privately-owned real and personal property from ranchers having grazing rights within the strip." According to the minutes of a public hearing in Phoenix on March 31, 1973, one rancher said "he would like to plead with the San Carlos Tribe that they work together to get this worked out before anything is done that someone might regret. He said that the ranchers have no quarrel with the Indians and expressed the opinion that the United States Government is fully responsible, but that they will not voluntarily leave without compensation" (Hayden Coll. 282/38).

Another rancher stated, "We are also of the opinion that the San Carlos Apache Tribe should recognize the fact that many of the affected ranchers on the Mineral Strip have dedicated their lives to improvements on this property." Many ranchers pleaded with the Apache for more time. Senator Paul Fannin of Arizona stated that "it was an arbitrary Federal action by Secretary of Interior Udall in 1969 that deprived the ranchers of their expectation to continue their livelihood of ranching on that land."

San Carlos Apache chairman Marvin Mull adopted a conciliatory tone and supported the use of federal funds to compensate the ranchers.

> It seems clear to us that the ranchers now living on the San Carlos Mineral Strip and their predecessors by direct authorization or acquiescence of the Government of the United States, under nonexistent but presumed authority of the Homesteading and Taylor Grazing Acts, and with their own bare hands built homes, developed water holdings, constructed fences, corrals, and developed from the raw land valuable and profitable ranching operations. There is nothing underhanded or criminal in what they have done. Similarly, the efforts of the San Carlos Apache Tribe and all those who have assisted to restore to them these lands which were part of their aboriginal domain and included in the reservation set aside for them by executive orders in 1871 and '72 were just and honest and appropriate.

Floyd Mull, another San Carlos Tribal Council member, stated:

> We recognize that in a real sense it is very difficult, if at all possible, to compensate a person who is forced to leave his home, to walk away from his possessions. From a purely financial sense, the goods can be paid for and in a sense replaced. But from an emotional standpoint, regardless of the size of the lump in his wallet, it is difficult to remove the lump in his throat.
>
> Unfortunately, the knife that cuts into the heart of the San Carlos Strip rancher has cut in two directions. As Marvin has said to you, just over a hundred years ago, the President of the United States set aside certain of our lands as a reservation for the Apache Indians in East Central Arizona. Our fathers, while not pleased with giving up the freedom to roam the lands totally as they wished, were pleased that the lands given them were part of our aboriginal home. They were familiar lands—lands where their hearts had also been planted. Some 20 or so

years later, their children were promised great wealth from the mineral deposits in certain portions of that reservation—wealth which they thought could be obtained by allowing the United States Government to take control of certain of these lands for disposal under the Mineral Land Laws. The San Carlos then, beginning to understand the value of the white man's dollar, allowed these portions of their lands to be separated from them for this purpose only.

These great riches, however, never materialized . . . Since 1931, we have spent more than 40 years in the attempt to have these restored to us. . . . I invite you to visit our reservation; to visit our homes and our schools; to see the unemployment and the poor living conditions of many of our people. (Dodge Coll. 2/13)

The situation remained volatile. A story in the *Los Angeles Times* on June 28, 1973, two days before the Apache's eviction deadline, stated the ranchers' intentions: "To stay put until they are compensated—not by the Indians but by the U. S. Government which they believe put them in their present pickle . . . Some of the ranchers reportedly have said they would have to be shot off the land. And some Indians, especially young ones, have been pressing their elders for direct action . . . Mull admitted that he had heard talk about a six-month extension. He said the council might even be willing to grant such an extension. 'But I feel they (the ranchers) should ask us, sit down with us,' he said. 'In the past, they've negotiated with congressmen but not with us. Neither they nor any congressman has asked us for any extension.' "

On July 6, 1973, the Tribal Council voted six to three, over Chairman Mull's objections, not to extend the eviction deadline. On September 18, a bill to compensate the ranchers was defeated in the House.

Only in the 1980s did most maps begin to include the Mineral Strip as part of the San Carlos Reservation. The issue has continued to simmer well into recent years.

The case of the Mineral Strip is an example of conflicting interest groups whose fortunes are subject to powerful external forces but who are placed at odds with one another. In 1896 the Apache were possibly as powerless as a group could be. Appropriation of their land—even for fictional coal fields—served the purposes of parties with far more access to the mechanisms of state power than they had. With cattle production for eastern markets a promising enterprise early in this century, the ranchers served the purposes of other powerful interests who had the leverage to invoke state authority, despite faint cries of outrage from the Apache and their advocates, even though the ranchers themselves were marginal producers of commodities allocated to the profit of interests far from the Arizona deserts.

By the latter half of the century, though, it seems that mineral prospects had risen again, while cattle ranching had fallen in its ability to move policy. Restoration of these lands to the San Carlos Apache, who continue to experience staggering poverty, removed the ranchers from the scene and reopened the possibility of mineral exploitation. The land is once again accessible to "developers," subject to the agreement of the Apache and their advisers. It remains to be seen what resources may be extracted from the Mineral Strip, or perhaps what wastes may be deposited there, and what the next round of negotiations might involve for the people of San Carlos.

CHAPTER 6

San Carlos after Mid-century

By mid-century San Carlos was dotted with small frame houses, often one or two rooms, built in clusters in the matrilocal joint family pattern. During the summer a few of the dome-shaped dwellings of bent poles covered with brush still appeared scattered here and there among the frame houses. The open-walled *ramadas* of flat roofs covered with brush sheltered an occasional hammock or cooking stove and provided relief from the blazing, baking Arizona summer sun—places of shade and breezes for visiting and for various chores.

The Southern Pacific Railroad track runs through Peridot north to the community of San Carlos and then westward toward Globe past a black water tower. On their westward sweep the tracks run near Dripping Springs Wash where, in 1864, troops attacked an Apache camp and where the Tribe now grows Christmas trees for sale.

In recent decades Apache men have worn their hair short and have dressed in jeans, western shirts, and cowboy hats. Middle-aged and older women in the early 1960s still commonly wore the long, full camp dresses based on nineteenth-century Mexican styles with bright shawls over their heads and shoulders in cold weather, but contemporary mass styles have made inroads. Younger peoples' clothes are more likely to coincide with current American fashions. In the late 1960s the miniskirts that made their appearance throughout the United States were much in evidence on young Apache women, and in 1988 many young women wore jeans. But almost any morning on the road past the tribal store and offices, older women continue to go about their business in the long, full, old-style dresses. Donna Searles comments that while the camp dress was "formerly worn by women of all ages, today it is primarily the daily dress of elderly women (Young and middle age women wear camp dresses at ceremonials or on special social occasions)" (1990:4).

The cradle board that the people acquired some time during the migration from the Subarctic to Arizona was evident in 1963. It had

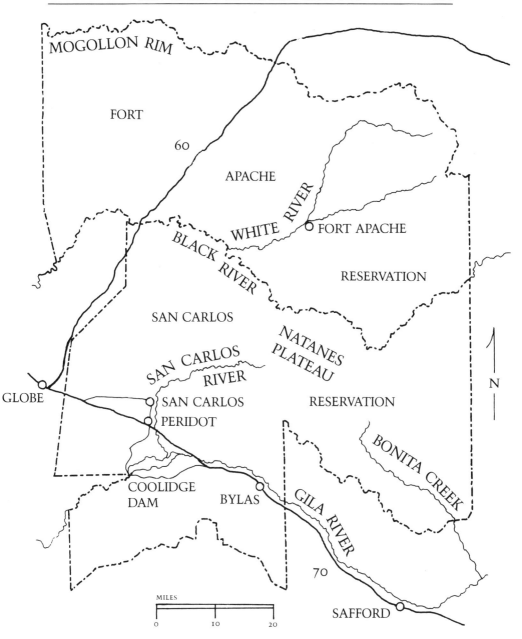

Map 4. The San Carlos and Fort Apache reservations

become less common by 1970. In the early 1960s, to see mothers breast-feeding their babies was not unusual, but one woman substantiated the impression that, since that time, many more women began to bottle-feed their infants. Ironically, this change came at a time when the importance of mothers' milk was being rediscovered in Anglo-American society.

Small churches dot the hillsides around San Carlos, many of them evangelistic. Most homes have access to electricity, but since the regional utility company in the mid 1980s refused to increase service to San Carlos, the only electrical access for many homes is through long extension cords between houses. The meager firefighting equipment and inadequate alarm system do little to lessen this danger.

Coolidge Dam generates electrical power to pump water from underground to storage tanks atop the surrounding mesas. Gravity provides water pressure for homes. The dam that flooded their farms produces hydroelectric power, but the federal government has refused to provide funds for new power lines that would allow the Apache to take advantage of it in their homes (Schmidt 1983:1). For many houses in 1970 the only access to water was from outdoor faucets. None had indoor toilets, although a sewer system was planned. Some now have running water indoors.

Private telephones are still rare in San Carlos. This is a hardship and a potential danger, since getting help quickly in an emergency may be difficult. The local telephone company took a somewhat puzzling position on this. Normal company practice has been to pay property owners for right-of-way when installing lines which, after all, are intended to result in profit for the company. But in San Carlos the company took the stance that to install such lines would be a favor to the community. The company has not been particularly interested in the project.

The tribal government collects trash, but a good deal of refuse is thrown into gullies and arroyos near the house clusters. The numerous dogs that belong to each cluster of dwellings quickly dispose of food scraps tossed outside. Most groups of houses have from two to a dozen dogs of various mixed breeds that not only take care of food scraps but help to maintain the security of the area. They are familiar with every member of their own family cluster and noisily set upon any stranger who ventures near enough to come to their attention.

Language as an Aspect of Apache Identity

The maintenance of the language is an important marker of the people's distinctness. In 1963 almost all but a few very old people were able to speak English, but among older adults, Apache was the normal medium of discourse. It seems clear that many people felt most at ease using this language and spoke it in their homes. Orations and spoken public announcements often are in Apache. Until recently, Apache had no standardized script, and public notices have been in English. In 1970, people in San Carlos showed interest in classes a missionary was conducting to teach them to read their own language written phonetically. English is essential for communication with non-Apache people, particularly for shopping and transacting business in Globe, and most people seemed to feel that a knowledge of English is a necessary tool for survival.

When researchers in 1981 asked parents on the Fort Apache Reservation for their views on a Comprehensive Education Plan, the parents indicated that one of their major concerns was continuation of their language and culture (Liebe-Harkort 1980). In 1982 about 75 percent of the population on both of the major Western Apache reservations were able to speak the language. According to Robert Young, "With about 12,000 speakers, the Western Apache dialect group was the most viable of all the Apachean languages in 1982" (1983:400).

Local non-Apache people have sometimes voiced the opinion that Apache is impossible for Anglo-Americans to learn. At least one missionary in San Carlos and the owner of a chain of stores in the region, however, mastered the language well enough to communicate easily. Apache seemed to consider this remarkable, and indeed, it was highly unusual, but they express little desire for non-Apache people to learn the language. Researchers in 1962 asked Apache children in Globe and San Carlos whether they would like their teachers to speak in Apache. Almost all of the teachers were non-Apache, and most of the students indicated that they often had difficulty understanding English, but overwhelmingly, their response to the question was negative (Roessel 1964). The language is something uniquely Apachean, and it is valued as a major aspect of identity.

In 1963 a schoolteacher in San Carlos observed that it still was common for Apache children to begin school speaking no English. In the primary grades, many would sit at their desks immobile and apparently terrified. After every recess, the teacher said, she had to search the bushes around the schoolhouse for hiding children. Through the 1970s, many Western Apache children began to use English extensively for the first time when they entered school, but this may be changing.

Some people now fear that soon no young children will be fluent in Apache, and many are concerned that the language will be lost. Older people of the Apache community were punished as children for speaking in Apache in government and missionary schools, but they retained the language. Now, it appears, the popular mass media threaten to bring about what an oppressive educational system could not. The frequency of marriages with non-Apache Native Americans may be equally significant. This results in households in which the parents' only common language is English.

Personal Bonds, Clans, and Individualization

Older patterns of kinship still direct and constrain interpersonal behavior. The matrilocal joint family remains the ideal basis for the social organization. Joking relationships among cross cousins and the strictures of mother-in-law avoidance associated with matrilocal residence, for example, continue to be part of life in San Carlos. On an evening in 1963 a man sitting outdoors suddenly broke off his conversation and stood up to leave, explaining hastily that "my mother-in-law's coming." Not everyone was equally scrupulous about such etiquette. People's personalities and their feelings about one another play a part, but it remains the ideal.

Joking relationships might extend to ribaldry and pranks. A child in 1963 pointed out a man some distance away, saying: "He's my father's cousin. Whenever he comes over they joke a lot. That's the custom." *Shi di ké*, a term of address used between people who enjoy a casual, jocular relationship, is not technically a kinship term but roughly means "my friend." This term is based on a relationship of mutual assistance and also refers to a woman who takes a special role in one's daughter's puberty ceremony (see Basso 1966:32; Goodwin 1969:548).

In earlier times people called upon far-flung networks of clan and other kinship bonds, and they could extend or activate them at will according to the needs of the moment. This was especially so with regard to people outside the joint family cluster who would not be in the sphere of face-to-face daily interactions. Much of the time these ties were dormant because the people were dispersed. In modern San Carlos society, they continue to be implicit until people call upon them. A man might approach his relatives for aid, but otherwise he might not come into contact with them for weeks or even months at a time.

Probably the main change in Western Apache social organization is that residence now is more stable, although many Apache people travel often and far. But social relationships that developed in the past to meet the dynamic needs of a fluid hunting-and-gathering population seem to continue in this relatively sedentary pattern of reservation life. One reason for the persistence of kinship networks is probably the flexibility that was inherent in the social organization all along. The system provides aid when it is needed, but otherwise it leaves people relatively free. The social organization in the past made it easy for matrilocal joint families to cluster into larger groups, as they do in the more sedentary context of the modern reservation. The society continues to function on the same principles that carried the Apache through the centuries. Older patterns have adjusted, but they have not disappeared.

These strategies now must cope with problems generated by contemporary circumstances. In one case, a couple with four children found that they could not provide adequately for all of them. They gave their youngest daughter to the mother's sister and her husband to raise. The latter couple had a good source of income and no children at the time, and the two families' dwellings were no more than twenty yards apart in the same family cluster. The child's original parents and siblings saw her constantly and interacted with her almost as closely as they had before. Everyone in the cluster understood the situation, and the little girl grew up referring to her adopted parents as "mommy and daddy." People seemed to accept the adoption as proper, although at times the original parents seemed to betray some ambivalence about it. In one conversation, the child's original mother indicated the little girl playing some distance away and said, "She's really mine, you know." On an earlier occasion when the child was quite small, her original father teased her by asking, "Who's your daddy?" The child merely laughed and ran off.

The social system in the past easily accommodated arrangements of this sort to cope with uncertain conditions. Normally the people all would have lived together anyway, and the kinship terms underscore the social equivalence of these alternatives. Since the child had moved into the home of her mother's sister, in Anglo-American terms she became a "cousin" to her biological siblings. But in Western Apache terms, the children of sisters are equivalent to children of the same parents, and therefore she remained "sister" to her siblings. Her change of residence and filiation was not a breaking of ties but an adjustment, which the kinship pattern easily accommodated.

Factors more peculiar to modern life in this case, though, did cause some stresses that might not have been as likely in the prereservation period. As the child grew up, the financial situation of her original parents improved. An employment opportunity some distance away led them to move out of the family cluster. They had another child later and continued to make frequent visits to their old family cluster, but the immediacy of living in the same group had changed. The child's increasing maturity and the years spent in her adopted home probably amplified this distance, although she continued to be "best friends" with her sister/cousin.

The clans continue to exist relatively unhampered by the current circumstances because of their normally free-floating nature. As always, they remain abstract categories rather than visible groups. Most people know to which clan they belong and which clans include likely marriage partners. Preferred marriage does not always take place now, but this was probably always the case. In the 1930s it still occurred with some frequency (Goodwin 1969:695–698).

Just as in the past, people belonging to the same clan may live in many different places. Clans are society-wide categories of people and do not depend on collective group expression or activity. Perhaps the only times large numbers of people gather and interact as members of particular clans is in the female puberty ceremonies. Their main effect, as before, is to help define ideal relationships among individuals.

The government and other agencies have applied considerable pressure to weaken the clan system, promoting change in the interest of modernization. To nullify this fundamental sinew of Apache social organization would be a major step in the process of individualization. No doubt it would promote the dissolution of Apache social organization and promote the absorption of individuals into the general milieu of the state. How the people might benefit from the loss of such a well-defined social order is not clear. Despite the relatively recent historic origins of many specific clans, the principles of the system have ancient roots in Apache traditions and values and provide a major theme in structuring interpersonal bonds. Certainly the wider social system of the United States, embarrassed by tens of thousands of homeless people who lack such connecting ties and sleep on the sidewalks of its major cities, has problems of its own.

But as tenacious as the clan system seems to be, there is some feeling among Apache and non-Apache alike that it may eventually disappear. In 1970 one elderly woman was confident that most of the people in San Carlos still kept track of clan membership. She estimated her age to be about eighty-five but qualified this with the observation that "old people here don't know how old they are" because of undependable birth records before the turn of the century. She asked whether "white people" have clans. Upon being told "No, they did once, but they sort of lost track of them," she replied that she thought that eventually that would happen in San Carlos too.

Despite this assumption, though, whether the clan networks will atrophy in the near future remains to be seen. They provide people with security through embeddedness in the social system. In a community confronted with external stresses and widespread economic deprivation, this value could well give them continued significance.

Pressures toward Change

Economic factors could undermine the system of relationships by creating difficulties in meeting kinship obligations. Occasionally, people cast aspersions regarding the apparent failure of some individuals to share their resources with relatives. The few people who have well-paying jobs are especially vulnerable to this social comment. How serious a sign of radical change this may be is not clear, though.

Individualism was inherent in the social system in the past, with wide options in the activities of small groups. But at the same time, considerable pressures still bear on people who are remiss in their behavior toward kin. One could even argue that the pressure of opinion is potentially even stronger now because of the greater concentration of people on the reservation. Reputation can be a powerful concern in a community in which every person knows everyone else. The population size in San Carlos has increased, but not enough to have produced a balancing effect of anonymity.

People may think less of a person who fails to be a good relative or to aid his or her kin. Just as in earlier centuries, such behavior now could make getting help from relatives at crucial times difficult. More than this, however, the deep significance kin ties hold for most people in San Carlos and the high value of sociability and gregariousness that characterize close relatives' interactions have powerful effects on the way most people manage their lives. If economic individuality is a potential factor in contemporary San Carlos, it is tempered by the strong situational demands of kinship, much as it has been in the past. Whether this amounts to any marked, qualitative departure from older patterns is questionable.

House ownership still is weighted in favor of women, although this may be changing. With the temporary bent-pole dwellings of former times, women did the work of gathering materials and construction. Contemporary homes are more permanent. They require carpentry and other work that usually is done by men rather than women and that consequently tends to give the builder a greater claim on the house. Nonetheless, houses still are usually built within the constellation of dwellings around the wife's mother's home, which bolsters the proprietary rights of the wife.

In one instance, a house that happened to be unoccupied was commonly referred to as the house of the man who had built it. He and his wife and their children had lived there several years earlier. But it was located within the wife's family cluster, and when the question arose of whether or not other people would be allowed to use it temporarily, the wife's permission was required. A woman still can divorce her husband publicly in a de facto sense in the old way, crossing two poles before the entrance and throwing his belongings outside.

Resilience of the Social Organization

The value on individual autonomy is moderated by sensitivity to reverberations on kin. One could say that the pattern involves a reciprocal individualism. Although each person is submerged in a network of relationships, the constraints are more flexible than rigid. They allow freedom of movement if obligations are met when the need arises.

This system entails some conflict with the ideal of interpersonal competitiveness that characterizes Anglo-American society. While Apache social organization is structured horizontally with ties linking each individual to many others, the mainstream Anglo-American social system is hierarchical. Children throughout the United States play games to determine who wins and who loses. Not everyone in school gets an A, and collaborating on tests is not acceptable. The rewards of hard work are supposed to be promotion over others. In large cities, young men wearing five-hundred-dollar suits step over homeless elders huddled over warm air ducts. American wealth is unevenly distributed, and in many ways the thrust of ideology entails that it should be.

In the confrontation of these two systems of values, some aspects may be irreconcilable. On the Apache side, the social rules require generosity. One shares available surplus with relatives. This is not necessarily applauded; it is expected. In Anglo-American society one strives to acquire wealth, to accumulate it, and to keep it. Sharing with relatives beyond a minimal degree is not expected. It may be applauded, but it may just as well be seen as foolishness.

Alcohol and Social Problems: The Effects of Poverty

Like any community, San Carlos has problems that are disruptive and detract from the personal happiness of individuals. Some of the more evident of these are legal problems because they are disruptive enough to be dealt with by legal agencies. To emphasize the resiliency of Apache social organization and the dynamics of cultural continuity is not to imply that the people enjoy an absolutely harmonious adaptation to their present circumstances.

Drinking is acknowledged to be a problem in many reservation communities. In San Carlos it may be one of the most serious and immediate threats faced by the society. Alcoholism heads the list of San Carlos health problems enumerated in a government report of 1981. Also near the top are "accidents including poisoning and violence" and cirrhosis of the liver. The report goes on to state: "Mental health problems and suicide gestures are major and significant areas of concern. The successful suicide rate for 1977 was the highest in years" (Bureau of Indian Affairs 1981:67).

Although habitual drunkenness is certainly a symptom of other factors, drinking in turn gives rise to violent crime, which occurs with greater frequency in San Carlos than on most reservations. In 1953–1954, tribal convictions for all crimes in San Carlos were almost ten times the national average and one fourth higher than the average of all Native American groups. At least 74 percent of these incidents were related to drinking (Stewart 1964:63). People of San Carlos attribute most homicides on the reservation to drunkenness, and this seems to be borne out. During the summer of 1963, three murders occurred between married couples when either one or both had been drinking heavily. In 1970 a man killed his brother in the course of a drinking party.

The Western Apache had used alcohol long before the reservation period. At prereservation summer encampments people made *tulpai* from corn sprouts. The Western Apache learned the technique for making *tulpai* from the Chiricahua Apache, who in turn had learned it from native peoples in Mexico. *Tulpai* contains what little alcohol can develop after a few days' fermentation in the open air. In the nineteenth century the use of *tulpai* was an integral part of the gathering cycle, a pleasant indulgence at one of the most enjoyable times of the year. It was an internal aspect of the social pattern rather than external to it.

With the curtailment of the gathering cycle at the beginning of the reservation period, people continued to make *tulpai* in many parts of the reservation. Since the subsistence pattern was disrupted, *tulpai* was no longer an integral part of it, but it continued to be a basis for sociability. An elderly woman, talking about a time when she had visited the area where she grew up, said: "When I went up there my relative asked me to have some *tulpai* with him and I said no. I don't

Law enforcement facilities in San Carlos, 1960s (National Anthropological Archives, Smithsonian Institution, 55138-D)

drink *tulpai* since I joined the church. I never did drink whiskey, but I used to have a glass of cold beer once in a while." She added that in earlier years "people used to sure drink *tulpai*. They make a five-gallon can full and then just drink it, they didn't even eat."

The Apache had some acquaintance with wine, beer, or distilled liquor at least from the time of the Gálvez reforms of the eighteenth century. By the end of the nineteenth century they could buy these beverages and avoid the laborious production of *tulpai*. The manufactured products were not linked with the seasonal cycle, and they had no special relationship to any aspect of traditional life. They had no particular social context, meaning, or value beyond their own properties, and their consumption tended to be external to the existing social system. Although people often consumed *tulpai* in large quantities, it is only mildly alcoholic. Most of the manufactured beverages have a much higher alcoholic content, and drinking them in such quantities often has disastrous effects.

Jack O. Waddell and Michael W. Everett suggest that mass-produced, cheap, sweet pink wine is the most important socially "external" source of alcohol among Apache, while cold beer, *tulpai*, and "home brew" still retain an important and relatively positive role in certain social and ceremonial contexts (1980:228; see also Everett 1980:148–177).

The pattern of drinking tends to be polarized in the sense that most individuals either drink heavily or never take a drink at all. Casual drinking is rare. Nondrinkers tend to be most numerous among those who are affiliated with one of the evangelistic churches, and some of those who do drink heavily often appear incapacitated. In the White Mountain community to the north, according to Michael Everett: "People either 'drink' or they do not. Potentially, it can be said of any individual 'he drinks' or 'she doesn't drink.' 'He used to drink' is also a common and quite meaningful description" (1980:153).

In 1963 and 1970, for the most part, nondrinkers did not abuse those who had been drinking heavily. If a man who was heavily intoxicated approached a home to ask for money, people might give him some change or send him away with the polite excuse that there was none. This nonconfrontational strategy might be due partly to the tendency for people who have been drinking to go for financial assistance to the homes of close relatives, where they could be sure of at least a moderately hospitable response. But a person who has been drinking may also be quite volatile, and an angry confrontation could be dangerous.

There is a general perception that a drunken person is not necessarily responsible for his or her behavior. With regard to the people of the Fort Apache Reservation, Everett notes: "Once drunkenness occurs, it is handled cautiously. Only rarely is the intoxicated person confronted directly, and then usually by another drunk." As for the importance of kin ties, "kinsmen can be expected to cooperate, and one kinsman is not likely to tolerate an act of ill will or aggression against a relative" (Everett 1980:165).

In San Carlos a rare instance of public verbal abuse directed at a person who had been drinking involved a small girl. She shouted, "Get out of here!" as a man walked up the road. He just laughed and shouted back: "This is a public road. Don't holler at me—I won't like you anymore."

Conflict associated with drinking in domestic settings often has serious consequences. One woman called the reservation police to have her husband and father jailed because of their unruly behavior. She kept them incarcerated for over a week in order to "teach them a lesson."

Just as in the wider society of the United States, relationships between spouses can be chronically turbulent when drinking is involved. One man in 1970 who appeared to get along well with his wife when he was not drinking threatened to kill her one evening after he had been drinking all day. He had borrowed money in anticipation of a check he was due to receive, and he became impatient when she failed to return home on time with the mail. He attempted to get a ride to where she was working late, brandishing a knife in each hand. He said that he had "had enough" and was going to teach her a lesson. After being stalled and dissuaded for a time, he forgot his intention and went home to bed.

In this case nothing serious probably would have come of the matter, even if he had succeeded in finding her. But situations of this sort do sometimes lead to bloodshed. Quarrels in the context of drinking seem most frequent among spouses, but other relatives may be involved, particularly where they are in frequent contact.

One older man who lived with his daughter and son-in-law became disgruntled one day, after drinking during the afternoon, when he discovered that no one was there to prepare his supper. They had gone to a cattle auction. He became belligerent when they returned, and he directed his anger at his daughter's husband. "I'm your father-in-law," he grumbled. "Why don't you feed me?" The daughter and her husband apologized, and the son-in-law pointed out that there was some canned food in the house. The father-in-law became antagonistic, and the son-in-law replied "You're not a baby. You can fix yourself anything you want to eat." The older man swung at him and hit him on the side of the face. The son-in-law hit him back and knocked him onto the bed. The older man tried to rise, and his daughter, becoming angry and perhaps frightened, shouted at her husband to stop. The son-in-law went outside, and the older man followed and grabbed him by the shirt. The son-in-law accused him of being drunk. He replied, "Okay, I'll fight you when I'm sober," and walked off to sit in the *ramada* in the dark. The younger man commented afterward that "he's mean when he's drunk" and claimed that the older man once had taken three of his jackets and his Polaroid camera and sold them to buy wine.

Several people have maintained that younger men in San Carlos sometimes beat up drunks at night and roll them. If people have no transportation to a nearby town, they can buy beer and wine at one of the several house clusters where clandestine "bootleggers" operate with little secrecy. The Tribal Council has made the sale of alcohol illegal in San Carlos, but the role of bootlegger is probably as old as the reservation itself and was well established in the 1870s, in the days of John Clum (Clum 1936:136). There are one or two favored places in Globe whose clientele consists mostly of people from San Carlos.

The aggressive behavior associated with heavy drinking is greatly at variance with Apache cultural ideals, and the people of the community recognize it as aberrant. It is a problem with some frequency, however, and is a significant part of life in San Carlos.

Everett describes one aspect of the "trouble" associated with this phenomenon: "[The chronic drinker is] part of the community at large, a position in an intricate kin network whose effective functioning depends upon relatively smooth interpersonal relationships, especially in economic terms. By his behavior, he abrogates familial and kinship responsibilities, something which can be especially disruptive when alternatives to cooperative kin relations are nonexistent or ineffective. For this, the [chronic drinker] is held responsible and, as a result, frequently becomes the target of domestic conflict and discord" (Everett 1980:173).

Drinking is a symptom of deeper problems faced by the society at large—the stresses and ambiguities, the bigotry and poverty that Apache have reaped from their contact with United States society. Drinking in turn tends to aggravate these problems and lead to others as well.

Ideological Continuities

There are striking differences between many of the problems that face San Carlos now and those that confronted the people in the past. Most notable, perhaps, are the external pressures of the state that penetrate the reservation community. But like the basic social organization itself, many ideological features have persisted. Nominal Christianity is common in San Carlos, but this has not resulted in the disappearance of older beliefs involving nonhuman reality. A movement known as the Holy Ground religion, inspired by a man named Silas John in the early part of the century, drew on a synthesis of traditional belief and innovation (Basso 1973; Spicer 1962:131–135). But more ancient patterns persist as well.

People still speak of owls with dread in San Carlos because of their association with death. One evening in 1963 an elderly woman asked, "Do owls speak to you in English?" Hearing that they did not, she said: "They speak in Apache real plain. One time an owl said to me 'I'm your grandfather.' I dreamed once that an owl was standing out there with the chickens. It said, 'You're going to cry.' A few weeks later my little niece died." In San Carlos, as among other Athapaskan populations, people consider owls to be messengers from the dead. To see or hear one is an omen of misfortune to come. They also can be a form taken by ghosts, which explains the owl's having said "I'm your grandfather." The very mention of owls always seems to provoke uneasy feelings. An elderly woman in 1963 warned: "We shouldn't be talking about owls. They hear everything we say."

Many people in San Carlos can relate some incident involving an owl as a supernatural messenger, and often such prophecies seem to have been fulfilled. A young woman related: "One time my cousin dreamed that an owl came and said, 'Your father's going to die.' She cried and cried, and the owl said, 'If you all go to church and pray real hard, he'll be hurt, but he won't die.' They all went to church, and their father had to leave on a long trip. Later they heard that he was in an accident, but he was okay."

In this case the owl acted as a proponent of Christianity. Apparently, many people in San Carlos find little difficulty in reconciling older features of Western Apache belief with Christianity, a religion to which they have been exposed since the 1600s. By the same token, they have incorporated features of other religious systems of the Southwest. Sand painting and masked dancers are prominent examples.

Anxieties about the dead and reluctance to travel about alone at night are quite evident, although some individuals who drink heavily may wander around at any time. One man in 1963 recounted having been followed down the road by a ghost. People also are reluctant to spend much time around the prehistoric ruins in the area. One man recounted his experience years earlier working with an archaeological crew in the high country Point of Pines site and recalled the uneasiness he had felt. Another man, examining a small masonry ruin in the niche of a cliff on the Nantac Rim, stayed outside the structure about ten feet away, saying, "I wonder where his bones are." A family of thirteen who moved into a large three-bedroom house near a major wash had barely settled in when one of the daughters "saw something." After some hesitation they moved out, feeling that to live there would be bad luck. Eventually they acquired a smaller and less comfortable house. Gossip about this incident was mixed. Some people felt it was too bad that they could not use the first house, but few people questioned their wisdom in moving.

Nowadays Apache dead are taken to funeral homes—a practice owing largely to state laws but also quite compatible with older patterns because it facilitates disposal of the body with a minimum of contamination or exposure. Funerals and even wakes are common now, however. Nonetheless, people avoid mentioning the names of the dead, although they might refer to them by kinship terms denoting the relationship: "my cousin," "my father," and so on.

Pollen still is used in some ceremonies and is thought to bring good luck. If a person is about to undertake some uncertain venture, a friend might jokingly advise him to take along some yellow powder.

People still take sweat baths, although probably more seldom now than in the past. In addition to their religious role in the female puberty ceremony, the sweat baths provide general good health and a feeling of well-being. Health, long life, and supernatural blessing are deeply associated in Apache thought, but as one man put it, often sweat baths are "just for sanitary purposes." This man, who was in his early twenties, said that he used to take sweat baths when he was younger. The men brought in hot rocks and covered all openings of the sweat house to retain the heat. They would stay inside as long as they could stand it and then run out and jump into the river.

He recalled being in a sweat house as a small boy with some of his friends and a lot of men. They sang continuously, with someone outside tending the fire. The boys did not last very long. "It was pitch dark and hot as an oven," he said. One of the boys yelled, "Let's get out of here!" and they ran out. He explained: "When you come out of the hut, the air really feels cold and the river looks cold, but when you jump in it's just right. It really makes you feel good." In the late nineteenth century, Lieutenant John G. Bourke described a similar experience in a sweat bath with Apache scouts. When Bourke's turn came to sing, the Apache graciously tolerated his rendition of an old army ditty in lieu of a more traditional Apache song (Bourke 1886:47–48).

Apache curers still are important in San Carlos also. One woman was so severely crippled with arthritis that she was bedridden. She had a curer sing over her for many hours, the name Jesus Christ occurring several times throughout the chant. The following morning, and for a few days afterward, the woman was able to walk about outdoors, although she eventually relapsed and died about three years later. Another man whose hand had become severely infected turned to an Apache curer after treatment by a doctor in Globe had proved to be ineffective. After seeing the curer, he said, his hand healed almost immediately. Such anecdotes abound, and it is clear that many people in San Carlos retain considerable confidence in Apache curers.

The Puberty Ceremony

The Western Apache continue to celebrate female puberty in cere-monies. There was a period several decades ago when the ceremony almost died out, but the Apache hold it now with a great deal of energy, enthusiasm, and investment. Ten or twenty years ago this ceremony, which is generally referred to in English as the "Sunrise Ceremony," was restricted to the summer, and the Fourth of July weekend was an especially favored time. With the recent resurgence, ceremonies now occur from Easter through November.

A young woman around the time of her first menstruation is the central focus. The aim is not only to enhance her health, strength, beauty, and long life but also to bring the blessings and benevolent power of the female deity Changing Woman to the community (see Basso 1966). In preparation for the ceremony the young woman's par-ents seek the assistance of each of their clans. The public ceremony can be very expensive, and usually the family must draw on the re-sources of many people. This is undoubtedly one reason why at one time very few were held.

In a ceremony held in San Carlos in 1963, a week or so ahead of time people began erecting dome-shaped brush-covered dwellings around the edges of a bare dance ground. The area was almost a hun-dred yards in diameter, surrounded by cottonwood trees. A few en-terprising families set up refreshment stands. On the final night of the ceremony, pickup trucks and brush dwellings ringed the open ground, and a bonfire shot flames and sparks into the night sky. A dozen or so men sat around the fire on logs or railroad ties and sang, beating small single-membrane drums in a persistent, unvarying rhythm.

The crowd was festive, and hundreds of people milled around far into the evening. "Social dancing" went on for hours with lines of dancers locked arm in arm encircling the fire, gently moving a few steps forward and back as the dust rose at their feet. The lines moved around the flames in a stately revolution, the faces illuminated in the firelight. When the number of dancers grew larger, they formed sev-eral concentric circles.

The young woman wore a deerskin dress trimmed with conical metal bells and fringe six or eight inches long. She had old-style deer-skin moccasins extending almost to the knees, with leather disks turned up at the toes. A flat, drop-shaped pendant of abalone shell on her forehead reflected the light. Her female companion, also finely dressed but in a costume of cloth, stayed beside her as they danced slowly in place for hours beneath a structure of poles ten to fifteen feet high.

Female puberty ceremony, San Carlos, 1963

Throughout the days of the ceremony, the young woman displayed her endurance by dancing far into the night and through the intense heat of the day. At one point she collapsed, but the older woman who supervised the proceedings helped her, gave her a drink of water through a reed, and encouraged her to go on. During the day an older woman massaged her to promote her strength.

On the last night, masked dancers impersonating the *gaan* appeared from out of the darkness. The first to appear was *tibahu*, or "the Gray One," sometimes referred to in English as the "clown." He leaped at the crowd, whirling a bull-roarer (a flat piece of wood that produces a buzzing sound) on a three-foot cord and sending children tumbling over one another to escape. The *gaan* dancers wore high moccasins and fringed, knee-length kilts decorated with small metal cones that jingled as they moved. Black cloth hoods topped with crowns of painted sotol stems about two feet high and with feathers suspended from the chins covered their heads. They uttered a high-pitched tremulo as they leapt from the darkness and gesticulated in the firelight. On the final morning of the ceremony the masked dancers encircled the area, leading the young woman and throwing a liquid made from corn sprouts on her and the crowd as a blessing.

Female puberty ceremony, San Carlos, 1963

The crown worn by the *gaan* varies among Apache groups. In San Carlos it usually radiates from the top of the head in a fan shape, although the headdress of the Gray One may be in the form of a cross. The dancers also carry three-foot wooden sticks, or wands, with double crossbars at the ends (see Ferg 1987 for examples).

In San Carlos the importance of this ceremony is complex. In part, it reaffirms clan ties, which are of major significance. As Basso points out, this is one of the few public occasions in which people's roles are defined on the basis of clan membership (1966). Its frequency may also have increased as a result of a relaxation of missionary opposition and the growth of the cattle industry in recent decades, which has made such ceremonies more feasible. Perhaps as important, the ceremony is a major recreational social event in San Carlos. It may be misleading in this case to draw a distinction between the "ideological" and the "social."

Much of the ceremony's significance lies in its spectacular reassertion of identity. It involves a periodic reinforcement and celebration of Apache self-definition, and in many ways the ritual is a proclamation. Through it, the Apache assert themselves, and this is an assertion which the Apache seem to be pleased to have outsiders witness. After generations of assaults on their sociocultural integrity and threats to their physical survival, the role of the ceremony has increased importance to the community.

The ceremony was always a means of articulating a central theme of Apache life by invoking the power of femaleness. For a beleaguered reservation population, it gained the additional role of asserting Apache ethnic identity vis-à-vis the wider arena, giving public display to Apache esthetics, symbols, and beliefs, strengthening kinship ties by exercising them, and giving specific roles to clans. It creates visible, tangible enactments of shared identity. It may be significant in this vein that the *gaan*, who play a central role in this ceremony and have potent meaning for the Apache in their own right, have now become a tribal logo, appearing on signs, stationery, and other such "presentations of self" to the outside.

The ceremony, with its connotations and affirmation of relationships, is not a cultural time capsule from the past but an ever-changing, dynamic aspect of Apache life. While it is rich with symbols and meanings that have been central to the people for many centuries, it remains part of the lives of Apache whose circumstances differ profoundly from those of their ancestors, even as they are affected by these ancient experiences. It has changed from the past, but what is the nature of these changes?

There is a growing disparity among the ceremonies themselves. In prereservation times when the population was scattered over fifty thousand square miles or more, fewer people could come together for these celebrations, and they were necessarily smaller in scale. The reservation brought about a different situation. The ceremonies became more costly because the circumstances brought more people within range. D. C. Cole suggests that on the Chiricahua Apache Reservation in the 1870s the need for supplies for these ceremonies was a major incentive for raids into Mexico (Cole 1988:20). He also notes that Cochise attempted to subsidize many of these ceremonies from his own raiding booty (Cole 1988:137).

In San Carlos, at one end of the scale are massive public extravaganzas that require a tremendous outlay of resources. At the other, some ceremonies are small unimposing affairs of "sixteen songs" presided over by a singer and attended mainly by the young woman's close relatives. Most ceremonies fall somewhere between. The differences tend to reflect the family's access to wealth, which means not only household income as such but also the extent to which the father's and mother's clan relatives can or will support the venture.

Old-style dwelling constructed for temporary use near dance ground, San Carlos

The recent upsurge in the number of ceremonies means that, once again, this experience has become a more typical part of growing up for Apache women. Old values and concepts continue, but the great disparity in elaborateness and the occasional conspicuous display of wealth may have profound implications. Such disparity may also be true of the series of gift exchanges that follow the ceremony.

The sociopolitical system of the United States, firmly articulated to the system of global capitalism, is among the predominant factors of the modern Apache environment. One aspect of this factor has been the promotion of values and an ideology appropriate to a capitalist system. The onslaught of American popular culture that flickers on the faces of Apache children from the television screen challenges beliefs in such entities as Changing Woman. The benevolent female power personified by the young woman dancing in her fringed buckskin dress with abalone shell on her forehead deeply affects many Apache people, but sometimes young women who normally wear designer jeans and listen to rock music are embarrassed to go through the ceremony, with its symbolic impregnation of Changing Woman by the sun. Older Apache values, moreover, stress shyness and modesty in people of that age.

Nonetheless, despite these factors, the ceremony has increased. It appears that the issue is not whether it will continue, but how its character and significance might change. It seems possible that the influence of the state, rather than uprooting the ceremony as a bastion of Apache ethnicity, may infiltrate aspects of it and turn it into something other than what it was.

There are several points in which the female puberty ceremony is especially at variance with prevailing American values. For one thing, there is little place in it, or the gift exchanges associated with it, for interpersonal competitiveness. But the very generosity that epitomizes Apache values provides a vulnerable point which, ironically, could begin to erode the ceremony.

In the contemporary Apache community some people have jobs. Many more do not. Of those who do, a few are fairly well off. If sharing with kin and giving generously at gift exchanges is good, giving more is even better. Ideally, gift exchanges are reciprocal interactions between members of the clans who participated in the ceremony and contributed to it. But in recent years, these exchanges themselves have escalated among families who happen to have more resources. Despite the noncompetitive ethic, there has been a tendency in many cases for people to give away more than they receive. These people are able to give more because they have more, and if they value traditional ways and place importance on their kinship ties, they may be particularly liable to give more than others. As it happens, this can undermine reciprocity because those relatives without such resources are unable to equal the gifts they receive. Among people who are well off, a sense of competition can creep in "through the back door" in the incentive to more than match one another in generosity.

The material root of this process is in the community's embeddedness in a capitalist system in which wage labor is the source of wealth. Access to this source is severely limited and uneven, and consequently, so is the wealth. As an ironic result, the greater the people's urge to fulfill traditional expectations of generosity, the more the disparity may result. The competitive potential can be exacerbated further by the public nature of the interaction. Because of this, the value placed on kinship may carry with it the potential for its own erosion.

The roles of clan members in helping with the ceremony are established and specified, and in a sense, the ceremony strengthens the clan system. But the economic situation of the present community means that people who are not clan relatives, but may happen to be co-workers and good friends, might have more in common in certain ways than members of the same clan.

This would not have been significant when there was little wealth differentiation. The present circumstances may cause good friends to help out with a puberty ceremony if they are in an economic position to do so. In contributing, they are acting "just like close relatives," but since they are not close relatives, the effect may be an inadvertent weakening of the older structure by the very people who value it. The level of wealth and the relationships associated with the workplace may tend to substitute for kin ties and thereby undermine them, even as they attempt to imitate them. The consequences of immersion in a capitalist system play on some of the strongest positive values in Apache life, and in the process, they could begin to turn the system against itself.

At present, however, the ceremony continues to be a central aspect of life in San Carlos. There is some reason to think that still another concern has fueled the resurgence in the number of ceremonies. There have been many reasons in the past for the Apache to believe that the government has sought to get rid of them. The state has tried to suppress, minimize, and reduce their population in a variety of ways. After voices of the nineteenth century no longer advocated genocide, the state in the twentieth century took children away and placed them in foster homes. It was revealed in the 1970s that the government had sterilized thousands of Native American women throughout the United States without their knowledge (see Kehoe 1981:539). And for generations, the government had undercounted the Apache population in census data.

Now the Apache have adopted a conscious policy of population expansion. This has been manifest in a variety of ways, including resistance to birth control programs. To older people the puberty ceremony, among other things, is a fertility ritual. This may not be a factor in the minds of young people who participate, but for many of their elders it is a means sanctified in ancient values not only to promote health, beauty, strength, and long life, but to perpetuate the life of the population itself.

Beliefs of External Origin

Apache people do not seem particularly bothered by personal conflict or a sense of contradiction between participation in traditional ceremonies and membership in one of the local Christian churches, despite the intolerance of a few clergy. One missionary in 1963 expressed poignant ambivalence when she said, "All my life I've wanted to see a Sunrise Ceremony, but I don't want to encourage paganism."

Those Apache people who attend church regularly seem to prefer the evangelistic type, in which displays of emotion are encouraged and both the minister and congregation often break into weeping. People in the congregation offer testimonials of salvation, and the ministers practice faith healing, generally through the laying on of hands, and sometimes with dramatic results. Some men attend these services, but women are more likely to constitute the majority of the congregation. The minister and his staff usually are from outside the community, although a few Apache men have been ordained. This type of church is characteristic of many rural areas of the United States, and in San Carlos it seems to fulfill some needs in a manner compatible with existing social and cultural patterns.

One particular service in 1970 can serve as an example. The church was a small cinder-block building with a poured cement floor and a low wooden platform at the front. The hall was brightly illuminated by fluorescent ceiling lights. Rows of metal folding chairs had been set up for the congregation, mostly women in long camp dresses who chatted quietly. A few men in jeans and cotton shirts sat motionless, gazing straight ahead.

Some non-Apache people were in charge. The men referred to themselves and each other as "brother." Brother A was a young, dynamic man who energetically introduced himself to everyone he had not already met and greeted those he had. Brother B was an older, white-haired man "from Modesto, California," who shook hands all around. A young non-Apache woman played the piano while the people sang hymns and more wandered into the building. Two Apache men, later introduced as newly ordained ministers of the church, walked up onto the platform and sat impassively facing the congregation.

Another Apache man mounted the platform and sat down to tune an electric guitar. He was introduced by Brother A as one who "has been here several times before . . . he shouldn't hide his light under a bushel." The Apache man gave a short account of his life in both English and Apache, with emphasis on the waywardness that preceded his conversion. He then played and sang two country-and-western style religious songs.

Brother A introduced an Apache child as a "healing miracle." He told the congregation that the boy had severely injured his leg, which had been "cut to the bone" by bicycle spokes. Doctors had given up hope, but the boy had been blessed at a meeting with prayers and hands laid on his head, and he had recovered with only a slight limp. The boy, who was about ten years old, smiled happily, although with apparent self-consciousness. Scattered voices from the congregation shouted, "Praise God," and the child's mother sobbed. Brother C, sitting in front with trembling chin, caught his breath in a sob and struggled to control his display of emotion.

Brother C was then introduced, and he described his religious conversion. He said that he had given up his business and saved many people and that he had worked with Indians in Canada, where he had prayed for an apparently barren woman who subsequently bore five children in five years. In a stentorian voice, Brother C discussed the Old Testament, sobbing with his face contorted and eyes welling with tears as he reached the crescendos. He announced that the Bible proves that Indians are descended from the seed of Joseph and that San Carlos is the Land of Rolling Hills mentioned in the scriptures. He closed with a supplication to the people in the congregation to open their hearts to Jesus and to stand up and tell everyone.

After a brief pause during which no one stood, Brother D took the floor. With a kindly smile, he told of a boy with no arms who became a fine carpenter, hopping on one foot with a crowbar under his chin and a hammer grasped between his toes. Brother D declared, "I love Indians," and added: "You all look beautiful to me here tonight. In fact, I'm in love with you, because you're filled with the spirit of Jesus." There were a few sidelong glances at this in the congregation and a muffled laugh, but for the most part the people appeared quiet and serious, occasionally nodding in agreement.

One of the two Apache men on the platform dozed off, his head slowly dropping toward his chest. The other, his eyes betraying amusement, bumped his knee to wake him.

An older non-Apache couple, also from California, gave an additional testimonial of conversion. People then came forward to be healed through prayer and the laying of hands on their heads. After more hymns, another Apache child was presented to the congregation as one who had been healed miraculously. The minister announced that she had not been able to walk at all until she was three years old. Then her mother had brought her to be prayed for, and later that same afternoon she was outdoors playing. The service ended with the people in the congregation shaking hands all around, saying "Bless you" to one another.

One major impetus for church attendance seems to be sickness, other ailments, or old age. During one church service a teenage boy was cured of ghost sickness. He had been brought to the service by his grandmother, who testified to the congregation that they had been walking down the road on the way to church Sunday morning when he was stricken with terrible pains in his head and was unable to go on walking. He told her that he believed he was sick because he had seen a man standing by his bed the night before, and he had been frightened by the apparition. The grandmother told the minister: "I want you to pray for him. He's a good boy and he believes in Jesus, because he said to me, 'Grandma, I want you to pray for me.'" Several people laid hands on the boy's head and prayed. When this was done, the boy got up without a word and walked out, apparently satisfied.

More than any other institutions, these churches have had some success in dealing with alcohol problems on an individual basis. Referring to the need for religious conviction for strength in overcoming alcohol, one man commented that "it's too much for a single mind by itself." Many individuals are able to stop drinking completely after being saved. Sometimes the conversion is dramatic, with fainting or ecstatic experience. Participation in these churches appears to represent a response to some of the problems of the San Carlos community, although their total effect on the society has yet to be seen.

Children

The principles and philosophy underlying child rearing seem to have changed very little among the Western Apache in San Carlos. The matrilocal extended family pattern of residence reinforces the stability of this pattern. Because this clustering keeps married sisters together, their young children spend most of their time playing with one another. The closeness of a child to the children of the mother's sisters and the relative lack of interaction with the children of the mother's brothers who have moved out to other family clusters is often quite obvious, even in the exceptional cases in which these relatives happen to live nearby.

In one instance, a man who had spent years away from San Carlos and married a woman from another state returned to live near the homes of his mother and married sisters. A flimsy wire fence separated his home from theirs. The fence was not an effective barrier, since people frequently stepped over it to visit, but it served the symbolic purpose of separating his home from the matrilocal cluster.

Children often run freely in and out of their maternal grandmother's dwelling. Usually this relationship is warm and relaxed, with a great deal of affection expressed in gentle joking. A grandmother spying her four- or five-year-old grandson might call out, "There's my boyfriend." In one case, as an older woman walked by, a little girl laughed and cried out: "The wind blew grandma's blouse up her back! You can see her T-shirt!"

Teasing of this sort reflects the warm and bantering tone of the relationship between these relatives, particularly when children are very young. Certainly the personalities of the people involved are

Apache children, San Carlos

important determinants of this, but older people in general seem to enjoy joking with children.

As little girls get older, their grandmothers may give them more serious training and make an explicit effort to teach them various skills. People may send even very small children to perform such chores as fetching water, but they seldom order them to do so. Rarely are children scolded, and spanking or other physical punishment is still rarer. If a child should create an intolerable situation, perhaps making enough noise to drown out a conversation or stirring up clouds of dust, he or she might be spoken to in the same tones that would be used to address an adult.

In one instance in 1970, two little boys somehow obtained some wooden kitchen matches and set fire to dry tumbleweeds in a gully behind their house cluster. The fire quickly spread to some dry mesquite bushes and threatened some of the nearby dwellings. People rushed to the scene with shovels, and with a good deal of effort they put the fire out before it did much damage.

The small boys were shocked at the result of their play. They tried to help extinguish the flames that roared into the sky over their heads by throwing stones at the blaze. The culprits were obvious, but no form of punishment or even scolding was directed at them. One man merely remarked in a matter-of-fact, nondirected way within earshot of the guilty two about the dangers of such a blaze and the damage it could have caused.

When Apache children play together, fighting seems rare compared to its frequency among many Anglo-American children of similar ages. Fights between adolescents are more frequent, and they tend to be more serious in their consequences. But at younger ages, before twelve or so, boys and girls generally play together freely. Older children tend to look after younger ones—not hovering over them, but keeping them in sight in case they get into trouble. Play might consist of running off and hiding from one another or of chasing each other around the area of the house cluster. Children climb about the hills and cliffs near their houses in apparently aimless exploring activities. Basketball is popular, and basketball hoops and backboards on poles rise over many house clusters.

At puberty, young people are likely to become "shy" in conformity with the expected pattern. This shyness seems quite genuine and is especially marked between teenagers of the opposite gender. A lack of shyness or an apparent familiarity between a young man and woman is liable to be interpreted by onlookers as an indication of sexual promiscuity.

In 1963, a little girl who was then nine years old said, "When you come back I'll be shy." In 1970, at the age of sixteen, she was, indeed, very properly shy.

As in all societies, children sometimes pick up moods and attitudes from adults, and often they are more candid, if less articulate, about expressing them. Often they have not yet learned to be cautious in revealing themselves to others through their thoughts. In 1970 some small children often played "Indians," which consisted of stalking from bush to bush and peering out at one another. Explaining why the children hid behind bushes when playing Indians, a little girl said that it was "because Indians are afraid of people." Another young child told a story, the beginning of which apparently comes from a child's book about a train: "Slowly, slowly, there was a train coming . . . but people didn't know what it was because it was an Indian train. There were all Indians inside, and they were afraid. And some cars came along and the Indians were afraid, but the train moved along so the cars couldn't catch them."

The society beyond the reservation is pervaded by forces that are powerful, unsympathetic, threatening, and all but impossible to influence or control. These forces intrude upon the reservation, and as the child sensed, they are not always friendly to Indians. Both the game and the story betray anxieties that probably stem from such perceptions.

Some of the apprehension children express also is associated with anxieties about school, which many small children throughout American society feel. The onset of the school experience is compounded by deep cultural differences in the Apache case. These anxieties for Apache children probably are quite strong. But the game and the story both suggest feelings that encompass but go beyond the particular school experiences of these children. They derive much of their tone from the attitudes and feelings more pervasive in the wider society. Surely this perception of reality is an important factor, both cause and effect, of the separatism of modern San Carlos.

Until recently, children in San Carlos had still other reasons to fear the society outside the reservation. County laws stipulate living standards considered necessary for suitable homes for children. They include such things as a minimum number of windows per dwelling, adequate plumbing and heating, the maximum number of children who sleep in the same bed, and other criteria deemed to be essential aspects of a healthy upbringing in the modern United States. The economic conditions in San Carlos often mean that many families cannot meet such living standards. As a consequence, social agencies in the past took many Apache children away from their families and placed them in foster homes outside the reservation.

Typically these children were taken in by non-Apache couples, often members of some of the more aggressively proselytizing religious denominations. Mormon families have taken many Native American children throughout the West. Having lost their territory and control of their resources, many Apache suffered the loss of their children to the state as well. In 1967 Congress passed a law known as the Indian Child Welfare Act which brought an end to this practice.

In recent years the San Carlos Apache population has grown significantly, after generations of relative stability. Probably there are many reasons for this, but perhaps one is that Apache children can no longer be taken away as easily as they were in the past.

Survival of the Reservation Community

The reservation is a place where a few thousand people face the many problems of human existence. They deal with birth and death. They ponder why things happen to people and explain them as best they can, often using the wisdom their ancestors developed over centuries of survival. They consider how they can control the annoyance, envy, needs, passion, and violence that spring from people living with one another; how they can get enough to eat; and how they can make things better for their children. Their heritage and social organization grew from strategies and premises refined and adapted over millennia of experience. But having lost control of their resource base, they are subject to a range of liabilities that stem from having been incorporated into a state system. They require money to survive in the contemporary United States. They are available for wage labor, but they have little access to jobs. They must rely on the government for such vital services as medical care and, in some cases, for food. They have a few resources. At one time they had more, but for the most part, they have not been able to benefit from them.

Part of the nature of a reservation is that, although the population is incorporated by the state, the community is not fully a part of that state. San Carlos remains an ethnic enclave, a body politic without control of resources or true sovereignty over significant aspects of its people's personal lives. As we will discuss in the next chapter, the corporate charter establishing the people of San Carlos as the "San Carlos Apache Tribe," with formal recognition by the government, has the effect of subsuming them within the state system while delimiting their access to power.

As a reservation community, the people are subject to special economic problems. Government agencies and various observers tend to attribute poverty to their maintenance of "traditional" patterns: the clan system, matrilocal extended families, and so on. This is the basic position underlying the concepts of underdevelopment and modernization. From this point of view, San Carlos is poor because the community is underdeveloped, and it is underdeveloped because the people cling to old ways and institutions that are neither modern nor appropriate to a capitalist system.

One aspect of becoming modern would be the greater individualization of the populace. If people ignored their kin ties, if the clans were forgotten, if the Apache language were no longer spoken, and if Apache ceremonies no longer were held, the people might well cease to constitute an ethnically distinct population. Instead, they would become relatively undifferentiated individuals within the larger state. They might very well be as poor as they are now, or even poorer, but they would be far less visible. They would, in that sense, disappear. Considerable pressures work toward this end in San Carlos. Some government programs designed to promote modernization are quite explicit in these aims.

But ironically, the loss of resources and the Apache's resulting poverty may have inhibited the process of individualization. For most people in San Carlos the main source of comfort, support, and assistance comes from relatives. The matrilocal extended family is a base of nurturance. Far-flung clan relatives are the people who ideally, at least, are obligated to help in times of need. The puberty ceremonies reiterate and dramatize principles that are nurturing and reassuring. The curing practices provide aid and confidence. The more difficult things become, the more the people are likely to seek these strengths.

Impoverished in economic terms, the Western Apache have resisted the rootlessness of the individual urban and rural poor scattered throughout the rest of American society. The state, unable as yet to dissolve the Western Apache, encompasses them almost as a tree grows around a nail.

CHAPTER 7

Political Economy in San Carlos

Formal Apache government on the San Carlos Reservation consists of an elected Tribal Council with a council chairman, but many decisions of the council are subject to the approval and sometimes the veto of the Bureau of Indian Affairs. The community passed a tribal constitution and by-laws in 1935, in compliance with the federal Indian Reorganization Act of 1934. This document not only specified the organization and powers of the Tribal Council but also enumerated issues "subject to the approval of the Secretary of the Interior or his representative" (United States Department of the Interior 1936). These were rather extensive.

Actions subject to federal control included such items as the Tribe's choice of legal counsel, expenditures of the tribal fund, management of the tribal cattle herd, passage of ordinances regarding local voluntary organizations, removal from the reservation of persons who are not tribal members and whose presence may be injurious to tribal members, prescription of the rules of inheritance, provision of guardians for minors and mental incompetents, and amendments to the tribal constitution. In practice this meant that the reservation superintendent, as representative of the Secretary of the Interior, could exert the pressure of the state in all of these matters.

The tribal constitution stipulated that any resolution or ordinance the Tribal Council might pass that was subject to review by the Secretary of the Interior should "be presented to the superintendent of the reservation." This official had ten days to approve or disapprove the resolution. But the constitution also required the superintendent to send a copy of the decision to the Secretary of the Interior, who could rescind approval "for any cause" within ninety days. To put it another way, the constitution empowered a political appointee in Washington who had never seen San Carlos to overrule, "for any cause," decisions reached by representatives of the community even if the local representative of the state had endorsed those decisions.

But the state made itself felt in subtler ways as well. The constitution specified, for example, that "all marriages shall be in accordance with the State [of Arizona] laws." It also stipulated that the federal government must be represented by a non-voting delegate in Tribal Council meetings, and with the council's approval that person, who normally would be the reservation superintendent, could act as secretary. Whether secretary or not, the government representative, the constitution stated, would be entrusted with "safekeeping in the agency, the records, and other books, documents, and related valuable papers of the council and the tribe." And according to Article III, Section V on "Conduct of Business," the normal voice vote or show of hands could be put to a secret ballot either at the discretion of the council chairman, at the request of *two* Tribal Council members, or at the demand of that single government official.

The Corporate Charter of 1940 certified that the San Carlos Apache Tribe was a "body politic," a corporate entity with political standing within the wider state system (United States Department of the Interior 1941). But the stipulations in the San Carlos constitution illuminate the role of state power. They suggest some of the reasons why an "Indian reservation" is not quite the same as other communities.

Interestingly, one of the first statements in the tribal constitution is an assertion that the Tribe wishes the continued presence of the government. One might view this statement in many ways, but in some respects it is not inconsistent with the people's ambivalence about the government. Just as they may be aware of the oppressive aspects of the state system in their community, they are concerned about the withdrawal of certain government services and protections. They have been deprived of most of their resources and many of the weapons that might allow them to survive economically. They have been disarmed, and the structure of their political relationship with the state cripples their ability to take radical steps to change the situation. As onerous as some aspects of the federal relationship with the reservation may be, it also stands between the people of San Carlos and forces that potentially may be more threatening.

Historically, the State of Arizona has not displayed a congenial or sympathetic stance toward its Native American populations. Local governments have tended to adopt the same posture. But numerous Supreme Court decisions have affirmed that the sovereignty of Indian tribes is prior to the United States Constitution and can be limited only through congressional actions (see Wilkinson 1987). This means that the federal government rather than the states has jurisdiction over reservation communities. It also means that Indian sovereignty remains intact except in matters that Congress has explicitly defined. One of these is in the area of criminal law. By congressional action, state laws regarding homicide and other major crimes are enforceable on reservations, although some may be tried in tribal courts. But the Supreme Court has ruled, for example, that states cannot impose sales taxes on reservations (see Deloria and Lytle 1983:205–208).

The tax issue is of some importance in Arizona, a state with one of the nation's largest Native American populations and roughly a third of its bounded territory consisting of reservations. The court decisions do not mean that there has been no effort to "get at" the reservation populations through taxes. In 1988 a state legislator argued for a general sales tax on food. Since most people buy their food off the reservations, this would certainly amount to taxation of the Native American populace.

Within the reservation community, Tribal Council offices come up for election regularly, but just as in other legislative bodies, there is a tendency to retain incumbents. Many council members stay in office for several terms. The role of council members as representatives of kin groups or other constituencies certainly is a factor in their election. The council member of a district is sometimes referred to as *nant'an*, a term that formerly referred to the leader of a local group.

Apache leaders have encouraged the people to register and vote in local and national elections. In 1970 the chairman addressed the people of San Carlos in Apache every Saturday morning over a local radio station, using this half hour to make public announcements and to offer advice relating to current reservation issues. The tone was very much like that taken by past leaders, whose primary role entailed counseling their local group rather than expressing authority. "The Apache Hour" also was broadcast regularly over a local station and usually consisted of recorded Apache music played by request, with dedications read on the air.

But Apache participation in the electoral process has encountered obstacles. Prior to the 1980 election, it was clear to some state officeholders that the San Carlos Reservation contained a bloc of potential voters with many common interests. The Arizona State Legislature attempted to nullify this by dividing San Carlos into three separate voting districts. Each of the three segments of the reservation was part of a larger district in which the majority of voters were non-Apache. This would have diluted the effect of the Apache vote and washed out whatever possibilities there might have been for them to exert pressure on particular issues or candidates. Despite the rhetoric of encouraging Native Americans to enter the "mainstream" of

American society, it appears, some politicians feared the effects of the Apache exercising that most fundamental American responsibility of voting.

Bruce Babbitt, then Democratic Governor of Arizona, vetoed the redistricting measure, but the Legislature overrode his veto. The courts remained the only recourse for the Apache. Before a panel of three judges in Federal District Court in 1982, a legislator who had been involved in the redistricting claimed that he had had no idea what the boundaries of the San Carlos Reservation were. San Carlos Tribal Attorney Joe Sparks compelled him to admit that in the glove compartment of his car he carried a road atlas with a map of Arizona and its Indian reservations. The defense unraveled, and the panel of judges ruled in favor of the plaintiffs (*Goddard* v. *Babbitt*, 536 F. Supp. 538 [1982]). As a consequence of this case, Arizona now is one of the states subject to federal monitoring under the Voting Rights Act of 1967.

Formal Education and the State

Many people in San Carlos make great efforts to encourage their children in school, but access to education has been difficult. In 1970, only 13.5 percent of the people in San Carlos over the age of twenty-five had graduated from high school, and none had graduated from college (Snipp 1989:202; see also Parmee 1968). The figures for 1980 show that 32.1 percent of high school–aged children were not enrolled, although by that time 43.6 percent of the adults in San Carlos were high school graduates, and almost 1 percent had graduated from college (Snipp 1989:203).

The busing of Apache children to the public school in Globe was a lively political issue in 1970. The government rationale behind busing was based on civil rights legislation regarding school segregation. Some Apache parents supported it, but many appeared to favor having the local San Carlos school, which then handled grades one through seven, expanded to accommodate students through the twelfth grade.

Apache parents objected that many of the children had to get up at 5:30 or 6:00 A.M. to meet the bus, which then traveled for some time around the scattered homes of the reservation before leaving on its twenty-mile trip to Globe. For the same reasons, many students were not able to get home again until five or six in the evening.

Many Apache parents wanted to keep their children out of the public school for other reasons, though. As one man put it: "We think that must be a high-class school. They give grades on the clothes the kids wear and on personal appearance." The public school system has tended to put Apache and, to a lesser extent perhaps, the poorer families of other ethnic groups at a disadvantage. Children and parents are vulnerable to humiliating incidents. Such an apparently minor issue as the need to pay for school pictures can be a financial crisis to many Apache families.

Yet despite the low level of income in San Carlos, Apache children leaving for school each morning tend to be strikingly well dressed and carefully groomed. On cold mornings, paradoxically, some have no coats to wear over their nice-looking clothes and stand along the road hugging themselves with breath steaming as they wait for the school bus.

By 1987 a good deal more had transpired. Because the reservation is under federal jurisdiction, it is not subject to state and local school taxes. The Johnson-O'Malley Act of 1934 authorized the Bureau of Indian Affairs to establish contracts with the various states for the education of Native American children within their boundaries. Edgar S. Cahn and David W. Hearne, in their devastating book, *Our Brother's Keeper*, note that many states "simply ignore the special needs of Indians while using Indian funds to subsidize the local state school system" (1969).

For many years the Globe school system had collected tuition for Apache children to attend school. The people of San Carlos, being members of the Globe school district, elected people from their community to the Board of Education. Eventually, Apache board members checked the books and found irregularities in the tuition charges. The Globe school administration relented and agreed to cease certain questionable practices in the future.

In the aftermath of this, many of the people of San Carlos developed plans to build their own school on the reservation. They explored procedures for establishing San Carlos as a separate school district, and a referendum showed a favorable response to the idea. They applied for federal funds to build a school, but the issue was complex. At a meeting to discuss the school project, members of the Tribal Council stated that on procedural grounds they would not permit the allocation of reservation land for a school for at least another four years. The people leading the move for the new school withdrew their proposal but resubmitted it a short time later. The designated site for the new school was on a high point of land on U.S. Route 70, near the turnoff for Peridot and San Carlos, although by 1990 no construction had begun.

Some people in Globe worried about the impending loss of federal funds from Apache students, especially considering the precarious local economy. And it seemed that things had begun to change a bit in recent years. A Chicana woman who grew up in Globe claimed in 1988 that, over the previous ten years or so, Apache children in the high school had taken a more active part in school life. This was particularly true in sports—"all sports except tennis," she noted. Students established a Native American Club, and in the late 1980s a few Apache students, apparently all of them women, were elected to student government.

On the other hand, there seems to be little social interaction after school hours between Apache students and their counterparts who live in Globe. The twenty-mile bus trip to and from San Carlos certainly has something to do with this, and perhaps history has more. The trajectory of local history will change once again if Apache students acquire their own high school out on Route 70.

The Federal Government in San Carlos

The federal government is a predominant aspect of life in San Carlos and other reservations, and no discussion of the reservation could be complete without considering the role of the agencies that represent power from outside. Of the agents of this state power, the Bureau of Indian Affairs and the Public Health Service (the BIA and the PHS) are the most visible. Much of the major decision-making within the community is dominated by the BIA, and the influence of both of these agencies pervades almost every level of Apache society from community governance to personal affairs.

The BIA has come under a great deal of scrutiny and criticism in recent years (see Cahn and Hearne 1969). Established under the War Department in 1824 as the Office of Indian Affairs, it was placed under the Department of the Interior in 1849 and has since become a large and complex bureaucracy. It shares the characteristics of many such bureaucracies including vested interests, internal factions, and old timers who have seen it all.

As a branch of the Department of the Interior, the BIA falls under the auspices of the executive branch of the federal government, although it must depend on Congress for its funding. Many Presidents have tried unsuccessfully to restructure, streamline, or otherwise radically change the BIA. The ponderous resiliency of the bureaucracy has thwarted even commissioners of Indian Affairs in their attempts at reform. Commissioners are appointed by presidents and generally lose their jobs when the presidents lose theirs. At the lower echelons, career people carry out their programs as parties win and lose elections, sometimes grumbling at the vagaries of the current administration and sometimes agreeing with it.

But the ultimate power of the BIA is not in the people who swivel in chairs behind the desks in local offices or grind gears in government vehicles over reservation dirt roads. These are the points of the BIA's articulation to reservation communities, but above all, the BIA is an organ of the state. Its public purpose is to promote assimilation and help the people of reservations enjoy the benefits of participation in American society.

At a fundamental level, many of its programs are directed at promoting individualization. In pursuing this, the BIA operates from a position of power as a representative of the same state system that in an earlier era brought these populations to submission through violence. It operates on the rationale of local populations' incompetence, perpetuating the myth that justifies administrating Native Americans' resources "on their behalf."

The BIA is hierarchically structured, so that workers in the field on the various reservations follow orders whose origins may not be visible up the convergent chains of command to Washington. "Washington," in turn, is a comprehensive shorthand for the network of power involving the Commissioner of Indian Affairs, the Secretary of the Interior, the President, Congress, and so on. Policies and decisions emanate from a variety of sources and stimuli, including various political action committees and other lobbying interests. Rarely are they dominated by a sensitivity to the needs of a small community of Native Americans living in the desert three thousand miles away. The Secretary of the Interior has many other responsibilities besides Native Americans, and many of these conflict.

The BIA's structure makes it almost impossible for it to contravene the imperatives of powerful interests. Even if the local employees are enlightened and well meaning, they may not be able to implement these qualities effectively. And BIA policies calling for the frequent transfer of personnel ensure that an official who develops a sensitivity to local issues will soon be sent elsewhere. The ones who oppose BIA policy will be frustrated, but the policies will not change on account of their frustration.

The Public Health Service, like the BIA, is also a government agency whose stated purpose is to benefit people on reservations. The Indian Health Service was taken from the jurisdiction of the BIA in 1955 and made a branch of the PHS under the Department of Health, Education, and Welfare. The PHS maintains hospitals in many reservation communities and carries out programs intended to alleviate conditions that are recognized as serious problems by the people of the community and the government alike. The people of San Carlos, like populations of many other reservations, have suffered in the past from a high incidence of tuberculosis and other infectious diseases that tend to be associated with severe poverty.

Throughout the United States, Native American populations have suffered an increase in degenerative diseases at the same time that infectious diseases have declined, and this probably is true of San Carlos as well. Infant mortality in the past was staggering, with infant diarrhea one of the main causes. It has improved a great deal in the last decade, possibly because of increased efforts including community health outreach programs, many of them involving Apache people. The infant mortality rate still exceeds the overall national average but by far less than it once did (Searles, personal communication, 1991). The mortality rate for children beyond the newborn stage, though, remains quite high, often involving pneumonia and influenza (Searles, personal communication, 1991).

The BIA reported in 1981 that "the obstetrical population has a high rate of preeclampsia and other complications of pregnancy" (Bureau of Indian Affairs 1981:67). Preeclampsia involves extreme hypertension in advanced pregnancy which endangers the lives of both mother and fetus. Normally, treatment involves abortion or delivery. The causes have not been established, but some doctors feel that preventative treatment through nutritional therapy is effective (Ammer 1983:335).

Pathological drinking among children has also become a tragic problem. Twenty-year-olds in San Carlos have died of cirrhosis of the liver. Fetal alcohol syndrome has become a concern. Compounding the tragedies of alcoholism and the homicide rate, suicides are terribly frequent, particularly among young people who in most societies of the world, as well as in Apache society in the past, would have been able to look forward to a long life stretching ahead of them.

A deep ambivalence runs through the relationship between the government and the people of San Carlos. To overstate the degree of historical distrust underlying this relationship would be difficult. In 1970, one man who was involved in a discussion of a controversial BIA program commented: "We've been living here for so many years under a certain kind of a system, and under like a dictatorship from the BIA . . . we just, you know, remain quietly." Yet it seems that most would not want the BIA to leave. One person felt: "The BIA used to be really good. They did a lot of things for the Indians, but now they never come around anymore." There is a feeling that the BIA should act as an advocate of the people and guardian of their rights, whereas in practice it often seems to have been foremost in usurping those rights.

Some of the tension in this relationship has sprung from interpersonal frictions. Some government personnel in the past have been ignorant and insensitive. Decades ago, a pair of government social workers who often made decisions to remove children from their parents and place them in foster homes made a habit of loudly discussing individual cases by name in the local cafe. Apparently they were oblivious to the Apache people sitting at tables on all sides of them, some of whom were relatives of the people being discussed.

In another case more than twenty years ago, a government psychiatrist treating a man with a severe drinking problem tried to convince his patient that the reason for his affliction was the "neurotic" importance he placed on matrilineal kinship ties. The psychiatrist's ignorance of the cultural context would seem almost comical if it were not for the severe confusion he generated in an individual who was already troubled, and who contemplated suicide after the visit. Such outside expertise over the years, with its implicit arrogance in treating Western Apache culture as something unworthy of an attempt to understand, let alone respect, has been a source of harassment and frequent tragedy for people in the Apache community. Coupled with the power implied by association with the government, it has constituted a significant threat.

On occasion the BIA has used improvement programs as levers to dislocate traditional culture patterns. In the 1960s the government initiated a housing program to give Apache people assistance in building homes of tufa stone and cement block. The head of the household, as recognized by the government, would be responsible for providing the labor, after which the family would own the property. Many people enrolled in the program to take advantage of this chance to provide their families with more solid, substantial dwellings. Adequate housing had been a problem in San Carlos since the nineteenth century. In 1970, even after the housing program was well underway, 69.4 percent of the houses had more than one person per room. By 1980 this was true of 55.1 percent of the houses (Snipp 1989:118).

It soon became apparent, though, that the government did not wish the houses built in family clusters but aligned along streets, somewhat in the manner of a Levittown in the desert. A major effect of this program might have been to weaken the ancient matrilocal joint family cluster. Certainly proponents of assimilation would have welcomed the establishment of an atomistic nuclear family structure characteristic of the Anglo-American middle class. The concept implies a community of individual homeowners with modest little yards around their houses. Apparently the government wished not only to provide better housing but also to undermine the basis for joint family ties by breaking them into isolated nuclear families.

But the strength of traditional relationships in San Carlos involved a powerful imperative for people to live near their relatives, and the joint family has great significance for the quality of life as people in San Carlos perceive it. In 1970, a few rows of new houses stood unoccupied in regimental order up hillsides and along dirt lanes, looking like strangely misplaced suburban ghost towns. Dark picture windows, still bearing their paper labels, stared vacantly at one another across empty roads.

By 1988, though, several more clusters of newly built houses stood on the reservation. Many of these allowed groups of matrilineal relatives to live near one another. Donna Searles notes: "In recent years several new housing subdivisions have been built through H.U.D. and other programs. These housing units have altered the settlement and residence pattern, yet Apache principles of family, kin, and clan have endured. Close relatives may reside in the same subdivision, or will visit one another to share news, share meals, and lend help and support" (1990:2). Some people, however, have reported sporadic problems of vandalism, which apparently arose when kin relationships conflicted with residence patterns.

Despite such initiatives as the housing program, some people in San Carlos believe that the ultimate goal of the government is to get rid of Indians in one way or another. When we consider the history of the Apache's interaction with the state, this suspicion does not seem entirely unwarranted. And although the need for health care on the reservation is great, in the past many distrusted the government health agencies. Some refused to go to the PHS hospital on the reservation except in the case of dire emergencies. This has changed a great deal, no doubt because of greater efforts to involve Apache in the extension of health care to the community and to introduce more preventative measures to alleviate health problems. Specialized clinics are now held with physicians from Phoenix. A satellite clinic has been established at Bylas, and Apache community health workers extend care more effectively to the population (Searles, personal communication, 1991).

Up until the early 1970s it was a common belief that one went to a hospital to die. People did die there, of course, as they do in any hospital. A feedback effect may have arisen when people refrained from going for treatment until it was too late to save them. But there was some suspicion in the community that Apache had been allowed to die in the PHS hospital because they did not receive medicines that could have saved them. Twenty years ago, some feared that pills and other medicines issued by the PHS were poisonous. Scores of pill bottles discarded by people on their way back from the hospital lay scattered and unopened in Gilson Wash.

One man in 1970 told of a case in which one of his relatives, a child, suddenly fell sick and was unable to swallow. He developed a purplish color around the mouth, and blisters appeared on his feet. "They took him to the PHS hospital here," the man said, "and all they did was leave him in a room and watch him for a few days." Apparently the boy grew worse until he, too, was flown to a hospital in Phoenix where his condition improved.

Simply to dismiss this as an Apache distrust of modern medicine would be misleading. Many Apache even in the early 1960s preferred to see doctors in Globe for medical treatment, where they had to pay for it themselves, rather than use the PHS facilities. On the other hand, there is no doubt that the PHS and its facilities have saved many lives in San Carlos. The government flew one elderly woman over one hundred miles from San Carlos to Phoenix for a gallbladder operation. She had been reluctant to have the operation, but according to a relative, the doctor told her, "If you don't go, you'll die." Several weeks afterward she appeared to be well on the way to recovery, and she said that the flying had not bothered her. "There wasn't much to it," she said. "Just like riding in a car."

The government now provides a thirty-six-bed hospital and a number of clinics for prenatal and well-baby care, obstetrics/gynecology, eye care, cardiology, orthopedics, chest and diabetic diagnosis, ENT, and internal medicine (Bureau of Indian Affairs 1981:68). There is a dental service, an alcohol prevention program, and a variety of other programs related to health issues. Although the hospital has placed an increased stress on prenatal care, it has no surgical facilities, and women with difficult pregnancies generally are sent to Phoenix hospitals (Searles 1990:6).

Many people in the Apache community in 1970 held that the PHS doctors are learning their trade and using Apache patients to practice on. "We're just guinea pigs to them," one man said. People cited instances of doctors' showing an apparent lack of concern or respect, smoking in Apache patients' rooms or laughing and joking loudly near the sick. The youth of many of these doctors may have been one basis for the distrust, since most Apache curers are much older. According to former Navajo Tribal Chairman Peter MacDonald, PHS doctors are often recent medical school graduates serving their first residency, and for this reason, many of them have tended to be young (quoted in The *Arizona Republic*, January 9, 1973). Many also may be overworked. During the period of military draft, PHS duty was a substitute for military service.

No doubt other cultural differences contribute to misunderstanding. A cheerful demeanor that Anglo-Americans consider a good bedside manner may be interpreted as callousness by Apache patients. The barren, sterile atmosphere of a hospital room isolates the patient from the social interaction so vital to most Apache people's feelings of well-being. It stands in stark contrast to the more traditional treatment of ailments in which a sick person is immersed in the familiar household setting and surrounded by close relatives.

Whatever the various causes and contributing factors, though, distrust of the government is clearly deep. In many ways, feelings in San Carlos toward the hospital have reflected the more general misgivings about the actions and motivations of the government. Since the early 1970s, though, the tribal government has contracted with the PHS to run the Tribal Health Authority, and preferential federal hiring policies have placed more Native Americans in government agencies (Searles, personal communication, 1991). Whether this will lead to a significant increase in control over community affairs remains to be seen. Certainly there is much to overcome.

In 1970, a program through which old people were sent to rest homes in Tucson and Phoenix was a major source of friction. Most of these people had been born in San Carlos, some of them in the early years of the reservation. Some spoke little English. The government sent these people to rest homes on the grounds of neglect.

Supposedly, their enrollment in the homes was voluntary, and the old person's relatives were required to sign a release. But some of these relatives claimed that social workers had put pressure on them to sign. One man claimed that government workers had threatened to take away his children if he refused. Apparently, old-age benefits to which these elderly people were entitled were applied to the costs of their maintenance in the home.

Apache vigorously denied the charge of neglect of old people. One man said: "We Indians are different. We like to keep the old people with us. I took care of my father when he became blind. I took care of him until the day he died." Other people who discussed the issue stressed the important place of elderly people in Apache society. A man pointed out that "with my own children, their grandmother takes it upon herself to teach them how to behave."

Isolation of older people probably is far rarer in San Carlos than in Anglo-American society. In the joint family setting, people ranging from infants to aged great-grandparents interact regularly and often. Apache view loneliness with a deep sense of dread, and there is little likelihood that individuals might become cut off from the wider social milieu.

Tribal leaders visiting elderly people in the institutions where they had been sent by the government found that although some of them spoke only Apache, they were kept apart from one another. The leaders told of seeing two elderly women of different tribes attempting to carry on a conversation in two mutually unintelligible languages. The tales of neglect in these institutions are similar to those told of some rest homes in other parts of the country. An old man in the institution who had been in a wheelchair for twelve months asked a visiting tribal official to turn him toward a window, saying that he had not seen the sun for a year.

In response to this program, the Tribal Council drew up an alternative proposal for maintaining elderly people in their own homes on the reservation. They planned to provide them with housekeeping assistance if necessary, food or transportation for shopping trips, and social visits by Apache volunteers to help maintain their morale. The estimated cost of this was $31,000. The BIA declined to fund the project, responding that this should be a matter for the state funding, and the State of Arizona reminded the people that they pay no state taxes.

This government program meant that in some cases people had to travel hundreds of miles to visit their elders. No longer were these old people a presence in the lives of their grandchildren, an integral part of the joint family structure. Their absence prevented them from effectively conveying traditional knowledge, beliefs, and values to the children. The program had a self-perpetuating effect as well. Due to economic stresses in San Carlos, once the expenses of caring for an elderly person were relieved, for family groups to resume care was often difficult. As a consequence, some elderly people remained away from their relatives even after the program ended.

Since the early 1970s, though, the Tribe established a residence called the Shelter Care Home for the elderly on the reservation, and an Older Adults Center offers hot lunches, group activities, and housekeeping assistance. Nearby in Globe, a nursing home which has some Apache staff also houses some elderly Apache people (Searles, personal communication, 1991).

Relocation: Individualization by Removal

The strategy of removing individuals from the reservation dates back to the boarding-school concept. In some ways it complements more collectively focused programs designed to incorporate the Apache as a population. The Employment Assistance Program, generally known as "relocation," was a set of BIA initiatives beginning on a nationwide scale in the 1950s to encourage people to leave reservations permanently and find a place in the wider society. It had some impact in San Carlos, although not necessarily the effects its proponents anticipated.

A substantial number of people in San Carlos participated in relocation over the years. In October 1970, for example, ten people enrolled in various government-sponsored off-reservation employment programs. They left San Carlos to go to Chicago for welding training, to Los Angeles for "direct employment," to San Jose for body- and fender-repair training, to Roswell, New Mexico, for police training and direct employment, to Madera, California, for direct employment, and to Albuquerque for nurse's training. Two others began work for the Inspiration Consolidated Copper Company in Miami, Arizona, although this is only about thirty miles from San Carlos. The rate of people leaving San Carlos that month was not much different from that of June, 1963, when twelve families or individuals left San Carlos for cities as far away as Cleveland.

By 1960 about 35,000 Native Americans throughout the United States had relocated from reservations to cities (Stewart 1965:502–503). By 1972 the number of participants had risen to 100,000 (Snipp 1989:269), although a large proportion of these people returned to reservations. Vicki Page notes that this was true of about half of the Navajo participants (1985:23). The emphasis was on voluntary participation in the program, but as one person pointed out at the 1960 Indian Chicago Conference, in most cases relocation was not truly voluntary but impelled by economic pressures (Lurie 1961). In a policy statement in 1956, the Association on American Indian Affairs described relocation as a means of "letting desperation force them to abandon their homes and destroy their communities, eliminating an ugly picture by the dissemination of Indian poverty, individual by individual, until it disappears in the slums of the nation" (Association on American Indian Affairs 1956).

Some of the problems people were likely to encounter when they relocated from reservations had to do with the rural nature of their backgrounds. Others stemmed from more specific cultural factors. Language can be troublesome for people from reservations like San Carlos. Conflicts of values and attitudes can be still more difficult. Anglo-American society's emphasis on competitiveness, which has long been a major source of trouble for Native American children in public schools (see Havighurst 1957), often made it difficult for people to adjust to urban society where interpersonal relationships seemed harsh and antagonistic.

Because many people from reservations lacked skills that might have been in demand in the labor market, any jobs they could find tended to be strenuous, boring, and low-paying. Relocated people often found that after meeting the costs of life in the city, they were no better off than they had been on the reservation (see Ablon 1964; Graves 1970). Many people keenly felt the absence of kin they could have depended on for assistance, companionship, good cheer, or merely predictable behavior. Culture shock and acute depression overwhelmed relocatees in the run-down sections of the city to which the impoverished segments of the urban population tend to be relegated. Problems were aggravated in many cases by bigotry on the part of people they encountered.

Relocatees often attempted to relieve depression and anxiety through heavy drinking. Arrest rates for Native Americans are often higher in cities than they are on reservations. An individual lying on the sidewalk or sitting on a curb is more likely to draw the attention of police and be arrested in a city than in the more rural reservation setting.

Altogether, these and other factors inhibited the success of relocation programs. In many cases, moreover, people have a genuine attachment to the reservation despite its many problems, since they have spent their lives in the community and are enmeshed in a network of relationships there.

Referring to the Western Apache community at Cibecue on the Fort Apache Reservation, Keith Basso notes: "In a very real sense, the Apache categorizes all other beings on the basis of whether or not they are related to him. As individuals with whom he lives, works, and participates in ceremonial activities, relatives stand fundamentally opposed to nonrelatives, who are generally distrusted and approached with cautious formality" (1966:164).

Relocatees also worried about whether the old people would be properly cared for in their absence. Kinship bonds imply obligations as well as expectations, and many elderly people rely on their relatives for care and sustenance. Generally, older people are attached to their grandchildren and great-grandchildren, and they view their important role in child rearing as a responsibility. For Apache and many other Native Americans, this is a profoundly important relationship, and the loss of grandchildren is a deprivation for both parties. Sometimes the elders exerted pressure to keep the family together. One older woman's eyes filled with tears at the prospect of her grandchildren moving away. "It's sure going to be quiet around here," she remarked.

San Carlos is physically and socially isolated from the surrounding society in many ways, and attitudes on both sides support continuing separatism. People are keenly sensitive to the attitudes of others, and they may view the prospect of living among strangers in a foreign setting, isolated from their close relatives, with misgivings. Reinforcing this is the reservation's pull as a place of refuge. People in San Carlos may travel to Phoenix or Tucson for short visits, but although the Apache style of life is gregarious, it is not urban. As one man put it, "The reservation is the Indian's home base."

Yet despite these considerations, large numbers of Apache living in San Carlos have had some experience living away from the reservation for one reason or another. To find an Apache adult between the ages of twenty and fifty who has not spent some time away is difficult. Many Apache men have gone into the military, with the Marine Corps apparently the most popular choice. Throughout the country the military has long been an option for young people with meager economic prospects. Recounting one person's experience in World War II, a man said: "A lot of guys from around here were captured by the Germans and the Japanese, but every one of the Apaches escaped except him. He said he sure tried plenty of times, but he couldn't get out, and he stayed in the camp all through the war. They sure kidded him when he first came back. They used to call him P.O.W."

Considering all of these factors, that the number of people who returned to the reservation almost equaled the number who left on relocation may not be surprising. Probably many of those who left San Carlos planned to return eventually in any case. The numbers involved are somewhat difficult to assess because in San Carlos and many other reservations people repeatedly leave and return to spend time with their kin, alternating between urban centers and the reservation for years.

Relocation did serve as a convenient catapult for some people. Most reasons for leaving had to do with economic pressures, the desire for a better standard of living and the wish to "give the kids a better chance." As a contrast to the economic problems on the reservation, the BIA made relocation sound attractive to encourage people to take part in the programs.

Many young people hoped to benefit personally from outside experience. This did not necessarily imply that they were alienated from the reservation community. On the contrary, many had a strong sense of self-identification as Apache but felt that they would remain disadvantaged as long as they stayed on the reservation and lacked wider experience. An apparent motive for seeking this experience was a desire to achieve greater social impact, both on and off the reservation, and to develop the ability to cope with the challenges and problems of contemporary life. This did not necessarily involve any diminished sense of themselves as Apache.

The experiences of particular people who left San Carlos on relocation reveal some things about the implementation of the program. One young woman left for vocational training but dropped out when she became dissatisfied with it. She remained in California working for an organization that provided free legal advice for Native Americans, but she returned periodically to visit her relatives in San Carlos. Her brother had enrolled in a training program in a technical field through the BIA in San Carlos in what he understood to be a college in California. When he arrived there, the officials told him that no such training was available. Instead, they enrolled him in another "college" that turned out to be a rundown schoolhouse set up for vocational training. The next time he saw his sister he told her that he was ashamed to let her know what he was taking and that he had no books, only work clothes.

His sister angrily called the man in the San Carlos BIA office who had enrolled her brother and demanded to know why he had been misled. She reminded him that her brother had been a capable student and said: "You think the Indians are so dumb because they're Indians. If they were white people you'd put them in college . . . He deserves something better."

The BIA counselor did not respond to this directly but asked her for her name and then "put her on hold" to check her file. Unintimidated, she told him that she worked for a legal service that already had brought suit against the BIA in many cases of this sort. She told him that she was determined not to let this happen to her brother. In parting, she promised to seek an attorney if the matter was not cleared up to her satisfaction.

This situation shows a blend of old ways and modern problems. The close, supportive ties between brother and sister are evident, and his tone of respect and deference was appropriate between siblings of the opposite sex. But perhaps more significant was their wish that he receive a more academic type of education and their frustration at being thwarted. She reacted strongly to the perceived implication that Native Americans should not have access to demanding academic work.

Joseph Jorgensen, in discussing the history of government policies of this sort, notes that "the focus in the education programs was on services, skills and trades; not on management, investments, or the professions" (1978). Nikos Poulantzas has pointed out the ways in which the distinction between intellectual and manual labor reinforces state hegemony (1980:54–62). In this case, the sister also demonstrated the ability to use the strategies of other interest groups within the Anglo-American state—an attorney, threat of suit, and the like—with dexterity as a lever against the BIA. This is likely to be an important trend in the future in San Carlos as the Apache succeed more and more in penetrating what Poulantzas has called a "state secret": access to the law (1980:90).

Bureaucratic errors probably account for some people's return from relocation, but people have come back for many other reasons as well. One man took his family to Oakland but stayed there only for one week. Once he was there, he found that the expected support from the BIA did not materialize, and he disliked his job and the living conditions in the city. Like many others, he found that despite his higher wages, the cost of rent, utilities, and other necessities whittled down his resources until his real standard of living was no higher than it had been in San Carlos. Another man in his forties with a family of four who owned some cattle in San Carlos went to Dallas. He was unable to hold his first job, and because of his age, lack of education, and ethnic background, he had difficulties finding another. His teenage daughter "got in trouble" as a result of "running around with the wrong crowd." After a year this family, too, returned to the reservation.

Individual reactions to the relocation experience were not uniform. Sometimes they manifested themselves in a tendency to drink more heavily following the return to San Carlos, perhaps generated by a feeling of hopelessness after an unsuccessful attempt to improve the quality of life for themselves and their families. In other cases, though, people resumed life in San Carlos with a greater sense of Apache identity.

Frequently the experience reinforced their negative assessments of Anglo-American society. Having viewed it from the reservation, some tended to develop inaccurate impressions of the wealth, prosperity, and general style of living of the non-Apache populace. Television perpetuates this misinformation on a continual basis. For most, urban living brought about a revision of these impressions. Relocatees often were low-wage earners who precipitated out to the lower economic strata and often found their way to "Indian ghettos," and in many cases life in the city was far less pleasant than anticipated. Some people came back to San Carlos with a greater regard for their own background, coupled with a more realistic awareness of contemporary Anglo-American society as the poor of the cities experience it.

Such episodes probably tended to increase resistance to assimilation, just as exposure to a weakened virus can stimulate resistance to future infection. Having lived in a city for a time and acquired some of the basic skills necessary to survive there, they were not so easily duped in dealings with outsiders. They understood more of the American socioeconomic structure, including some of the leverage points at which they could deal with it most effectively. As in the past, many Apache acquired skills useful for survival in their contemporary environment.

One man who had spent several years as a migrant farm worker off the reservation was a proponent of voter registration in San Carlos. In his personal life he scrupulously observed traditional patterns. He usually spoke in Apache rather than in English, although he was fluent in both, and he carefully honored Apache patterns of etiquette. This man easily accommodated an adherence to Apachean cultural forms and participation in the external political system, observing that the development of more political consciousness in San Carlos is essential to the ultimate survival of the people.

Potential voters in San Carlos number only a few thousand, but they were enough to lead to the gerrymandering of the Arizona State Legislature which the Federal Court overturned. The total Native American population in the Southwest is large enough to constitute a major voting bloc on issues of common interest. People do take a strong interest in tribal elections, and the Tribal Council recently changed their election date to coincide with state and national elections in order to increase voting participation.

Ambiguities in the Role of the Government

Clearly, to understand life on a reservation without considering the extent to which the government is involved in the lives of the people would be impossible. But involved to what end?

The central rationale for government policies is that the people of reservations need help and that the government has a responsibility to assist them. Health, economic, educational, and social problems have all been targets of government programs over the years. Many individuals who have worked as agents of the government have devoted their lives with genuine good will to addressing these problems.

We might consider why it is that reservation populations need this help. Government programs have been based on the assumption that the people are unable to solve their own problems; but the actions of that same government have much to do with why these problems became unmanageable in the first place. The state has confiscated resources and divested the people of most significant decision-making power over their own affairs. Government employees on the reservation are in no position to address this fundamental problem. They may counsel people on immediate concerns and crises, but the programs they implement are not designed to strengthen the sovereignty of people on reservations and allow them to reclaim control over their resources. This severely constrains the extent to which they can, in the end, truly help.

Bigotry and incompetence on the part of a few government agents on various reservations also precipitate many individual tragedies. Senator James Abourezk, in a letter to the *New York Times*, observed: "[The BIA's] approach of oppressive paternalism and unimaginative programs make solution of Indian problems impossible. But the bureau has become adept at one thing—survival management. Survival of the bureau and the jobs of those who so miserably manage the lives of Indians results in such high disregard for the Indians, and the concomitant problems with which they must live" (December 21, 1987). But these are more symptoms than causes of the deeper problem.

To the extent that government programs are intended to induce assimilation, bringing Native Americans "into the mainstream," they undermine the capacity of the people to act in their own interest. They inhibit the impact of Native American communities as interest groups competing with other, powerful interest groups within the state. At the same time, the very appropriation of resources and power keeps people on reservations from being incorporated into the state in any capacity except as additions to the disenfranchised, impoverished underclass. Resisting this, the people remain a tiny, beleaguered enclave within the global system.

Subsistence in a Cash Economy

In late summer, people in San Carlos still journey to the areas where acorns of the Emery's oak grow in abundance. In the 1960s they returned with their distinctive fringed burden baskets loaded with the acorns. Now they are likely to use other containers ranging from gunnysacks to coffee cans (Searles, personal communication, 1991). People use the acorns in many dishes, but this variety is also tasty out of the shell. People in San Carlos also still hunt. To assess the impact of such activities on the food supply is difficult, but it does not seem likely that they amount to any large proportion of the total subsistence needs for most people in San Carlos. Their major value seems to be that they are enjoyable, and the food they produce is a welcome addition to the regular fare. The Western Apache, immersed in a cash economy, can no longer subsist on wild foods without money.

The cattle industry, a major enterprise in the State of Arizona, is one of the most important sources of income in San Carlos. During the early years of the reservation a few people had tried to raise cattle, but although the government apparently encouraged them, the results were disappointing. The reservation superintendent's report of 1913 states: "About three years ago 500 head of cattle were issued to Indians. But approximately half of these cattle can be rounded up at this time. A surreptitious slaughter of these animals has been going on, and some of it has been due to stern necessity—the need for food" (quoted in Getty 1963:27).

There had been no experience of raising livestock before the reservation years, although raiding for horses, mules, and cattle had been an important part of Apache subsistence. But since the people easily adopted many other cultural innovations, it does not seem likely that a simple conservative cultural resistance to change would account for the early failures of the cattle herds.

Part of the problem was also that the government had leased most of the best grazing land on the reservation to non-Apache ranchers. Adding to this problem, outsiders sometimes encroached illegally on other Apache lands. In 1922, a prolonged dispute over the southern boundary of the reservation culminated in the fence being moved to allow a non-Apache rancher to graze his cattle on what had been considered reservation land. After a good deal of correspondence with constituents about this issue, Congressman Carl Hayden of Arizona wrote to the Secretary of the Interior: "In regard to the elimination of certain lands from the San Carlos Indian Reservation. Could this be accomplished by executive order?" Commissioner of Indian Affairs Charles H. Burke responded on April 20, 1922, stating that a resurvey of the boundary adjusting the boundaries to eliminate "said lands" had already been carried out in 1915 and approved in 1916 (Hayden Coll. 622/8).

The cattle-raising enterprise now has become the largest single economic activity on the reservation, although many economic problems remain. It began as a means of alleviating some of these problems and involving the Apache in the market system of the United States. Proponents offered it as a major step in the acculturative process. As a government pamphlet from the early 1960s expressed it, "since the

Indians are now living in a country predominantly non-Indian in culture and economy, they must be assisted in making the necessary adjustments to these environmental conditions and equip themselves to handle their own affairs" (Bureau of Indian Affairs n.d.:1).

By 1963 the cattle industry was sufficiently well established for the San Carlos Tribal Council chairman to write that "the economy of the San Carlos Apache Reservation is primarily devoted to the production of livestock" (Mull 1963:1). This statement requires some elaboration, however. Many people draw some income from cattle sales, and for a few, the enterprise has been lucrative. But cattle raising has not had the pervasive social and economic impact in San Carlos that some predicted a couple of generations ago. Despite its status as the largest single subsistence enterprise, fewer than half of the families in San Carlos own any cattle at all. Of these who do own some, the income for most is small. Cattle raising is a major source of income in San Carlos partly because income sources overall are meager.

The Tribe and a handful of cattle associations, whose recruitment is based largely on kinship, carry out most cattle raising. Association cattle herds totaled fourteen thousand head in 1962 (Herbert and Herbert 1963). This was a substantial increase over the tribal herd of 1921, which amounted to 4052. In that year, the superintendent estimated that forty-five to fifty thousand non-Apache cattle were grazing under permit on the reservation (Hayden Coll. 622/8). Cattle sales in 1963 paid $633,000 to owners, with an additional $293,000 to the Tribe for grazing fees and sales tax (Herbert and Herbert 1963). But grazing range is limited and much in demand.

In 1970 the Tribal Council had a long list of individuals waiting to be issued cattle, but sufficient participation in the cattle enterprise has been a chronic problem. Owning cattle brings income on sales, just as it would anywhere else, whether or not the owner does any work with the herd. Many owners do not, and some cannot.

Range work is difficult, with long hours and few material rewards. Many people are reluctant to undergo the isolation that may last a month or more at a time. Cattle roam free on the grazing ranges during most of the year, but periodic roundups are necessary for branding calves, selecting stock to sell, finding strays, and driving herds to the auction pens. Associations fine their members who fail to take part in this work, but in most cases the fines are not enough to compel people to participate. The funds are used to hire additional help, but not many young men are available for this type of work.

Handling cattle requires a complex set of skills which take considerable experience to acquire. Good horsemanship is not the least of these, but only a small minority of Apache own or have access to horses. And the pay for this work is extremely low. In 1963 it amounted to between five and seven dollars a day, and in that part of Arizona outside the reservation, ranch owners routinely paid Apache cowboys a dollar or two less per day than Anglos.

Some owners have complained that young men who participate in roundups run the cattle too hard, possibly because of their inexperience. This causes weight loss and creates mavericks, cattle that leave the herd and go wild. In 1970 a cattle owner mentioned that the cowboys had killed one of his steers by being too rough with it, choking it too tightly with the lariat. "They're supposed to pay me for it," he said, "but I don't know when they're going to do it."

By taking a personal part in this activity the owner could have saved the price of a fine and prevented the loss of his cattle. But he was an older man, and he was no longer physically capable of range work. If he could participate in the roundup he could see that calves that "mothered up" to his cows were branded, and he could chase down mavericks bearing his brand and bring them back to the herd. But many cattle owners, because of age, illness, or other reasons, are unable to take part in such strenuous activity. Despite the relative importance of the cattle enterprise in the San Carlos economy, raising cattle is not a predominant activity in the lives of most people.

One cattle owner in late middle age who no longer participated as much as he once had in cattle raising gestured toward his wife's relatives and said: "I used to feed all these people when I was young, just married. I was the only one that owned cattle." He reminisced about the days when he sometimes would slaughter a steer among the dwellings and divide up the meat. But he said that he could no longer do that without a five-dollar permit from the Tribe. He grumbled that the regulation requiring an owner to secure permission to slaughter his own beef was unreasonable.

This man said that he had given his son fifteen heifers a few years earlier to start his own herd, but the son had left for three years in the Marines and now had a job in Phoenix, where he had let his hair grow long "like a hippie" and apparently had no interest in raising cattle. The older man claimed that the expenses involved in cattle raising were burdensome, and he enumerated corral repair fees, grazing fees, branding fees, and other costs.

During the past decade or so the cattle industry in general also suffered from a decline in the consumer demand for beef. Although the 1960s and 1970s boded well for beef producers, in the 1980s beef prices dropped as middle-class Americans from Los Angeles to Long

Island turned to white wine, chicken breast, and fillet of sole. Cattle raisers found themselves dealing with an indifferent market, and during those years the San Carlos cattle enterprise waned. In the late 1980s there has been an attempt to revise and reorganize, and recovery of the Mineral Strip may increase the available grazing land.

Employment and Unemployment

Although there are varied sources of income in San Carlos, no single source can support more than a small proportion of the population. A few people from San Carlos have worked for wages off the reservation in the open-pit copper mines and smelters of the Inspiration Consolidated Copper Company in Miami, a few miles west of Globe, or in the local lumbering industry. An asbestos mine operated on the reservation for a few years, but the market for asbestos dropped precipitously. The Bureau of Indian Affairs employs some Apache people, and a few more are smoke jumpers for the Bureau of Land Management and parachute from airplanes to fight brush fires during the dry season. Still more have had jobs in the tribal enterprises or private businesses that operate on the reservation—stores, service stations, and a small restaurant.

In recent decades the total employment resulting from these several sources has involved from a quarter to a third of the labor force. Some women also collect peridot, a semiprecious gem, for sale to dealers in nearby towns, and some make cradleboards or baskets for sale. In 1963, an article in *Arizona Highways* magazine noted that "according to figures prepared by the Bureau of Indian Affairs, the labor force on the San Carlos Reservation is 1,500 persons, of whom 75%, or 1,225, are unemployed" (Herbert and Herbert 1963).

In 1969, the unemployment figure based on an estimated total labor force of 2,200 was 1,560 (Confederation of American Indians 1986:26). Based on U.S. Census data, C. Matthew Snipp calculates this in terms of labor force participation, which includes individuals over the age of sixteen who were recorded either as employed or having actively sought employment within four weeks of the date of the survey (1989). In 1969 these amounted to 33.5 percent of the adult population, of whom 13.1 percent were unemployed (Snipp 1989: 226). These numbers indicate that 20.4 percent of the adult population at the time of the survey had jobs. Unemployment figures reflect the number of people who register at the employment office, but as one observer put it: "Apaches aren't stupid. They know there aren't any jobs, so they don't always bother to show up at the employment office to register first thing Monday morning." In 1979 the labor force participation in San Carlos had risen to 59.1 percent, of whom 21.1 percent were unemployed, which suggests a total unemployment rate near 50 percent of the potential work force (Snipp 1989:226).

At one time in the 1970s the official unemployment figure dropped to an incredible 19 percent, although the basis for this calculation is not clear. Certainly this anomalous statistic did not reflect the true state of affairs. The BIA figures show unemployment from 1970 to 1974 fluctuating between 60 percent and 70 percent (Bureau of Indian Affairs 1981:65). By the mid 1980s, according to the tribal chairman, the rate was back around 70 percent. Whatever the causes for fluctuations in these figures, they reveal a persistent dearth of jobs.

The average income per family in 1963 was twelve hundred dollars (Herbert and Herbert 1963). In 1969 it had increased only to $2,626, with an average yearly income per capita of $525.20 (Confederation of American Indians 1986:26). The *median* family income for that year, presumably reflecting a few disproportionately high cases, was $7932, with 62.3 percent of the families below the poverty line (Snipp 1989:260). By 1979 the median family income in San Carlos had risen only to $7986, for a gain of fifty-four dollars in ten years (Snipp 1989:260). That year the census figures showed 53.6 percent of the families in San Carlos below the poverty line.

The *average* family income in San Carlos in 1982, based on combined sources including such things as peridot collecting, part-time work, and social assistance, was about five thousand dollars (Schmidt 1983). This included a broad range of variation. Most of the people with full-time employment worked for the Bureau of Indian Affairs, and their salaries were above the average. Others made a good deal less. By contrast, the average non-white American family income in 1982 was $15,211. For white families, it was $24,603. The average income *per person* in the United States that year was $11,100—more than twice as much as the average for an entire Apache family (*Information Please Almanac Atlas and Yearbook* 1983:50).

The few Apache jobs in the open pit copper mines dried up in the early 1980s when the price of copper fell on the world market. Unemployment in Gila County as a whole, which includes Globe and Miami, was 34.9 percent in 1983 (Schmidt 1983). In the late 1980s the Inspiration Consolidated Mine all but closed its doors and retained only a skeleton work force. In September, 1987, the previous year's Christmas greeting still hung across the face of one of its buildings. This cutback staggered the economy of the local region, but the on-again, off-again nature of copper mining has many facets in the local area. In general, the Apache were not much affected by those layoffs. Despite the fact that the copper mines are on land that once was within the reservation boundaries, the Apache never had benefited much from the copper. The layoffs did not much affect Apache who had not been hired in the first place.

One might suspect that as miners were laid off, they might take up alternative jobs in the region and crowd Apache workers out. But according to the perceptions of many people in the area, local businesses have an understanding with mine management not to hire out-of-work miners. When miners are out of work in Globe or Miami, they often look for jobs in the Phoenix area a hundred miles to the west. The few jobs available to Apache are not particularly threatened by laid-off miners, and the copper company labor force, unable to find alternative local employment, are held in reserve until they are needed once again.

There have been very few jobs in Globe for Apache at any time. Until a few years ago, Apache women in their long dresses could not be reasonably certain of courteous treatment in many of the stores, although now a few work as clerks in a couple of the local supermarkets.

The asbestos mine that had operated for years closed down when the dangers of asbestos became a matter of public concern. In the early 1980s, a privately owned sawmill that had operated on the reservation for decades closed down with very little warning, and seventy-five Apache workers lost their jobs. As Council Chairman Buck Kitcheyan noted, that meant over "400 hungry mouths." The diner and one of the trading posts also closed.

Commercial timber interests cut trees in the high country of the reservation for many years, and the ecological effects became more and more severe as erosion took a heavy toll. In the 1980s, two consultants, one federal and one hired by the Tribe, both concluded that further timber cutting on the reservation would bring soil erosion to a critical state. But the tribal government was in a dire financial situation and desperately needed the income. As a result, they agreed to another multiyear lease allowing timber cutting over additional thousands of acres. Since the sawmill on the edge of the reservation had fallen idle, the Apache timber went elsewhere to be cut into lumber.

The Tribe has run or endorsed a long list of enterprises ranging from a Christmas-tree farm to a resort area near Coolidge Dam. But the resort faltered when the government ruled that the buildings were substandard. A bowling alley closed down because of chronic vandalism. An irrigation project to develop cotton farming fell through,

Small business, San Carlos

and land under cultivation in San Carlos fell from seven hundred to three hundred acres by 1988 (Kitcheyan, personal communication, 1988). The late 1970s brought some optimism about marketing the jojoba beans from a shrub that grows in abundance among the rocky hills of San Carlos. The seeds of the plant contain an oil marketable to the cosmetic industry. In 1981, San Carlos sold $250,000 worth of jojoba seeds to a Japanese cosmetic firm, but in the following year the Japanese buyers found a better deal in Mexico, and the budding jojoba bean enterprise foundered (Schmidt 1983).

In 1981 and 1982, welfare payments in San Carlos rose 25 percent. In the same period, the federal government cut funding for economic development and job training by 30 percent (Schmidt 1983). The Community Action Program office closed. The Internal Revenue Service filed a claim against the Tribe for over a million dollars in taxes it had failed to withhold from employees' paychecks. In the midst of all this, President Ronald Reagan declared that Indian communities needed to be more self-sufficient. Secretary of the Interior James Watt announced on television that the poverty on Indian reservations demonstrated the "failure of socialism" (Schmidt 1983).

Tribal store, San Carlos

The Regional Economic Environment

Although the San Carlos Reservation includes 1,827,421 acres of land (Bureau of Indian Affairs 1981:65), most of the population is clustered in the small communities of San Carlos and Peridot and along Seven Mile Wash and Gilson Wash, which lie approximately twenty miles to the east of Globe. The settlement at Bylas to the east is closer to Safford. The reservation boundary on the west is only a few miles from Globe. This town is the primary buying center for the people of San Carlos, since it is the nearest commercial center to San Carlos and is accessible by a paved highway. Despite the ambivalence in relations between San Carlos and Globe, they are strongly linked by economic bonds.

Although the tribe has operated a store on the reservation for decades, many consumer items are not available in San Carlos. Even when they are, prices there tend to be higher than they are in Globe. Alcoholic beverages are another incentive for travel to Globe. The Tribal Council has ruled that no alcohol can be sold on the reservation, and the illegal bootleggers there tend to charge twice the normal price. The purchase and service of cars and pickup trucks, clothing, groceries, and movies all draw Apache money into Globe and, to a lesser extent, Safford.

Since the reservation brings thousands of additional consumers into a market that would otherwise serve about six to eight thousand, the economic importance of San Carlos to Globe is substantial. A few merchants recognize this. In the 1960s some of them advertised in the monthly tribal newspaper. One grocery store owner proclaimed himself "Friend of the Apaches." Another announced that "We Welcome Apache People" (*Apache Drumbeat*, July 1963). Many area businesses more recently advertised in the San Carlos weekly newspaper *Moccasin*.

Globe has lost population in recent years, largely because of its economic problems. The San Carlos population, however, has increased. Although the Bureau of Indian Affairs in 1981 listed the number of Apache in San Carlos as a little over six thousand, in 1987 some Apache estimated that the population was closer to ten thousand. Whatever the causes for this difference, it means that San Carlos now is at least as large as Globe, and the impact of the Apache on the economy of Gila County is even greater than before.

This economic importance of San Carlos remains unrecognized by many people in Globe, however. The relative poverty of the Apache is evident to residents of the town, and Apache purchasing power tends to be low compared with that of people off the reservation. Yet although most people from the reservation have little income, their spending is proportionately higher than it is among most of the population of Globe, since the Apache have little cash surplus. Close to 100 percent of Apache income is necessarily directed toward consumption and poured back into the market.

Interpersonal Relationships

Apache are forced to participate in the external market because older means of subsistence are no longer adequate or possible, and some cash is necessary for survival. But despite numerous collective enterprises, there is little evidence of entrepreneurial competitiveness at the individual level. The poverty of the reservation, with little surplus cash, is certainly one of the most salient features of this, but various leveling mechanisms tend to reinforce it.

Social censure, usually in the form of gossip, discourages hoarding and inhibits conspicuous consumption. The strength of kinship obligations also makes the accumulation of wealth difficult. Regarding the nature of such leveling mechanisms, one community leader

stated, "Every day people come to me . . . they try to put down somebody else, and, . . . you know, somebody is getting ahead over here
and then they want to put him down, or her down." Another man
recounted the pretensions of a relative who had acquired a high-
paying seasonal construction job and purchased a new car. "We're
really getting high up now," the relative had gloated. "Well," replied
the other, with some pleasure in the retelling, "if you're so high up,
you'd better be careful you don't fall."

These statements reflect only one side of an ethic that stresses and
rewards the generous distribution of resources and the recognition of
strong reciprocal kin relationships. The imperative of generosity conflicts with the standard capitalistic prescription of saving and rein-
vestment. But one could argue that by following the pattern of generosity, people in San Carlos are investing in personal relationships
worth a great deal to them in enhancing the quality of their lives.

Beyond its necessity for survival, cash becomes capital for purposes that are less clearly materialistic. When surplus or windfall
money becomes available, perhaps through cattle sales, people often
use it to promote traditional and celebrative activities. The female puberty ceremony is a major example. At times people have advertised
ceremonies in the newspaper. Pit-barbecued beef, beer, cigarettes,
candy, and cases of pop are lavished on the crowd. This involves a
tremendous expense for the family and their relatives. The magnitude
of the cost is especially numbing when one considers the average annual income per family. Rather than being allocated to individual
capital or savings, cash becomes a means of reaffirming and establishing solidarity between the spender and his or her relatives. As a result
of this, large sums of money may seem to disappear within a few
days, spent on kin and friends.

These expenditures and more general expressions toward money
suggest that neither the cattle industry nor other programs or innovations in San Carlos have generated a profit-maximizing ethic on the
Euro-American model. Returns from cattle sales feed into other aspects of life in San Carlos and, in turn, incorporate the cattle industry
into the existing social structure. Cattle sales have come to support
older Apache patterns and have become a means of strengthening
some aspects of tradition rather than inducing radical change. The
major criterion for recruitment into the cattle associations is kinship,
and cattle sales underwrite the puberty ceremonies which epitomize
the reassertion of Apache cultural identity.

With regard to the Navajo, David Aberle states: "It is my belief that
traditional Navajo kinship organization is maintained because of,
rather than despite, changes in the Navajo economy—that, indeed,

traditional kinship organization, oriented earlier to the multiple, fluctuating resources of the traditional economy, preserves that same orientation now that the Navajo are marginal participants in the larger United States economy (see Aberle 1963, 1969). Relying on multiple fluctuating resources, which include flocks, farms, crafts, wage work, and welfare, most families have no single source of livelihood sufficient in quality or reliability to induce them to give up the others" (1980).

The interplay between the overall scarcity of resources, the value system that developed earlier in Apache history, and the uneven initial distribution of what little wealth does exist all stimulate redistribution. Where this takes place, kinship ties constitute the most common avenues. The ancestors of the Apache, as mountain-dwelling hunting-and-gathering people, developed social and cultural strategies to deal with a sparse and uncertain subsistence base. The nature of that subsistence base has changed, but it continues to be sparse and uncertain, and the distributive mechanisms continue to operate. As thinly as profits from cattle are spread, they reach more people in this manner than they otherwise might.

Perspectives on the Present

The present situation of the San Carlos Apache is rife with serious and often life-threatening problems. Do they stem from the cultural system's incapacity to provide for human needs? When we consider the resiliency and the success of the people through thousands of miles and hundreds of years from Alaska to the Southwest, this seems unlikely. What, then, is at the root of these problems? What is different about the present situation?

One difference is the loss of autonomy and the corresponding loss of control over land and other resources. The relationship between San Carlos and the state prevents the community from becoming entirely viable and self-sufficient. San Carlos is not economically "underdeveloped." It is locked into a situation in which the state has appropriated decision-making power. Resources and energies are tapped for the benefit of people elsewhere to whom the word "Apache" conjures little more than the image of a wild-eyed warrior in a mediocre movie about the "winning of the West."

Mineral deposits that could have provided an important economic resource for the Apache, had they not been excised from the reservation when their worth became known, provide the economic base for the surrounding towns of Clifton, Morenci, Globe, Miami, and Claypool to the east and west. The owners of these mines manage their wealth in the distant board rooms of major copper corporations. For a few dollars a day, young men on the San Carlos Reservation herd cattle whose prime ribs grace the menus of restaurateurs in cities from coast to coast. Apache who raise and sell the steers can rarely afford to eat prime cuts of beef. Some writers have referred to this situation as neocolonial.

CHAPTER 8

Trajectories and Trends

> Capitalism did not develop by accident; its expansion was not left to chance. The drive to accumulate capital and to create the political and institutional framework necessary for its security, expansion, and perpetuation form a dominant theme in North American history. (Katz, Doucet, and Stern 1982:2)

The American state entails a set of conditions. These conditions have their own history, and they constrain the choices of individuals. With regard to the reservation system, they have created similar phenomena in multiple cases. Although this discussion has focused on the San Carlos Reservation in Arizona, much of it applies to other reservations despite the profound differences in the cultural backgrounds of Native American populations. Some years ago Edward Spicer wrote: "As one goes from reservation to reservation, the feeling grows that what one sees today is what one saw not long before on some other reservation . . . In other words, 'culture contact' feels very much the same in these two widely separated places where people have had such different historical experiences. The sense of coming repeatedly into the same situations intensifies as one goes from, let us say, the San Carlos Apache Reservation in Arizona to the Rosebud Sioux Reservation in South Dakota and so on throughout the country" (1961:1–2).

The details of local history differ, but in many ways they represent the same process of state incorporation, with similar results. In *Apachería*, early motives for Anglo-American incursions sprang from the dynamics of a monetary system and the concept of property ownership. In that context, the need for money and a prevailing system of values that applauded the quest for wealth furnished an underlying impetus to bring outsiders into the territory. The possibility of finding wealth in the lands the Apache occupied and the self-justifying view depicting Native American populations as cultural anachronisms added to this set of conditions.

The apparatus of government, serving constituencies motivated by their own perceived interests, acted accordingly. Policies favored some over others and, when necessary, effected compromises among competing interests. The individuals made decisions within the contemporary sense of what would be right, justifiable, feasible, and desirable. They evaluated and applied such criteria in the context of a developing system of industrial capitalism.

In the early phases of the Arizona Territory, the government's presence in the form of the army was relatively innocuous. As the population of settlers increased and the conflict with Apache became more acute, the army came to the settlers' assistance in a more concerted way. Eventually the local citizenry, who had become dependent on selling supplies to the military and had an interest in perpetuating a state of chronic warfare to justify the army's continued presence, came into conflict with copper interests. Those interests were manifestations of a burgeoning industrial capitalism, and they required pacification of the area to get on with the large-scale appropriation of its resources.

In this phase the local settlers, the army, industrial interests, and factions within the federal government operated in a push-and-shove whose outcome eventually was to neutralize the Apache, forcibly removing them from their resource base and establishing hegemony over their territory. Industrial interests, the most powerful of the lot, prevailed in influencing the policies of the state. Viewed at higher magnification, we can see this played out in the series of presidential decisions and executive orders that repeatedly removed valuable lands from Apache possession to offer them up to the "public." The sector of the public most capable of exploiting this were corporate interests with sufficient capital to acquire the lands and extract their minerals.

Throughout all of this, the state was not a mystical, faceless entity with a life of its own. There were plenty of faces and plenty of individuals who made a variety of choices. Still, to see these historical processes as the result of a few crucial decisions made here and there by key people for idiosyncratic reasons would be a mistake. People chose courses of action within the context of relationships and motivations based on the ground rules of capitalism, and given the circumstances, they acted in a rational, pragmatic manner. The situations they confronted set limits on the range of feasible and effective choices, and the ideology of the times afforded a rationale.

Certainly many individuals made choices that diverged from prevailing views. In any age, there usually are people willing to swim against the tide. But often, such choices were ineffective. Vincent Colyer's peace initiatives were a dismal failure, at least partly because they were in conflict with too many more-powerful interests. While historical processes ultimately reduce to individual behavior, collectively such behavior has its own trajectory, channeled and deflected by preconditions. These circumstances favor some choices over others. The process of state encroachment and the establishment of hegemony over the Apache was such a phenomenon.

Throughout this process, the state has prevented the San Carlos population from adapting by disallowing all options but assimilation. Adaptation implies a group's continued existence through active adjustments to altered circumstances. Assimilation is an end to the group itself, as surviving individuals lose their identities through immersion in the wider and essentially foreign milieu.

The history of Apache relationships with the American state has entailed a series of attempts to remove them in one way or another. At the outset, the army removed the people from most of their land. In the reservation period the government removed more large tracts of land from the people. The local government removed children from their parents, sending them to boarding schools and foster homes. The relocation programs removed families from the reservation. The housing program endeavored to dismantle joint family clusters. And the Public Health Service separated elders from grandchildren. For the Apache in the twentieth century, much of the problem has been to survive these dislocations.

To assume that the personal tragedies caused by government policies have all been the result of malevolent people would be unjust, incorrect, and simplistic. Certainly such people have found a place in American history, but it seems that the more significant causes lie in the nature of the institutions that have engaged the Apache. At the local level, BIA employees in the reservation communities are constrained by their employer and policies arrived at by powerful consensus. In some cases they may be compelled to carry out programs against their better judgment. The power, as in any federal bureaucracy, flows from Washington down to the many local branches, and the organizational distance between the two ends of the structure may be very great indeed. The BIA is a ponderous bureaucracy with strict accountability to Washington, a seat of authority where powerful interests lobby in marble halls remote from the sun-baked, dusty roads of San Carlos.

Probably most individual BIA employees do not see themselves as agents of a capitalist state. Many are people with humanitarian concerns for the indigenous communities where they work. But they often accept the ideology of the state which implies that individualization is preferable to ethnicity. A corollary to this axiom is that such ethnicity, rather than state appropriation of resources and decision- . making power, is the cause of poverty and its related problems. And if one accepts this, then the way to solve problems is by helping to eradicate ethnicity.

The stated goal of the BIA is to "work itself out of a job" by bringing Native Americans "into the mainstream" of middle-class English-speaking America. Consequently, the formal posture of the Bureau entails an unrelenting attack on many of the things that make life worth living for human beings in any society: their heritage and the sense of who they are.

Although the government's stated aims may be to alleviate social problems, the strategy to achieve this has generally been to eradicate the indigenous social organization and culture, incorporate the individuals into the general populace, and open the reservation lands to "productive use." At least two major postulates contribute to this. The first has to do with identification of the root causes of social problems. The idea that "traditional" culture patterns are the basic cause of many problems in reservation communities has been a working assumption on the part of most government agencies. This is one of the fundamental assumptions of the underdevelopment perspective. In this view, it is necessary to do away with the culture patterns that generate these problems in order to solve them. By continuing to live and act as Indians, the argument goes, the people are preventing themselves from developing a "better way of life."

The second and related supposition is that Native American cultures are dying anyway and that it is only a matter of time before the old ways disappear altogether. This view has strong roots in the nineteenth century. A generation or two ago, this assumption justified taking children from their parents and sending them to boarding schools. More recently, it underlay a number of government programs ranging from relocating individuals and families in cities away from the reservation to attempts to undermine the matrilineal structure of the society by altering the residence pattern.

The severe problems that oppress the people of San Carlos—high infant mortality, self-destructive violence, alcoholism—are not features of traditional culture. They are problems that the Apache share with most Native American reservation communities, to some degree, and with impoverished people in the interstices of global capitalism everywhere. This spectrum of communities involves an array of different cultural backgrounds. What they all do have in common is poverty, powerlessness, and immersion in the hegemony of the state.

If the goal of the state were truly to benefit the people rather than to incorporate them, the situation might be different. Every community produces its own leadership, and ideas generated from within the local populace derive from far deeper insights into internal needs and dynamics than any outsider can develop. What is lacking in such cases, very often, is technical expertise, the financial capacity to carry out projects, and the power to implement them. If the BIA could function as a resource agency providing assistance to the community when requested, rather than imposing its own programs, the community probably could accomplish a great deal more. But the BIA is not structured to operate in that way. The policy of "self-determination" instituted in the 1970s, despite the implications of the term and the positive intentions of its initiators, is essentially a matter of allowing reservation communities the option of accepting or declining government programs (Deloria 1983:103).

Even if local resources are developed on reservations, the capital investment generally comes from powerful interests outside the community who then, in all important senses, control and reap the benefits of the enterprise. Local resources—whether minerals, timber, labor, grazing land, or water—typically are extracted to benefit larger interests with minimal return to the local populace.

The Fort Apache community to the north offers an interesting example of alternative possibilities. They recently won a suit against the BIA for mismanagement of the reservation (*White Mountain Apache v. BIA*). Over the past few years they have developed a tremendously successful program of fish and wildlife management and recreational facilities. According to Joseph P. Kalt, they appear now to have one of the finest elk herds in the world.

Kalt notes: "By turning fish and game into *economic* resources for the Apaches, incentives were created to preserve, protect, and invest in these resources. The results are remarkable by any standards and leave the Apaches teaching the rest of the world how to manage multiple-use forests" (1987:45). The White Mountain Apache issue trophy-elk hunting licenses at $10,000 to $15,000 apiece, and the herds "show steady growth under tribal management" (1987:45, 46).

In assessing the positive results of White Mountain Apache tribal enterprises, Kalt observes that "it is conventional wisdom that in or-

Copper company in former Apache territory, Miami, Arizona

der to be truly sovereign polities and economies, Indian reservations
need strong economies and good business environments." He notes
that the Apache case suggests, however, that "to develop strong
economies, tribes need true sovereignty" (Kalt 1987:57; see also Cornell and Gil-Swedberg 1990).

The Fort Apache Reservation does have certain advantages over
San Carlos in having forested high country, and the community itself
is less diverse in terms of historic band membership than San Carlos.
This may have meant fewer obstacles in achieving consensus for concerted efforts toward the development of resources. But far more significant, it seems, has been the capacity of the people of Fort Apache
to make and implement crucial decisions themselves—including the
judicious use of outside consultants—rather than merely following
the lead of government agencies.

Such an example of economic success stands out partly because it
is unusual. It does, however, dispel the stereotypical view that Native
American communities have opposed development of their resources
in principle. As Marjane Ambler puts it in her study of Native American energy development: "No one could assume that tribes would

Billboard between Globe and Miami, Arizona, near Bloody Tanks Wash

meet romanticized expectations and protect 'Mother Earth' at any cost. With staggering unemployment and poverty rates, tribes had even more interest than states in encouraging economic development. Yet tribes had a unique relationship with their lands: They could not relocate. They knew that if they made mistakes or if they were influenced by economic considerations, their grandchildren would be faced with the resulting problems" (1990:202).

Louise Lamphere discusses the example of the Navajo, whose reservation has been the scene of strip-mining for coal: "Peabody, one of America's largest coal companies and a subsidiary of Kennecott Copper, leased rights to strip-mine 13 million tons of coal a year over a period of 35 years on the Black Mesa, a remote plateau in the heart of the Navajo and Hopi Joint Use Area. The Navajo and Hopi receive 25 cents a ton for the coal (12.5 cents for each Tribe for coal mined in the Joint Use area). Peabody resells the coal to a power plant at $4.00 a ton and there are provisions for the payments to increase to 30 cents a ton, if the resale price exceeds $4.00 a ton" (1976:11).

Joseph Jorgensen summarizes the recent history of the development of the Navajo coal enterprise:

[Mining is an] example of BIA and Department of Interior steward-
ship . . . Between 1957 and 1965 the BIA let all but one Navajo coal lease
to multinational corporations at *fixed* royalties between 15¢ and 37½¢
per ton. The national average price for coal in the late 1970s was over
$20 per ton, up over 400 percent in less than a decade. Peabody Coal
and other extractors who have held the leases have not had to renego-
tiate, so they have not renegotiated, and they have reaped windfall
profits from the extraordinary profits they were already making as the
price of coal has risen. Furthermore, many of the BIA-arranged leases
waive the tribe's right to tax the producers, so the tribe has no way to
adjust for their give-away rents and royalties. (1978:53)

The material benefit to the Navajo community in the form of royalties and the few jobs created for individuals have been far too small
to have any significant impact on their needs. In the meantime,
Navajo families were scheduled to be dislocated to make way for the
mining activities, and the estimated 37 billion gallons of water to be
used over the next thirty-five years to transport the coal to power
plants threaten to disastrously lower the water table in an already dry
area (Jorgensen 1978:26).

Reservations are not poor simply because they have failed to progress far enough along the path of development, or because they lack
resources, or because of backward traditional cultures. They are poor
because they are legally powerless to manage their resources and
benefit from them and because they stand in a sociopolitical relationship that all but ensures that whatever resources they do have will be
used to benefit interests that have far more influence over government policies than they do. Social programs to eradicate their traditional cultures are not, for the most part, designed to give Native
Americans power but to incorporate them into the wider society at
the lower socioeconomic strata.

Jorgensen points out that in the 1950s, when the dominant political
rhetoric was toward a disengagement of the government to "free" the
Indian, a familiar pattern prevailed. "The Secretary of Interior, the
Congress, and the BIA continued to settle Indian heirship problems,
lease Indian lands, approve tribal budgets, and let oil and mineral
leases to multinational corporations on behalf of their powerless
wards, while pointing out that Indians were *not* wards of the government" (1978:28).

In 1966 an omnibus bill was proposed to promote assimilation by
doing away with "the old ways and the old paternalism." Nonetheless: "[This bill] vested all final authority over tribal land transactions, mortgages, 99 year leases and the like, in the hands of the
Secretary of Interior. The proposed legislation, like the General Allot-

Copper mine tailings, Miami, Arizona

ment Act and the termination legislation before it, would have dissolved Indian tribes and sent potential wage earners to the city" (Jorgensen 1978:26).

Many reservations have addressed their economic problems in innovative ways, but whether they can avoid the longstanding exploitative relationships remains to be seen. The upsurge in gambling operations on many reservations is an interesting recent development. In some cases, at least, it seems to be still another version of outside interest groups acquiring Native American resources. In this case one resource seems to be the legal ambiguities in state and federal jurisdiction over reservation lands, ambiguities which afford a niche for high-stakes gambling operations. Such enterprises require a large capital outlay. Often the investors are not from the reservation but have addresses in Reno and Las Vegas. As always, the holders of capital, as owners of the means of production, stand to profit most.

The economic needs of reservation communities also make them vulnerable to hazardous waste disposal. Vast areas of reservation lands under federal jurisdiction may appear to be unoccupied or "undeveloped." Reservation communities may find it difficult to resist the possibility of deriving income by accepting the deposit of American society's poisonous wastes, tainting their soil and ground water and putting their health still more at risk.

Considering the history and structure of the relationship between Native American communities and the political apparatus of United States society, the survival of Apache cultural integrity seems tenuous. Considering what the people have already been through, though, their maintenance of cultural continuity into the present is remarkable. Predictions of an end to the Apache cultural continuum seem premature.

The development of San Carlos has been a complex episode in the human experience, and we could view it from a number of perspectives. In many ways it is a product of the flow of past events and reflects processes that continue in the present. The Apache of San Carlos may or may not survive as a people, but administrative policies assuming the demise of indigenous cultural systems clearly err insofar as they view this as a "natural" process. As the history of San Carlos and other reservations has shown, policies based on that assumption are likely to generate a good deal of tragedy. Given the tendencies of cultural systems to adapt and survive, policies that inhibit their abilities to do so are more accurately viewed as destructive than benevolent. People whose indigenous heritage shapes their existence and comprises an essential component of their identity are not likely to abandon it willingly or without serious laceration.

Government programs to induce change often are justified on the grounds that the traditional culture has already changed, which implies that part of it already has been lost. But this is to confuse culture change with "deculturation." Such a rationale rests on the archaic assumption that some stable, "true," or pristine Apache culture existed before the change process began. If this concept of a stable pre-European culture were valid, then any subsequent changes might well be considered changes away from the true culture and seen as "culture loss." But such a perspective rests on a misleading concept of culture, which is inherently dynamic and tends always to be in a state of change. "Traditional" Western Apache culture at any time in the long history of the people was a product of changes and adaptation over millennia. Among human populations, culture change in response to new circumstances is a universal means of maintaining cultural continuity.

Certainly this cultural identity represents more than a simple tendency for traditional patterns to persist as anachronistic remnants from the past. These patterns have changed, altering in response to shifting circumstances, even while they remain distinct. The continued integrity of Native American communities has operational value, both in permitting these communities to act in their own interest within the state and in providing support within the community under stressful conditions. For people who find themselves immersed in the competitive arena of state hegemony, there is a great deal at stake in retaining their identity.

Viewed from the perspective of the long span of Athapaskan culture history, the unique aspects of the present situation are not a simple reaction of the Apache people to exposure to novel culture patterns or modern ideas. The people have always selected ideas and items from other cultures when these appeared to be of some value or use to them. This process strengthened and enriched their cultural repertoire without threatening it. The uniqueness of the present circumstance is in the loss of autonomy and the drastic usurpation of decision-making power that had its inception in their status as prisoners of war in the early years of San Carlos.

Western Apache culture is the product of generations of people transmitting ideas of the nature of the universe and of human beings, of the way things should be done and why they happen, to their children and grandchildren over the centuries. Those ideas—the culture of the people—changed and persisted to allow them to survive in circumstances that ranged from the tundras, mountains, and conifer forests of Siberia and Alaska down the slopes through the continent into the Southwest, where the Apache came upon sedentary farmers with their elaborate ceremonial cycles, encountered the Spanish of the seventeenth century, and where little more than a century ago, they were inundated by growing numbers of English-speaking Americans who eventually came to restrict their movements and administer their communities.

As individuals, people can leave San Carlos and do what they please in the wider society, within the constraints of limited access to wealth and power experienced by most of the populace—particularly those with discernible ethnicity. During the past decades many young people from San Carlos have spent years away from the community in places as diverse as Washington, D.C., Chicago, San Diego, Japan, Vietnam, and various places in Europe. Fluency in Apache may be dropping. Whether these people retain their ties to older traditions remains to be seen—but many people in the earlier generations also left for extended periods. Few of them remained away. The ancient way of dealing with reality may not disappear. The network of interpersonal bonds, patterned in the old way and valued as they were in generations past, continues to affect the choices people make and to color their concepts of the way things should be and people should act.

Like most of the western reservation communities, San Carlos is a society confronted with crushing problems, severely beleaguered, and deeply in trouble. But in the face of problems that for some have made life impossible to bear, occasionally one can still sense the attitude that to be Apache is better than to be anything else. Despite the predictions of an end to Apache cultural integrity over the past century or more, there is little reason to think that such a disappearance is any closer now than it was then. This is not an allusion to Apache culture as a mysterious, self-perpetuating entity but merely a recognition of the preference of individuals on a collective scale for a way of life that to them, often having tried alternatives, appears to be preferable to any other. Clearly this is only the most recent, current manifestation of an ancient continuum. The Western Apache of San Carlos have been incorporated into the global system, but so far, they have not disappeared within it.

References Cited

ABERLE, DAVID F.

1963   "Some Sources of Flexibility in Navajo Social Organization." *South-western Journal of Anthropology* 19:1–8.

1969   "A Plan for Navaho Economic Development." In *Toward Economic Development for Native American Communities*, pp. 223–276. Compendium of Papers Submitted to the Subcommittee on Economy in Government of the Joint Economic Committee, 91st Congress, 1st Session, Joint Committee Print. Washington, D.C.

1980   "Navajo Exogamic Rules and Preferred Marriages." In *The Versatility of Kinship*, edited by Linda Cordell and Stephen Beckerman, pp. 105–143. New York: Academic.

ABLON, JOAN

1964   "Relocated Indians in the San Francisco Bay Area: Social Interaction and Indian Identity." *Human Organization* 23:296–304.

ADAMS, WILLIAM Y.

1971   "The Development of San Carlos Apache Wage Labor to 1954." In *Apachean Culture History and Ethnology*, edited by Keith H. Basso and Morris E. Opler, pp. 116–128. Tucson: University of Arizona Press.

ADAMS, WILLIAM Y., DENNIS O. VAN GERVEN, AND RICHARD S. LEVY

1978   "The Retreat from Migrationism." In *Annual Review of Anthropology*, edited by Bernard J. Siegel, A. R. Beals, and S. A. Taylor, pp. 483–532. Palo Alto: Annual Reviews.

AMBLER, MARJANE

1990   *Breaking the Iron Bonds: Indian Control of Energy Development*. Lawrence: University Press of Kansas.

AMMER, CHRISTINE

1983   *The A to Z of Women's Health: A Concise Encyclopedia*. New York: Everest House.

ANDERSON, BENEDICT

1983   *Imagined Communities: Reflections on the Origin and Spread of Nationalism*. New York: Verso.

ARIZONA TERRITORIAL LEGISLATURE

1871   *Memorial and Affadavits Showing Outrages Perpetrated by Apache Indians, in the Territory of Arizona, during the Years 1869 and 1870.* San Francisco: Francis and Valentine, Printers.

ASCH, MICHAEL

1984   *Home and Native Land: Aboriginal Rights and the Canadian Constitution.* Toronto: Methuen.

ASSOCIATION ON AMERICAN INDIAN AFFAIRS

1956   "This Way Lies Freedom: A Statement of Policy of the Association on American Indian Affairs." *The American Indian* 8(3):1–4.

BALL, EVE

1980   *Indeh: An Apache Odyssey.* Provo: Brigham Young University Press.

BANCROFT, HERBERT HOWE

1889   *History of Arizona and New Mexico.* San Francisco: History Company.

BARRERA, MARIO

1979   *Race and Class in the Southwest: A Theory of Racial Inequality.* South Bend, Ind.: University of Notre Dame Press.

BASSO, KEITH H.

1966   *The Gift of Changing Woman.* Bureau of American Ethnology Bulletin 196. Washington, D.C.: Smithsonian Institution.

1970   *The Cibecue Apache.* New York: Holt, Rinehart and Winston.

1973   "A Western Apache Writing System: The Symbols of Silas John." *Science* 180(4090):1013–1022.

1979   *Portraits of "the Whiteman": Linguistic Play and Cultural Symbols among the Western Apache.* New York: Cambridge University Press.

1990   *Western Apache Language and Culture: Essays in Linguistic Anthropology.* Tucson: University of Arizona Press.

BENAVIDES, ALONSO DE

1965   *The Memorial of Fray Alonso de Benavides, 1630,* translated by E. E. Ayer. Albuquerque: Horn and Wallace.

BENEDICT, JAMES E

1975a   "The Murray Site: A Late Prehistoric Game Drive System in the Colorado Rocky Mountains." *Plains Anthropologist* 20:161–174.

1975b   "Scratching Deer: A Late Prehistoric Campsite in the Green Lakes Valley, Colorado." *Plains Anthropologist* 20:267–278.

BISHOP, CHARLES A., AND SHEPARD KRECH III

1980   "Matri-Organization: The Basis of Aboriginal Sub-Arctic Social Organization." *Arctic Anthropology* 17(2):34–45.

BODLEY, JOHN H.

1982   *Victims of Progress.* Palo Alto: Mayfield.

1983   *Anthropology and Contemporary Human Problems.* Palo Alto: Mayfield.

BOLT, CHRISTINE

1987   *American Indian Policy and American Reform: Case Studies of the Campaign to Assimilate the American Indian.* London: Allen and Unwin.

BOLTON, HERBERT E.

1916   *Spanish Explorations in the Southwest, 1542–1706.* New York: Charles Scribner's Sons.

BOURKE, JOHN G.

1886   *An Apache Campaign in the Sierra Madre: An Account of an Expedition in Pursuit of the Hostile Chiricahua Apaches in the Spring of 1883.* New York: Charles Scribner's Sons.

1892   *The Medicine Men of the Apache.* Bureau of American Ethnology Ninth Annual Report, 1887–1888. Washington, D.C.: Smithsonian Institution.

1971 (1891)   *On the Border with Crook.* Lincoln: University of Nebraska Press.

BROWNE, J. ROSS

1864   *Adventures in Apache Country.* New York: Harper & Bros.

BRYSON, REID A., AND WAYNE M. WENDLAND

1967   "Tentative Climatic Episodes in Central North America." In *Life, Land, and Water,* edited by William Mayer-Oakes, pp. 271–298. Winnipeg: University of Manitoba Press.

BURCH, ERNEST S., JR.

1972   "The Caribou/Wild Reindeer as a Human Resource." *American Antiquity* 37:339–368.

BUREAU OF INDIAN AFFAIRS

n.d.   "Facts about—San Carlos Agency." U.S. Department of the Interior. Mimeograph.

1966   "A Followup Study of 1963 Recipients of the Services of the Employment Assistance Program, Bureau of Indian Affairs." Mimeograph.

1968   "1968 Followup Study of 1963 Recipients of the Services of the Employment Assistance Program, Bureau of Indian Affairs." Mimeograph.

1981   *Information Profiles of Indian Reservations in Arizona, Nevada, & Utah.* Phoenix: Bureau of Indian Affairs, Phoenix Area Office.

BURAWOY, MICHAEL

1983   "The Function and Reproduction of Migrant Labor: Comparative Material from Southern Africa and the United States." *American Journal of Sociology* 81:1050–1087.

BUSKIRK, WINFRED

1986   *The Western Apache: Living with the Land before 1950.* Norman: University of Oklahoma Press.

CAHN, EDGAR, AND DAVID W. HEARNE

1969   *Our Brother's Keeper: The Indian in White America.* New York: World Publishing Company.

CLARK, ANNETTE MCFADYEN

1970   "Koyukon Athabascan Ceremonialism." *Western Canadian Journal of Anthropology* 2(1):80–88.

1977   "Trade at the Cross Roads." In *Problems in the Prehistory of the North American Subarctic: The Athapaskan Question,* edited by James W. Helmer, S. Van Dyke, and Francois J. Kense, pp. 130–134. Calgary: University of Calgary.

1981   "Koyukon." In *Handbook of North American Indians,* vol. 6, *Subarctic,* edited by June Helm, pp. 582–601. Washington, D.C.: Smithsonian Institution.

CLUM, WOODWORTH

1936   *Apache Agent.* Boston: Houghton Mifflin.

COLE, D. C.

1988   *The Chiricahua Apache, 1846–1876: From War to Reservation.* Albuquerque: University of New Mexico Press.

COLYER, VINCENT

1971 (1871)   *Peace with the Apaches of New Mexico and Arizona: Report of Vincent Colyer, Member of Board of Indian Commissioners.* Freeport, N.Y.: Books for Libraries Press.

CONFEDERATION OF AMERICAN INDIANS

1986   *Indian Reservations: A State and Federal Handbook.* Jefferson, N.C.: McFarland.

CONNER, DANIEL ELLIS

1956   *Joseph Reddeford Walker and the Arizona Adventure.* Norman: University of Oklahoma Press.

CORNELL, STEPHEN, AND MARTA GIL-SWEDBERG

1990   "Sociocultural Factors in American Indian Economic Development: A Comparison of Three Apache Cases." Harvard Project on American Indian Economic Development, Project Report Series, John F. Kennedy School of Government. Cambridge: Harvard University (photocopy).

CORTÉS, JOSÉ

1989   *Views from the Apache Frontier: Report on the Northern Provinces of New Spain.* Edited by Elizabeth A. H. John. Norman: University of Oklahoma Press.

CREMONY, JOHN C.

1969 (1868)   *Life among the Apaches.* Glorieta, N.Mex.: Rio Grande Press.

CROOK, GEORGE

1946   *General George Crook: His Autobiography.* Norman: University of Oklahoma Press.

CZAPLICKA, M. A.

1914   *Aboriginal Siberia: A Study in Social Anthropology.* Oxford: Clarendon Press.

DALE, EDWARD EVERETT

1949   *The Indians of the Southwest: A Century of Development under the United States.* Norman: University of Oklahoma Press.

DAVIES, D. M.

1973   *The Last of the Tasmanians.* London: Frederick Miller.

DAVIS, BRITTON

1951 (1929)   *The Truth about Geronimo.* Chicago: Lakeside Press.

DAVIS, MICHAEL G.

1988   "The Cultural Preadaptation Hypothesis: A Test Case on the Southern Plains." Ph.D. dissertation, University of Oklahoma, Norman.

DE LAGUNA, FREDERICA
1975   "Matrilineal Kin Groups in Northwestern North America." In *Proceedings: Northern Athapaskan Conference, 1971*, edited by Annette McFadyen Clark, pp. 120–190. Mercury Series Paper no. 27. Ottawa: National Museum of Man.

DE LAGUNA, FREDERICA, AND CATHERINE MCCLELLAN
1981   "Ahtna." In *Handbook of North American Indians*, vol. 6, *Subarctic*, edited by June Helm, pp. 641–663. Washington, D.C.: Smithsonian Institution.

DELORIA, VINE, JR., AND CLIFFORD M. LYTLE
1983   *American Indians, American Justice.* Austin: University of Texas Press.

DOBYNS, HENRY F.
1971   *The Apache People.* Phoenix: Tribal Indian Series.
1983   *Their Number Become Thinned: Native American Population Dynamics in Eastern North America.* Knoxville: University of Tennessee Press.

DUTTON, BERTHA P.
1976   *Navajos and Apaches: The Athabascan Peoples.* Englewood Cliffs, N.J.: Prentice-Hall.

DYEN, ISIDORE, AND DAVID F. ABERLE
1974   *Lexical Reconstruction: The Case of the Proto-Athapaskan Kinship System.* London: Cambridge University Press.

ELKIN, A. P.
1951   "Reaction and Interaction: A Food Gathering People and European Settlement in Australia." *American Anthropologist* 53: 164–186.

ELLIS, FLORENCE
1974   *American Indian Ethnohistory*, vol. 1, *Navajo Indians*, edited by David Agee Horr. New York: Garland.

EVERETT, MICHAEL W.
1980   "Drinking as a Measure of Proper Behavior: The White Mountain Apaches." In *Drinking Behavior among Southwestern Indians*, edited by Jack O. Waddell and Michael W. Everett, pp. 148–177. Tucson: University of Arizona Press.

FERG, ALAN, ED.
1987   *Western Apache Material Culture: The Goodwin and Guenther Collections.* Published for the Arizona State Museum, University of Arizona. Tucson: University of Arizona Press.

FLETCHER, ALICE C.
1888   *Indian Education and Civilization. A Report Prepared in Answer to Senate Resolution of February 23, 1885.* Bureau of Education Special Report, 48th Congress, 2nd Session. Senate Ex. Doc. No. 95. Washington, D.C.

FOLEY, DUNCAN
1983   "Commodity." In *A Dictionary of Marxist Thought*, edited by Tom Bottomore, pp. 86–87. Cambridge: Harvard University Press.

FORBES, JACK D.

1959   "Unknown Athapaskans: The Identification of the Jano, Jocome, Jumano, Manso, Suma, and Other Indian Tribes of the Southwest." *Ethnohistory* 6:97–158.

1960   *Apache, Navaho, and Spaniard*. Norman: University of Oklahoma Press.

FOWLER, WILLIAM R., JR.

1977   "Linguistic Evidence for Athapaskan Prehistory." In *Problems in the Prehistory of the North American Subarctic: The Athapaskan Question,* edited by James W. Helmer, S. Van Dyke, and François J. Kense, pp. 102–105. Calgary: University of Calgary.

FRANK, ANDRÉ GUNDER

1972   "Introduction." In *Dependence and Underdevelopment: Latin America's Political Economy,* edited by James D. Cockcroft, A. G. Frank, and Dale L. Johnson, pp. ix–xxix. Garden City, N.J.: Doubleday.

FRAZER, ROBERT

1885   *The Apaches of the White Mountain Reservation, Arizona*. Philadelphia: Indian Rights Association.

FRIED, MORTON

1968   "State: The Institution." *International Encyclopedia of the Social Sciences,* pp. 143–150. New York: Macmillan and The Free Press.

FRISON, GEORGE C.

1962   "Wedding of the Waters Cave: A Stratified Site in the Bighorn Basin of Northern Wyoming." *Plains Anthropologist* 7:246–265.

1965   "Spring Creek Cave, Wyoming." *American Antiquity* 31: 81–94.

1978   *Prehistoric Hunters of the High Plains*. New York: Academic.

GETTY, HARRY T.

1963   *The San Carlos Apache Cattle Industry*. Anthropological Papers no. 7. Tucson: University of Arizona Press.

GILLESPIE, BERYL C.

1981   "Territorial Groups Before 1821: Athapaskans of the Shield and the Mackenzie Drainage." In *Handbook of North American Indians,* vol. 6, *Subarctic,* edited by June Helm. Washington, D.C.: Smithsonian Institution.

GODDARD, PLINY EARLE

1916   "The Beaver Indians." *Anthropological Papers of the American Museum of Natural History* 10(4):201–293.

GOODWIN, GRENVILLE G.

1935   "The Social Divisions and Economic Life of the Western Apache." *American Anthropologist* 37:55–64.

1938   "White Mountain Apache Religion." *American Anthropologist* 40: 24–37.

1969   *The Social Organization of the Western Apache*. Tucson: University of Arizona Press.

GOODWIN, GRENVILLE G., AND KEITH H. BASSO

1971   *Western Apache Raiding and Warfare*. Tucson: University of Arizona Press.

GOUGH, KATHLEEN
   1962   "Variation in Residence." In *Matrilineal Kinship,* edited by David M.
           Schneider and Kathleen Gough. Berkeley: University of California
           Press.

GRAMSCI, ANTONIO
   1971   *Selections from the Prison Notebooks.* New York: International Pub-
           lishers.

GRAVES, THEODORE D.
   1970   "The Personal Adjustment of Navajo Indian Migrants to Denver,
           Colorado." *American Anthropologist* 72:35–54.

GRIFFEN, WILLIAM B.
   1988   *Utmost Good Faith: Patterns of Apache-Mexican Hostilities in Northern
           Chihuahua Border Warfare, 1821–1848.* Albuquerque: University of
           New Mexico Press.

GUNNERSON, DOLORES A.
   1974   *The Jicarilla Apaches: A Study in Survival.* DeKalb: Northern Illinois
           University Press.

GUNNERSON, JAMES H.
   1969   "Apache Archaeology in Northeastern New Mexico." *American An-
           tiquity* 34:23–39.

GUNNERSON, JAMES H., AND DOLORES A. GUNNERSON
   1971   "Apachean Culture: A Study in Unity and Diversity." In *Apachean
           Culture History and Ethnology,* edited by Keith H. Basso and Morris
           E. Opler, pp. 7–33. Tucson: University of Arizona Press.

HALL, E. RAYMOND, AND KEITH R. KELSON
   1958   *Mammals of North America.* New York: Ronald Press.

HALL, THOMAS D.
   1989   *Social Change in the Southwest, 1350–1880.* Abilene: University of
           Kansas Press.

HAMMOND, GEORGE, AND AGAPITO REY
   1953   *Don Juan de Oñate, Colonizer of New Mexico, 1595–1628.* Albuquer-
           que: University of New Mexico Press.

HARP, ELMER, JR.
   1978   "Pioneer Cultures of the Sub-Arctic and the Arctic." In *Ancient Na-
           tive Americans,* edited by Jesse D. Jennings, pp. 95–129. San Fran-
           cisco: W. H. Freeman.

HAVIGHURST, ROBERT J.
   1957   "Education and American Indians: Individual and Cultural As-
           pects." *Annals of the American Academy of Political and Social Sciences*
           311:105–115.

HEARNE, SAMUEL
   1911   *A Journey from Prince of Wales's Fort in Hudson's Bay to the Northern
           Ocean in the Years 1769, 1770, 1771, and 1772.* Toronto: Champlain
           Society.

HELM, JUNE
   1981   "Dogrib." In *Handbook of North American Indians,* vol. 6, *Subarctic,*

edited by June Helm, pp. 291–309. Washington, D.C.: Smithsonian Institution.

HERBERT, LUCILLE, AND CHARLES W. HERBERT
1963   "Land of the San Carlos Apaches." *Arizona Highways* 39(5):8–35.

HOBSBAWM, ERIC
1989   *Politics for a Rational Left: Political Writing 1977–1988.* New York: Verso.

HOCKETT, CHARLES F.
1977   "Review of *Lexical Reconstruction* by Dyen and Aberle." *Current Anthropology* 18:84–91.

HOIJER, HARRY
1971   "The Position of the Apachean Languages in the Athapaskan Stock." In *Apachean Culture History and Ethnology,* edited by Keith H. Basso and Morris E. Opler, pp. 3–6. Tucson: University of Arizona Press.

HOLMES, CHARLES E.
1971   "A Northern Athapaskan Environmental System in Diachronic Perspective." *Western Canadian Journal of Anthropology* 5(3–4):92–124.

HONIGMANN, JOHN J.
1946   *Ethnography and Acculturation of the Fort Nelson Slave.* Publications in Anthropology no. 33. New Haven: Yale University Press.

1964   *The Kaska Indians: An Ethnographic Reconstruction.* Publications in Anthropology no. 51. New Haven: Human Relations Area Files, Yale University.

HOSLEY, E. H.
1981   "Environment and Culture in the Alaska Plateau." In *Handbook of North American Indians,* vol. 6, *Subarctic,* edited by June Helm, pp. 533–555. Washington, D.C.: Smithsonian Institution.

HOWARD, O. O.
1978 (1907)   *My Life and Experiences among Our Hostile Indians.* New York: da Capo.

HOXIE, FREDERICK E.
1984   *A Final Promise: The Campaign to Assimilate the Indians, 1880–1920.* Lincoln: University of Nebraska Press.

INFORMATION PLEASE ALMANAC ATLAS AND YEARBOOK
1983   37th edition. New York: A. & W. Publishing, Inc.

INSTITUTE FOR GOVERNMENT RESEARCH
1928   *The Problem of Indian Administration.* Baltimore: Johns Hopkins University Press.

JENNESS, DIAMOND
1937   *The Sekani Indians of British Columbia.* Canada Department of Mines and Resources Bulletin no. 84. Ottawa: National Museum of Canada.

1943   *The Carrier Indians of the Bulkley River: Their Social and Religious Life.* Bureau of American Ethnology Bulletin no. 133, pp. 469–586. Washington, D.C.: Smithsonian Institution.

JORALEMON, IRA B.
1973   *Copper: The Encompassing Story of Mankind's First Metal.* Berkeley: Howell-North Books.

JORGENSEN, JOSEPH G.
1978   "A Century of Political Economic Effects on American Indian Society." *Journal of Ethnic Studies* 6(3):1–82.
1980   *Western Indians. Comparative Environments, Languages, and Cultures of 172 Western American Indian Tribes.* San Francisco: W. H. Freeman.
1983   "Comparative Traditional Economics and Ecological Adaptations." In *Handbook of North American Indians*, vol. 10, *Southwest*, edited by Alfonso Ortiz, pp. 684–710. Washington, D.C.: Smithsonian Institution.
1984   *Native Americans and Energy Development II.* Forestville, Calif.: Anthropology Resource Center and Seventh Generation Fund.

KALT, JOSEPH P.
1987   *The Redefinition of Property Rights in American Indian Reservations: A Comparative Analysis of Native American Economic Development.* Discussion Paper Series, John F. Kennedy School of Government, Energy and Environmental Policy Center. Cambridge: Harvard University (photocopy).

KATZ, MICHAEL B., MICHAEL J. DOUCET, AND MARK J. STERN
1982   *The Social Organization of Early Industrial Capitalism.* Cambridge: Harvard University Press.

KAUT, CHARLES R.
1956   "Western Apache Clan and Phratry Organization," *American Anthropologist* 58:140–161.
1957   *The Western Apache Clan System: Its Origins and Development.* Publications in Anthropology no. 9. Albuquerque: University of New Mexico Press.
1974   "The Clan System as an Epiphenomenal Element of Western Apache Social Organization." *Ethnology* 13:45–70.

KEESING, ROGER M.
1987   "Anthropology as Interpretive Quest." *Current Anthropology* 28:161–175.

KEHOE, ALICE B.
1981   *North American Indians: A Comprehensive Account.* Englewood Cliffs, N. J.: Prentice-Hall.

KELLEY, CLARA B.
1980   "Navajo Political Economy before Fort Sumner." In *The Versatility of Kinship*, edited by Linda Cordell and Stephen Beckerman, pp. 307–332. New York: Academic.

KRAUSS, MICHAEL E.
1973   "Na-Dene." In *Current Trends in Linguistics*, vol. 10, *Linguistics in North America*, edited by Thomas A. Sebeok, pp. 903–978. New York: Humanities Press.
1979   "Na-Dene and Eskimo-Aleut." In *The Languages of Native North*

America: Historical and Comparative Assessment, edited by Lyle Camp-
bell and Marianne Mithun, pp. 803–901. Austin: University of
Texas Press.

KRAUSS, MICHAEL E., AND VICTOR K. GOLLA
1981   "Northern Athapaskan Languages." In *Handbook of North American
Indians,* vol. 6, *Subarctic,* edited by June Helm, pp. 67–85. Washington, D.C.: Smithsonian Institution.

KRECH, SHEPARD, III
1978   "Disease, Starvation, and Northern Athapaskan Social Organization." *American Ethnologist* 5:710–732.

LAMPHERE, LOUISE
1976   "The Internal Colonization of the Navajo People." *Southwest Economy and Society* 1(1):6–13.

LEVITAN, SAR, AND WILLIAM B. JOHNSON
1975   *Indian Giving. Federal Programs for Native Americans.* Baltimore: Johns
Hopkins University Press.

LIEBE-HARKORT, M. L.
1980   "Recent Developments in Apachean Language Maintenance." *International Journal of American Linguistics* 46(2):85–91.

LURIE, NANCY O.
1961   "The Voice of the American Indian: Report on the American Indian
Chicago Conference." *Current Anthropology* 2:478–500.

MARINSEK, E. A.
1960   *The Effect of Cultural Difference in the Education of Apache Indians.* Albuquerque: University of New Mexico Press.

MCCLELLAND, M., AND D. WINTER
1969   *Motivating Economic Achievement.* New York: Free Press.

MCDONNELL, ROGER F.
1984   "Symbolic Orientations and Systematic Turmoil: Centering on the
Kaska Symbol of Dene." *Canadian Journal of Anthropology* 4(1):
39–56.

MCGRATH, G. D., ROBERT ROESSEL, BRUCE MEADOR, G. C. HELMS-
TADTER, AND JOHN BROWN
1962   *Higher Education of Southwestern Indians with Reference to Success
and Failure.* Cooperative Research Project no. 938. Tempe: Arizona
State University.

MCKENNAN, ROBERT
1965   *The Chandalar Kutchin.* Technical Paper no. 17. Washington, D.C.:
Arctic Institute of America.

MIKESELL, RAYMOND
1979   *The World Copper Industry. Structure and Economic Analysis.* Baltimore: Johns Hopkins University Press.

MOORHEAD, MAX
1968   *The Apache Frontier. Jacobo Ugarte and Spanish-Indian Relations in New
Spain, 1769–1791.* Norman: University of Oklahoma Press.

MORICE, A. G.
1914   "Northwestern Denes and Northeastern Asiatics: A Study of the

Origins of the Former." *Transactions of the Royal Canadian Institute* 10:131–193.

MORSE, BRADFORD W.

1984   *Aboriginal Self-Government in Australia and Canada.* Aboriginal Peoples and Constitutional Reform Background Paper no. 4. Kingston, Ontario: Institute of Intergovernmental Relations.

MULL, MARVIN

1963   "Tribe Requests Service Corps." *Apache Drumbeat* 17 (July).

NAYLOR, THOMAS N.

1981   "Athapaskans They Weren't: The Suma Rebels Executed at Casas Grandes in 1685." In *The Protohistoric Period in the North American Southwest, A.D. 1450–1700,* edited by David R. Wilcox and W. Bruce Masse, pp. 275–281. Anthropological Research Papers no. 24. Tempe: Arizona State University.

NELSON, RICHARD K.

1983   *Make Prayers to the Raven: A Koyukon View of the Northern Forest.* Chicago: University of Chicago Press.

OFFICER, JAMES E.

1987   *Hispanic Arizona, 1536–1856.* Tucson: University of Arizona Press.

OGLE, R. F.

1970   *Federal Control of the Western Apache, 1848–1886.* Albuquerque: University of New Mexico Press.

OPLER, MORRIS E.

1936   "A Summary of Jicarilla Apache Culture." *American Anthropologist* 38:202–223.

1938   *Dirty Boy: A Jicarilla Tale of Raid and War.* Memoirs of the American Anthropological Association no. 52. Menasha, Wis.: American Anthropological Association.

1941a   *An Apache Life-Way: The Economic, Social, and Religious Institutions of the Chiricahua Indians.* Chicago: University of Chicago Press.

1941b   "A Jicarilla Apache Expedition and Scalp Dance," *Journal of American Folklore* 54:10–23.

1972   "Cause and Effect in Apachean Agriculture, Division of Labor, Residence Patterns, and Girls' Puberty Rites." *American Anthropologist* 74:1133–1146.

1973   *Grenville Goodwin among the Western Apache: Letters from the Field.* Tucson: University of Arizona Press.

1975   "Problems in Apachean Culture History, with Special Reference to the Lipan Apache." *Anthropological Quarterly* 48:182–192.

OSGOOD, CORNELIUS

1932   *The Ethnography of the Great Bear Lake Indians.* Canada Department of Mines and Resources. Bulletin no. 70. Ottawa: National Museum of Canada.

1933   "Tanaina Culture." *American Anthropologist* 35:695–717.

1936   *Contributions to the Ethnography of the Kutchin.* Publications in Anthropology no. 14. New Haven: Yale University Press.

1959   *Ingalik Mental Culture.* Publications in Anthropology no. 56. New Haven: Yale University Press.

1971   *The Han Indians: A Compilation of Ethnographic and Historical Data on the Alaska-Yukon Boundary Area.* Publications in Anthropology no. 74. New Haven: Yale University Press.

PAGE, VICKI

1985   "Reservation Development in the United States: Periphery in the Core." *American Indian Culture and Research Journal* 9(3):21–35.

PARMEE, EDWARD A.

1968   *Formal Education and Culture Change: A Modern Apache Indian Community and Government Education Programs.* Tucson: University of Arizona Press.

PERRY, RICHARD J.

1977   "Variations on the Female Referent in Athapaskan Cultures." *Journal of Anthropological Research* 33:99–118.

1980   "The Apachean Transition from the Subarctic to the Southwest." *Plains Anthropologist* 25:279–296.

1989   "Matrilineal Descent in a Hunting Context: The Athapaskan Case." *Ethnology* 28:33–51.

1991   *Western Apache Heritage: People of the Mountain Corridor.* Austin: University of Texas Press.

PLANTZ, MARGARET C., AND FREDERICK S. STINSON

1987   *Indian People in Indian Lands, 1980: Profiles of American Indian and Alaska Native Populations in Various Settings.* Department of Commerce. Washington, D.C.

PORTER, JOSEPH C.

1986   *Paper Medicine Man.* Norman: University of Oklahoma Press.

POTTINGER, RICHARD

1985   "Indian Reservation Labor Markets: A Navajo Assessment and Challenge." *American Indian Culture and Research Journal* 9(3):1–20.

POULANTZAS, NIKOS

1980   *State, Power, Socialism.* London: Verso.

REYNOLDS, JNO.

1896   *Letter from the Acting Secretary of the Interior* . . . House of Representatives, 54th Congress, 1st Session, Document no. 320. Washington, D.C.

ROESSEL, R. A.

1964   *San Carlos Apache Indian Education.* Tempe: Indian Education Center, Arizona State University.

ROTH, H. LING

1890   *The Aborigines of Tasmania.* London: Kegan Paul.

SAVISHINSKY, JOEL S.

1974   *The Trail of the Hare.* New York: Gordon and Breach.

SCHMIDT, WILLIAM E.

1983   "Economy Carves New Trail of Tears for Apache Tribe." *New York Times,* January 31.

SCHROEDER, ALBERT H.

1974a   *A Study of the Apache Indians.* Vol. 1. New York: Garland.

1974b   *A Study of the Apache Indians.* Vol. 4. New York: Garland.

SEARLES, DONNA B.

1990   "Common Ground, Varied Lives: San Carlos Apache Women and Birth." Paper presented at the Eighty-ninth annual meeting of the American Anthropological Association, December 2, 1990, New Orleans, La.

SHARP, HENRY S.

1981   "The Null Case: The Chipewyan." In *Woman the Gatherer*, edited by Frances Dahlberg, pp. 221–244. New Haven: Yale University Press.

SHINKWIN, ANNE D.

1977   "The 'Archaeological Visibility' of Northern Athapaskans in the Tanana River Area, Central Alaska." In *Problems in the Prehistory of the North American Subarctic: The Athapaskan Question*, edited by James W. Helmer, S. Van Dyke, and Francois J. Kense, pp. 40–45. Calgary: University of Calgary.

1979   *Dakah de'nin's Village and the Dixthada Site: A Contribution to Northern Athapaskan Prehistory.* Mercury Series Paper no. 91. Ottawa: National Museum of Man.

SJOBERG, ANDREE F.

1953   "Lipan Apache Culture in Historical Perspective." *Southwestern Journal of Anthropology* 9:76–98.

SLOBODIN, RICHARD

1975   "Canadian Subarctic Athapaskans in the Literature to 1965." *The Canadian Review of Sociology and Anthropology* 12:278–289.

1981   "Kutchin." In *Handbook of North American Indians*, vol. 6, *Subarctic*, edited by June Helm, pp. 514–532. Washington, D.C.: Smithsonian Institution.

SNIPP, C. MATTHEW

1989   *American Indians: First of This Land.* New York: Russell Sage Foundation.

SPICER, EDWARD H.

1961   *Perspectives in American Indian Culture Change.* Chicago: University of Chicago Press.

1962   *Cycles of Conquest.* Tucson: University of Arizona Press.

STEWART, KENNETH M.

1965   "American Indian Heritage: Retrospect and Prospects." In *The Native Americans: Prehistory and Ethnology of the North American Indians*, edited by Robert F. Spencer, Jesse D. Jennings, et al., pp. 490–506. New York: Harper & Row.

STEWART, OMER C.

1964   "Questions Regarding American Indian Criminality." *Human Organization* 23:61–66.

SUMNER, WILLIAM GRAHAM

1906   *Folkways.* Boston: Ginn.

TANNER, ADRIAN
1979   *Bringing Home Animals.* St. John's: Institute of Social and Economic Research, Memorial University of Newfoundland.

THRAPP, DAN
1967   *The Conquest of Apacheria.* Norman: University of Oklahoma Press.

TILLER, VERONICA
1983   *The Jicarilla Apache Tribe.* Lincoln: University of Nebraska Press.

TOWNSEND, JOAN B.
1963   "Ethnographic Notes on the Pedro Bay Tanaina." *Anthropologica* 5:209–223.

TRAVIS, ROBERT
1968   *Tasmanians.* Melbourne: Cassell.

UNITED STATES DEPARTMENT OF THE INTERIOR
1936   *Constitution and By-Laws of the San Carlos Apache Tribe, Arizona.* Washington, D.C.
1941   *Corporate Charter of the San Carlos Apache Tribe, Arizona.* Washington, D.C.

WADDELL, JACK O.
1980   "Alcohol Use in the Southwest." In *Drinking Behavior among Southwestern Indians: An Anthropological Perspective,* edited by Jack O. Waddell and Michael W. Everett, pp. 1–32. Tucson: University of Arizona Press.

WAGONER, JAY
1970   *Arizona Territory, 1863–1912: A Political History.* Tucson: University of Arizona Press.

WALLERSTEIN, IMMANUEL
1974   *The Modern World System: Capitalist Agriculture and the Origins of the European Economy in the Sixteenth Century.* New York: Academic Press.
1975   *World Inequality: Origins and Perspectives on the World System.* Montreal: Black Rose Books.

WASHBURN, WILCOMB E.
1973   *The American Indians and the United States: A Documentary History.* New York: Random.

WATKINS, FREDERICK M.
1968   "State: The Concept." *International Encyclopedia of the Social Sciences,* vol. 15, pp. 150–157. New York: Crowell Collier & Macmillan.

WILCOX, DAVID R.
1981   "The Entry of Athapaskans into the American Southwest: The Problem Today." In *The Protohistoric Period in the North American Southwest, A.D. 1450–1700,* edited by David R. Wilcox and W. Bruce Masse, pp. 213–256. Anthropological Research Paper no. 24. Tempe: Arizona State University.

WILKINSON, CHARLES F.
1987   *American Indians, Time, and the Law: Native Societies in a Modern Constitutional Democracy.* New Haven: Yale University Press.

WILLIAMS, ERIC
1944   *Capitalism and Slavery*. Chapel Hill: University of North Carolina
        Press.

WOLF, ERIC R.
1982   *Europe and the People Without History*. Berkeley: University of Cali-
        fornia Press.

WORCESTER, DONALD
1979   *The Apaches: Eagles of the Southwest*. Norman: University of Okla-
        homa Press.

WRIGHT, GARY A.
1978   "The Shoshonean Migration Problem." *Plains Anthropologist* 23:
        113–137.

1984   *People of the High Country: Jackson Hole before the Settlers*. New York:
        Peter Lang.

YOUNG, ROBERT W.
1983   "Apachean Languages." In *Handbook of North American Indians*,
        vol. 10, *Southwest*, edited by Alfonso Ortiz, pp. 393–400. Washing-
        ton, D.C.: Smithsonian Institution.

Manuscript Collections

THOMAS H. DODGE COLLECTION, Arizona Room, Hayden Library, Arizona State University, Tempe, Arizona.

CARL HAYDEN COLLECTION, Arizona Room, Hayden Library, Arizona
State University, Tempe, Arizona.

MORRIS K. UDALL COLLECTION, University of Arizona Library, University
of Arizona, Tucson, Arizona.

Index

Osgood, Cornelius, 35
Oury, William S., 110–111

Page, Vicki, 204
Paiute, 85
Papago, 87, 110, 111
Parmee, Edward A., 194
Peabody Coal Company, 229–230
Pecos Pueblo, 46
Pedro, 133
Peridot, Arizona, 2, 160, 218
Perry, Richard J., x, 34, 35, 36, 39, 80
Phelps Dodge Corporation, 146
Phoenix, Arizona, x, xi, 148, 150,
 156, 201, 202, 206, 216
Pima, 56, 66, 149, 150
Pinal Apache, 66, 90, 95, 106, 136,
 153, 154. *See also* Western Apache
Pinal County, Arizona, 150
Pinal Creek, 119
Plantz, Margaret C., 17
Point of Pines, Arizona, 174
Pomponio, Alice, xii
Porter, Joseph C., 105, 107, 121, 125,
 126, 128, 137
Poulantzas, Nikos, 8, 9, 119, 130,
 208
Prescott, Arizona, 114
Price, Hiram, 151–152
Proto-Athapaskan, 20, 73. *See also*
 Apache, Athapaskan
Public Health Service, 3, 196–197,
 200–203, 225. *See also* Indian
 Health Service
Pueblo Revolt of 1680, 50, 52
Pueblos, 20, 41, 44, 46, 48, 49–55,
 59, 78, 94
Pueblo Viejo, 146
Pullman, George Mortimer, 128
Pullman Strike of 1894, 128

Racism, 11, 12, 67, 94, 95–96, 104,
 106, 109–116, 140, 173, 205
Railroads, 140, 146, 148, 160
Reagan, Ronald, 217
Reclamation Act of 1902, 26
Reisch, Jen, xii

Relocation programs, 203–209, 225,
 226, 231
Reservations: abolishment of, 7, 231;
 characteristics of, ix, 3–7, 129;
 economic problems of, 6, 7, 16–
 17; establishment of, 113, 129;
 federal governance of, 10, 15–16;
 gambling on, 232; hazardous
 waste disposal on, 231–232; history of, 4, 5, 129; internal governance of, 10, 129; rationales for,
 6, 7, 123, 129; relocation programs on, 203–209; resource
 expropriation of, 10, 16, 129,
 229–230; taxes on, 193, 203; trust
 relationship, 16. *See also* San Carlos Reservation
Reynolds, Jno., 150, 153, 154
Rio Grande, 44, 49, 50, 51, 52, 67,
 97, 98
Robert, H. M., 119
Roberts, James E., 131, 132
Roessel, R. A., 163
Rosebud Sioux Reservation, 223
Roswell, New Mexico, 204
Roth, H. Ling, 10

Sabe Mucho, 154
Sacaton, 109
Safford, A. P. K., 113–115, 146
Safford, Arizona, 1, 146, 218, 219
Salmon, 31
Salt River, 56, 66
Salt River Cave, Battle of, 104
San Carlos Reservation: administration of, 125, 129–130, 133–136,
 140–141, 152, 189, 191–193, 196–
 214, 225–228, 232; agriculture on,
 120, 121, 127, 130, 137–139, 146–
 149; cattle on, 138, 147, 153–154,
 155–157, 159, 211–214, 220–222;
 changing boundaries of, 119–120,
 145–146, 152–159, 211, 216, 225;
 children on, 160, 162, 185–188,
 198, 225, 226; churches in, 162,
 169, 171, 182–185; crime rate on,
 18; economy, 26, 140–143, 146,